BRITAIN'S HIDDEN RAILWAYS

Published by Times Books
An imprint of HarperCollins Publishers
Westerhill Road
Bishopbriggs
Glasgow G64 2QT
www.harpercollins.co.uk

First edition 2018
© HarperCollins Publishers 2018
Text © Julian Holland

The Times® is a registered trademark of Times Newspapers Ltd

A catalogue record for this book is available from the British Library

ISBN 978-0-00-824909-0

10 9 8 7 6 5 4 3 2 1

Printed in China by RR Donnelley APS Co Ltd

If you would like to comment on any aspect of this book,
please contact us at the above address or online.
e-mail: times.books@harpercollins.co.uk

www.timesbooks.co.uk

With special thanks to

MIX
Paper from
responsible sources
FSC™ C007454

This book is produced from independently certified FSC™ paper
to ensure responsible forest management.

For more information visit: www.harpercollins.co.uk/green

THE TIMES

BRITAIN'S HIDDEN RAILWAYS

JULIAN HOLLAND

Contents

Notorious for its 1-in-39 gradient near the coast, the 279-yd curving Ravenscar Tunnel was always a problem for drivers of steam engines hauling trains between Fyling Hall and Ravenscar stations on the Whitby to Scarborough line.

Introduction

It is well over fifty years since the publication of the Beeching Report (full title: *The Reshaping of British Railways*), in which Dr Richard Beeching recommended the closure of thousands of miles of railway across the length and breadth of Britain. Politicians of both hues rapidly put these closures into effect and by the mid-1970s around 4,500 route miles of railway and 2,500 stations had been closed along with the loss of 68,000 rail workers' jobs. Even before Dr Beeching's axe was wielded, around 3,000 miles of uneconomic railway across the country had already been closed since 1948, the year in which Britain's railways had been nationalized. With hindsight many of these closures should never have been implemented but, with a few recent exceptions (the Borders Railway reopening between Edinburgh and Tweedbank in 2015 is undoubtedly the highlight), it is unlikely that any of these routes will be reopened in the near future, if at all.

What has happened to these closed railways? Fortunately, many have been reborn as footpaths and cycleways – the latter forming part of the extensive traffic-free National Cycle Network (NCN) – providing important green corridors where insects, small mammals, birds, trees and wildflowers all flourish. In *Britain's Hidden Railways* I tell the fascinating story of fifty of these long-closed railways, which can be found scattered around the country – even the Channel Islands and the Isle of Man are not forgotten. I am lucky to have travelled on many of these lines before closure and have also explored them more recently in their new life as footpaths and cycleways. Inevitably a few of these routes escaped my undivided attention before closure as I was either a) not born or b) too young!

Without exception, all of these routes have their own unique character and, despite the passage of time, many still carry reminders of their illustrious past in the shape of stations, platforms, bridges, viaducts and tunnels – in many cases all that is missing from today's scene is the track and trains. Some of the more popular routes, such as the well-established and beautiful Camel Trail in Cornwall, contribute much to the local economy, while all, without exception, allow walkers and cyclists to enjoy peace and tranquility away from our noisy, polluted and increasingly dangerous roads.

I am often asked which of these hidden gems are my favourites. This is an impossible question for me to answer as I love them all. Instead, I will highlight a few routes from around Britain that will hopefully whet your appetite and encourage you, dear reader, to get out there and discover the delights of *Britain's Hidden Railways*.

Starting in the southwest of England, the aforementioned Camel Trail runs alongside the beautiful Camel Estuary between Padstow and Wadebridge and up ever-narrowing wooded valleys to Bodmin and Wenford Bridge. On Dartmoor the trackbed of the long-closed branch line to remote Princetown follows the contours around the rugged moorland tors and disused granite quarries, while in East Devon the Exmouth to Budleigh Salterton route winds through tranquil woodland only a stone's throw from busy and narrow country roads. Special mention must be made here of the old Somerset & Dorset Joint Railway route, which climbs up from Bath through two tunnels to Midford and Radstock; it was closed in 1966 but the section up through Devonshire and Combe Down Tunnels and across Tucking Mill Viaduct was reopened to walkers and cyclists in 2013. I have very many happy memories of this route as I travelled on the old 'Slow and Dirty' as a child while en route to family summer holidays in the 1950s and as a teenage trainspotter in the 1960s.

In southern England the trackbed of the Longmoor Military Railway (closed in 1969) through woodland and across heathland between Liss and Longmoor is now a popular footpath and cycleway. At the other end of the scale is the fascinating Parkland Walk between Finsbury Park and Alexandra Palace in North London – reopened as a footpath in 1984, this route is an oasis of calm amidst suburbia as it wends its way up through wooded cuttings to Highgate and Muswell Hill before ending at the glorious Victorian pile of 'Ally Pally'.

Across in Eastern England part of the long-defunct Midland & Great Northern Joint Railway can be walked and cycled along what is now known as Marriott's Way, between Norwich and Aysham. Further north the wide open spaces of Lincolnshire can be enjoyed as the Water Rail Way makes its way alongside the Witham Navigation between Lincoln and Boston.

Ranging from the Forest of Dean to the Derbyshire Dales, Central England has much to offer explorers of hidden railways. The highpoint must be the Monsal Trail

Undisturbed for years, the railway track lies hidden in the undergrowth alongside the Colliers Way between the outskirts of Radstock and Great Elm, near Frome.

as it makes its way across viaducts and through tunnels between Topley Pike and Bakewell in the Peak District National Park, while to the east the National Cycle Network now makes use of the substantial half-mile-long Fledborough Viaduct, which formerly carried the Chesterfield to Lincoln line over the River Trent.

Wales is no exception as it suffered greatly from railway closures in both the pre- and post-Beeching eras. The London & North Western Railway's Heads of the Valleys route between Llanfoist, near Abergavenny, and Brynmawr is especially dramatic as it clings to the slopes of the Clydach Gorge in a region rich in industrial archaeology. Equally dramatic is the Mawddach Trail, which crosses Barmouth Bridge before following the shoreline of the stunningly beautiful Mawddach Estuary to Penmaenpool and Dolgellau – apparently I travelled on this route while on a holiday to Barmouth in 1948 but unfortunately I have no recollection!

On the Isle of Man no fewer than three of the former 3-ft-gauge railway routes are now designated footpaths, affording a peaceful way of exploring this beautiful island. Over on the mainland the former electrified coal-carrying main line railway between Manchester and Sheffield now forms part of the Trans-Pennine Trail between Hadfield and Wortley, although a diversion is necessary around the famed 3-mile-long Woodhead Tunnels. Over in East Yorkshire the winding coast-hugging railway between Scarborough and Whitby is now a highly popular footpath and cycleway that ends at the dramatic Larpool Viaduct.

Finally to Scotland, which has suffered its fair share of railway closures, although the Far North lines to Kyle of Lochalsh, Wick and Thurso were fortunately reprieved from Beeching's recommendations for closure. Of particular note is the Formartine & Buchan Way, which follows the route of the Dyce (north of Aberdeen) to Peterhead and Fraserburgh railway route. Serving two important fishing ports, much of the infrastructure is intact along this 54-mile footpath and cycleway, making it an excellent candidate for possible reopening in the future. Finally, our journey of exploration ends in the Highlands where the Dava Way, once part of the Highland Railway's main line, crosses remote Dava Moor on its 22½-mile route between Forres and Grantown-on-Spey.

So put your walking boots (or cycle clips) on, pack some refreshments and an Ordnance Survey map into your rucksack and go forth and discover the delights of *Britain's Hidden Railways*.

Key to maps

▬▬▬	Route open as footpath/cycleway
▬▬▬	Route now inaccessible
───	Railway line open (selected only)
- - - -	Nearby heritage railway of interest
═══	Footpath/cycleway alongside open railway
▬ ▬ ▬	Footpath/cycleway alongside heritage railway
○	Station open
●	Station closed

Most of the historical maps in this book come from Bartholomew's Half-Inch Series from the early 1960s. Due to the age of the source material, quality is variable.

SOUTHWEST ENGLAND
and the
CHANNEL ISLANDS

Jersey Railway

St Helier to La Corbière

Open to passengers 1870–1936 | **Original length** 7¾ miles
Original route operator Jersey Railway
Length currently open for walkers & cyclists 7¾ miles

The Jersey Railway had an eventful life, first being opened in 1870 as a standard-gauge line then being converted to 3-ft-6-in-gauge and merging with an unfinished industrial line of the same gauge in 1884. After a succession of owners and bankruptcy the railway went on to achieve some success by operating an intensive service for tourists in the early 1920s. Serving no less than seventeen stations along its 7¾-mile route, it finally succumbed to competition from motor buses and cars and closed in 1936. It was resurrected as a metre-gauge line during the German Occupation of the Second World War to transport sand and stone used in the building of fortifications but was dismantled in 1945. Today the entire length of the railway can be followed on foot or cycle along the southern seafront and coastline from St Helier to La Corbière.

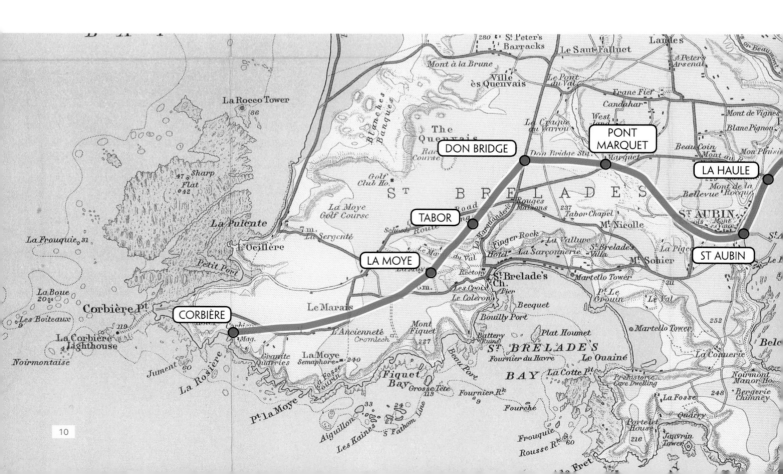

The Jersey Railway was one of two public railways on the Channel Island of Jersey – the other was the 6¾-mile standard-gauge Jersey Eastern Railway, which ran from St Helier (Snow Hill) to Gorey from 1873 until 1929. The Jersey Railway eventually extended to a length of 7¾ miles and had an extremely chequered career.

It originally opened as a standard-gauge (4 ft 8½ in) line between the capital St Helier (Weighbridge) and St Aubin in 1870 but was not successful and the company was declared bankrupt in 1874. However it continued to operate under several other owners until 1883. In the meantime, construction started on the 3-ft-6-in-gauge St Aubin & La Moye Railway, which was built to transport stone from a quarry at the southwestern end of the island. Before it was even completed or started operating this railway company was declared bankrupt in 1878.

Then in 1883 a new company was formed and the Jersey Railway amalgamated with the St Aubin & La Moye Railway – the former was then converted to 3-ft-6-in-gauge and the latter extended to La Corbière. The railway opened in March 1884 but ran as two separate sections until the two lines were connected through a short tunnel at St Aubin, with the first through trains running in August 1885. In its final form the single-track line served fifteen intermediate stations of which three, Millbrook, St Aubin and Don Bridge, had passing places. The terminus

at St Helier (Weighbridge) and the former terminus at St Aubin were grand buildings with overall glass roofs, while the impressive workshops were located at the former station. Between St Helier and St Aubin the line ran along the seafront but after the latter station it turned inland through a tunnel and then climbed steeply to the summit near Don Bridge before heading downhill to La Corbière.

The five steam locomotives built on the mainland for the original standard-gauge line were all sold when the line was relaid in 1884, finding new homes as far apart as the Tunis Railway and the Weston, Clevedon & Portishead Railway.

Financial problems continued for the new railway and in 1895 it entered voluntary liquidation. The following year a new company was formed – the Jersey Railways & Tramways Company – which took over the ailing business and, helped by the growing number of tourists visiting Jersey, was reasonably successful in keeping the railway operating until 1914. However, with the storm clouds of the First World War enveloping Europe, traffic on the

PREVIOUS SPREAD: The Camel Trail between Padstow, Wadebridge, Bodmin and Wenford Bridge in Cornwall is a highly popular level and traffic-free route for both walkers and cyclists (see pages 14–19). Here a group of cyclists are crossing the three-span girder bridge over Little Petherick Creek, 1 mile from Padstow.

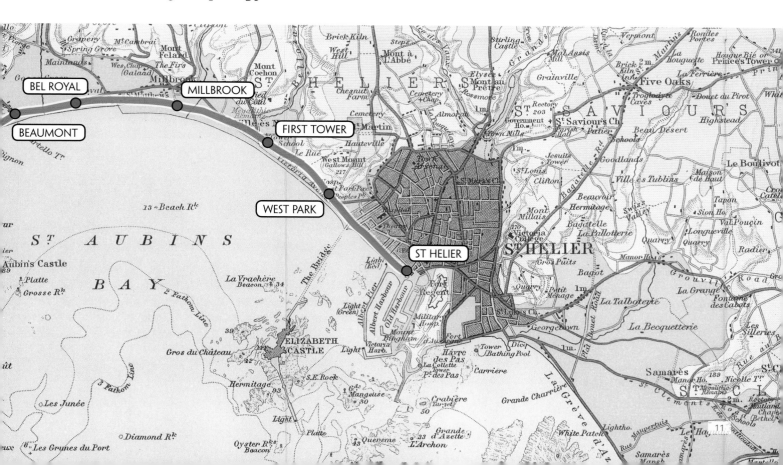

little line declined rapidly. After the war economies were made in operating costs by introducing steam railcars – between 1923 and 1925 four of these Sentinel-built vehicles were introduced on the line, with some success. They helped revitalise the line, which carried just over one million passengers in 1925, but more clouds were already appearing in the shape of motor cars and buses. By 1932 the winter service had been suspended and then, in October 1936, a fire broke out at St Aubin's station consuming the roof and most of the railway's passenger carriages, which had been stored there. The line never reopened, the track was soon lifted and the remaining locomotives and railcars scrapped. The entire trackbed was bought by the States of Jersey and the Jersey Railway was confined to the dustbin of history . . . or was it?

On 1 July 1940 the island was occupied by invading German forces and much of the route of the Jersey Railway was relaid to transport sand and stone for the construction of massive fortifications that were part of Hitler's 'Atlantic Wall'. The metre-gauge railway eventually extended from St Helier to Corbière with several branch lines, one of which extended northwards for six miles to Ronez Quarry. Jersey was liberated in May 1945 and the railway track soon lifted.

The pre-war purchase of the trackbed by the States of Jersey fortunately saved the route and it is now possible to cycle or walk along its entirety between St Helier and La Corbière, taking in dramatic views of the coastline along the way. Between St Helier (located in Liberation Square) and St Aubin the route follows the seafront promenade and at both of these former stations the station buildings have fortunately been preserved while the intermediate station at Millbrook is now a café. Beyond St Aubin the trackbed – known locally as the 'Railway Walk' – climbs inland where the tunnel (now used as a shop), bridges, embankments and cuttings still survive before emerging at the site of Don Bridge station. From here it heads downhill to La Corbière where the station building and platform survive as a private residence (complete with modern glass extension). Beyond are magnificent views of the rugged and often treacherous coastline and La Corbière lighthouse – completed in 1874, the latter was the first to be built in concrete in the British Isles and can be reached on foot at low tide. Nearby are the massive German fortifications, a megalith and a striking sculpture by Derek Tristram commemorating a recent sea rescue.

Pallot Heritage Steam Museum

Amechanical heritage museum located on Rue de Bechet, Trinity, Jersey. A former private collection of farm machinery, road vehicles, vintage bicycles, musical instruments and steam locomotives that is now open to the public. Included in the exhibits is a standard-gauge railway that runs round the site. Trains are hauled by a diminutive 0-4-0 saddle tank hauling restored North London Railway railway carriages dating from the 19th century. Open from early April to the end of October.

OPPOSITE: The former terminus station at St Aubin now houses the St Brelade parish hall.

LEFT: Between St Aubin and La Corbière the old Jersey Railway route is known as the Railway Walk. Here a road overbridge has survived on the climb out of St Aubin.

BELOW: Edwardian employees of the Jersey Railway pose for a photographer in front of a 2nd Class carriage next to the running shed at St Helier (Weighbridge) terminus.

Camel Trail

Padstow to Bodmin and Wenford Bridge

Open to passengers 1899–1967 | **Original length** 18 miles
Original route operator London & South Western Railway
Length currently open for walkers & cyclists 17½ miles | **NCN** 3 & 32

Padstow, the most westerly destination of the London & South Western
Railway's far-flung empire, had to wait until 1899 before a railway arrived.
In its relatively short life the railway opened up markets for local fishermen
and was responsible for Padstow's growth from a sleepy fishing village to a
thriving holiday destination. From 1927 until its demise in 1964 Padstow
was also the final destination of the famed 'Atlantic Coast Express' from
London Waterloo. Since closure in 1967 the railway route has been reborn
as a popular multi-user trail that runs alongside the Camel Estuary
to Wadebridge and thence to Bodmin and Wenford Bridge.

The first railway to operate steam locomotives in Cornwall was the standard-gauge Bodmin & Wadebridge Railway. It opened in 1834 and ran from a quay on the River Camel at Wadebridge to Wenford Bridge with a branch to Bodmin. The railway carried sea sand for agricultural use up to Wenford Bridge and granite in the opposite direction but passenger traffic (the railway only owned one carriage) between Bodmin and Wadebridge was of minor importance. Seeking to gain access into Cornwall, the London & South Western Railway (LSWR) purchased the railway in 1847 but it remained isolated from the growing national network for another forty-one years. Finally, in 1888, it was connected to the Great Western Railway's branch from Bodmin Road via a spur from Boscarne Junction to the Great Western Railway station at Bodmin General.

The LSWR, however, did not reach Wadebridge via its long and roundabout route from Halwill Junction and Launceston until 1895. Now with a direct connection to Waterloo station in London it served a sparsely populated rural region of West Devon and North Cornwall carrying seasonal holiday traffic, livestock, agricultural produce and slate from Delabole Quarry. Nowhere along this route did the railway reach the coast – Port Isaac Road station was 3 miles from the fishing village it purported to serve! Finally, in 1899, the LSWR opened the 5¾-mile single-track line from Wadebridge, alongside the River Camel Estuary, to the fishing village of Padstow. Before long through trains were running from Waterloo along what became known rather unkindly as the 'Withered Arm', so named because of its shape on the route map of the LSWR.

The coming of the railway transformed sleepy Padstow – it became a popular holiday destination and for the first time fishermen could transport their catches to London's markets by rail overnight. The introduction of the multi-portioned 'Atlantic Coast Express' (ACE) in 1927 from Waterloo was the crowning glory even though nearly half the journey west of Exeter was made at slow

LEFT: Ex-LSWR 2-4-0WT Class 0298 No. 30585 crosses the A389 at Dunmere Junction with the 1.20 pm goods train from Wenford Bridge on 19 August 1954. Built in 1874 and withdrawn in 1962, this veteran locomotive is now preserved.

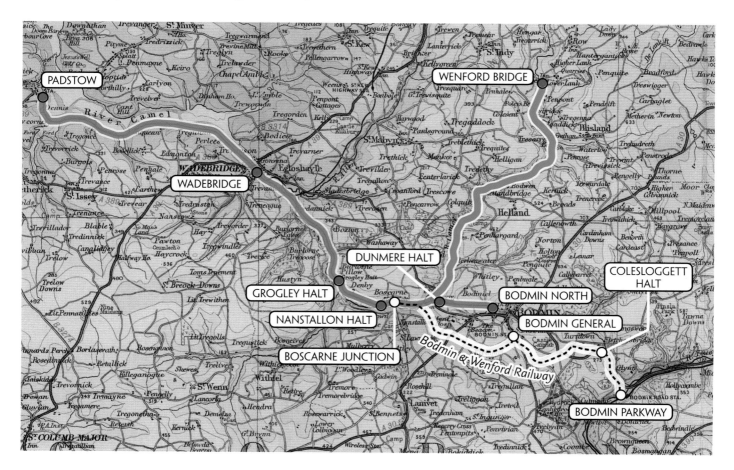

speeds along sleepy country railway byways – it last ran in September 1964 and even then the 259¾-mile journey to Padstow behind Oliver Bulleid's air-smoothed 'Pacifics' took six hours.

In the meantime, china clay had been transported from Wenford Bridge down to Wadebridge by veteran Beattie 2-4-0 well tanks since 1895. Because of the short wheelbase of these locos, built in the 1870s, and the sharp curves on the branch they remained in service until 1962, being replaced by ex-GWR Class 1366 dock tanks until diesel shunters took over this work.

By the 1960s the writing was on the wall for the railways of North Cornwall. The year 1963 not only brought the publication of the Beeching Report, in which all lines serving the area were recommended for closure, but it also saw the transfer of control of these lines away from the Southern Region to the Western Region of British Railways. Soon all vestiges of its illustrious past owners – the LSWR and its successor the Southern Railway – were erased. The through trains from Waterloo including the 'ACE', the goods services, the locomotives and rolling stock and most of the railway staff, were made redundant. They were replaced by basic diesel multiple units and the line from Okehampton via Halwill Junction, Launceston and Wadebridge to Padstow was on the railway version of death row – and there was to be no last-minute reprieve. First to go was the long and winding Okehampton to Wadebridge section, which closed completely on 3 October 1966, while the surviving service from Padstow to Bodmin Road via Wadebridge and Bodmin North went on 30 January 1967.

Freight trains continued to operate to Wadebridge until 1978, while the china clay trains from Wenford Bridge to Bodmin Road via Boscarne Junction and Bodmin, now in the charge of 0-6-0 diesel shunters, soldiered on until 31 October 1983 when they ceased.

Since closure the trackbed of the railway from Padstow to Bodmin and Wenford Bridge via Wadebridge has been reborn as a level multi-purpose trail known as the Camel Trail – so named after the river and estuary that it runs alongside. Purchased by Cornwall County Council for £1, it has been a huge success, attracting around 400,000 walkers, cyclists and disabled users annually and generating an income for the local tourist industry estimated at £3 million per year. Cycle hire shops are provided at Padstow, Wadebridge, Bodmin and Wenford

LEFT: Restored Dunmere Halt can be seen on the Camel Trail to the west of Bodmin.

BELOW: Another view of ex-LSWR 2-4-0WRT Class 0298 No. 30585 hauling a freight train on the Wenford Bridge branch in the early 1960s.

Bridge, while car parking is available at Padstow, Wadebridge, Hellandbridge and Poley's Bridge. The Trail is managed and maintained by Cornwall County Council with bike hire shops paying a fee to help fund the latter, and its entire 17½-mile length is traffic-free apart from a short section which is shared with road users in the centre of Wadebridge.

The scenery is particularly enjoyable as the Trail skirts the wonderful Camel Estuary for 5 miles before reaching Wadebridge. From here onwards there is a change of scenery as the Trail winds up the narrowing river valley to Boscarne Junction, which is served nowadays by the Bodmin & Wenford Railway (see box on page 19) during the summer months. Beyond here the Trail splits, with the shorter section ending at the site of Bodmin North station and the other section delightfully winding up to Wenford Bridge through Dunmere and Pencarrow Woods.

There are also many buildings and structures that are of interest to lovers of closed railways along the Camel Trail. In Padstow itself the station building and platform survive in the midst of the car park while 1 mile further on stands the impressive three-span girder bridge over

Little Petherick Creek, the only major engineering structure on the route. In Wadebridge the station building and canopy have been restored and named the Betjeman Centre in honour of the poet laureate Sir John Betjeman who loved to travel on this line before its closure. Beyond Wadebridge stand Shooting Range Platform, Grogley Halt and Nanstallon Halt, where the platforms still survive in various states of repair. Close to the site of Boscarne Exchange platform is a simple station known as Boscarne Junction that is served by the Bodmin & Wenford Railway, with trains to and from Bodmin General during the summer months. Beyond here the Trail branches off to Dunmere Halt where the platform survives in good condition before ending at the site of Bodmin North station, where all traces of the railway have long gone. Returning to Boscarne Junction the other part of the Trail heads off through the woods to the hamlet of Wenford Bridge but as this was a freight-only line there were no stations on this section. The appropriately named Snails Pace Café provides refreshments and cycle hire at this end of the Trail.

LEFT: Ex-GWR Class 4500 2-6-2T No. 4552 awaits departure from Wadebridge with a train for Bodmin on 3 September 1960. Built in 1915, this locomotive was withdrawn in 1961 and cut-up at Swindon Works.

BELOW: Fortunately preserved, the three-arch girder bridge over Little Petherick Creek lies on the Camel Trail, 1 mile from Padstow.

Bodmin & Wenford Railway

A steam heritage railway that has operated from Bodmin Parkway (for the national rail network and formerly named Bodmin Road) to Bodmin General since 1990. Trains also operate to Boscarne Junction (for the Camel Trail) in the summer months. The line was opened by the Great Western Railway in 1888 but was closed to passengers in 1967. Freight services continued until 1983 when the line closed. Operates from Easter to the end of October and during the Christmas period.

Tarka Trail
Barnstaple to Meeth

Open to passengers 1848/1925–1965 | **Original length** 24¾ miles
Original route operators Taw Vale Railway/Bideford Extension Railway/
London & South Western Railway/North Devon & Cornwall Junction Light Railway
Length currently open for walkers & cyclists 24¾ miles | **NCN** 27

What started life in 1848 as a short freight-only horse-drawn tramway along the south shore of the Taw Estuary eventually ended up seventy-seven years later as a 35-mile standard-gauge railway serving the small towns, villages and scattered farming communities of North Devon. During its life it was in part converted from broad- to standard-gauge and in part converted from 3-ft-gauge to a standard-gauge light railway. After losing its passenger service in 1965 the route soldiered on carrying milk until 1978 and clay until complete closure in 1982. Since then it has reopened as a level, traffic-free, footpath and cycleway known as the Tarka Trail.

FREMINGTON

BARNSTAPLE JUNCTION

INSTOW

BIDEFORD

TORRINGTON

WATERGATE HALT

YARDE HALT

DUNSBEAR HALT

PETROCKSTOW

MEETH HALT

21

The first railway to open in North Devon was the Taw Valley Railway, a horse-drawn tramway that operated between Barnstaple and Fremington Quay. Opening in 1848, its sole purpose was to carry freight but soon the merchants of Bideford were clamouring for it to be extended to their town. Although a start was made on this, it was soon suspended due to lack of finance following the period known as 'Railway Mania'. Eventually the Bideford Extension Railway (BER) was built, initially as a broad-gauge line (7 ft 0¼ in) and passengers were able to travel from Barnstaple to Bideford for the first time in 1855 – the line was worked by the North Devon Railway (NDR), which had opened from Crediton (reached from Exeter in 1851) to Barnstaple a year earlier.

Both the NDR and the BER were converted to mixed gauge (standard and broad) in 1863 and absorbed by the London & South Western Railway (LSWR) in 1865. In 1872 the LSWR extended the Bideford line to Torrington and by 1877 the last of the broad-gauge track had been removed.

A 3-ft narrow-gauge railway opened between Torrington and Marland (Clay Moor) in 1880, primarily to transport ball clay from quarries but it was also used to occasionally carry passengers. At Torrington the clay was trans-shipped

onto standard-gauge wagons, which then went to Fremington Quay where it was loaded onto ships. The line had a life of forty-five years and was then converted to a standard-gauge light railway by Colonel H. F. Stephens, the owner of many light railways in England and Wales. It was extended to Halwill Junction where it met the Southern Railway's (SR) lines to Bude and Padstow and opened throughout in 1925. Although worked by the SR, the North Devon and Cornwall Junction Light Railway, as it was known, remained an independent company until nationalization of the railways in 1948. As a light railway it was restricted to a maximum speed of 20 mph between Torrington and Dunsbear Halt and 25 mph from there to Halwill Junction.

Freight provided much of the traffic on this route with the transport of clay from Marland and milk from a creamery at Torrington lasting well beyond the end of passenger services. There were no through passenger trains between Barnstaple and Halwill Junction – passengers had to change trains at Torrington and they ran as mixed (passenger and freight) along the light railway section, taking about 1 hr 30 minutes for the 20-mile journey! Torrington even had through coaches

from London Waterloo that were conveyed with the Ilfracombe section of the 'Atlantic Coast Express', until its demise in 1964.

Apart from the Exeter to Barnstaple route all remaining railways in North Devon were recommended for closure in the Beeching Report (1963). On 1 March 1965 passenger services between Torrington and Halwill Junction ceased

with the Barnstaple to Torrington line losing its passenger trains on 4 October of that year. The milk trains from Torrington ended in 1978 although clay traffic from Marland continued until 1982, after which the track was lifted and the route was slowly overtaken by nature.

Today the former railway route between Barnstaple and Meeth forms part of the Tarka Trail, a 180-mile network of footpaths and cycle paths centred on Barnstaple, and the Devon Coast to Coast Cycle Route. It also includes the section from Barnstaple to Braunton on the former Ilfracombe line. Between 1986 and 1989 the Barnstaple to Meeth section with its numerous bridges was purchased by Devon County Council before being converted into a well-surfaced trail suitable for walkers, cyclists and in some places for horse riders. The section from Barnstaple to Bideford opened in 1991 and the entire route to Meeth in 1997. It has proved very popular with locals and visitors alike ever since.

PREVIOUS SPREAD: Set amidst unspoilt Devon countryside, the Tarka Trail crosses the River Torridge on this curving railway bridge near Torrington.

LEFT: Ivatt Class 2 2-6-2T No. 41298 approaches Watergate Halt with the 10.38 am Halwill Junction to Torrington mixed train on 28 September 1956.

BELOW: Ivatt Class 2 2-6-2T No. 41248 on shunting duties at Torrington on 10 June 1964 while a train departs for Barnstaple Junction.

The section from Barnstaple to Instow follows the south shore of the Taw Estuary and thence along the wooded valley of the River Torridge to Torrington before meandering through the peaceful, bucolic countryside of North Devon to Meeth. There are also plenty of car parks, cycle hire shops and cafés located strategically between Barnstaple and Torrington.

There is much of interest to lovers of old railways along this traffic-free route. In addition to the many bridges (and even a short tunnel at Instow) most of the stations, platforms and infrastructure have also survived. Travelling in a southerly direction from Barnstaple: Fremington station at Fremington Quay is a cycle hire shop and café; Instow station has a restored signal box, level crossing gates and platform; Bideford station has a

short length of track, signal box and café in an old British Railways coach; bridge over the Torridge at Pillmouth; stone arched bridge over the river just north of Torrington; Torrington station (now a pub), platforms, track and goods shed, now a cycle hire shop. South of here the small halts and platforms at Watergate, Dunsbear and Meeth have all survived.

TOP LEFT: The platform of Watergate Halt can be seen alongside the Tarka Trail, to the south of Torrington.

BOTTOM LEFT: All that seems to be missing at Instow is a train! Today the restored level crossing gates, signal, signal box and platform can be seen along the Tarka Trail at this delightful location close to the sea.

BELOW: The remains of a concrete lineside milepost is a lucky survivor alongside the coastal stretch of the Tarka Trail between Instow and Fremington.

Lynton & Barnstaple Railway

Financially backed by the publisher Sir George Newnes, this narrow-gauge railway opened between Barnstaple Town station and Lynton in 1898. It was built to a gauge of 1 ft 11½ in and featured stations built in a Swiss-chalet style and the 70 ft-high Chelfham Viaduct. It was modernized by its new owners, the Southern Railway, from 1923 but was closed in 1935. Today a 1-mile section of the line between Woody Bay station and Killington Lane is once again open for business. The owners, the Lynton & Banstaple Railway Trust, have ambitious plans to extend it southwards to Blackmoor Gate station and Chelfham and northwards to Lynton. Open most weekends and daily from April to October.

Princetown Branch

Yelverton to Princetown

Open to passengers 1826/83–1956 | **Original length** 10½ miles
Original route operator Plymouth & Dartmoor Railway/Great Western Railway
Length currently open for walkers & cyclists 9 miles

Built along the route of an early horse-operated tramway, the standard-gauge Dartmoor Railway opened in 1883. Serving granite quarries on Dartmoor it climbed up from Yelverton and meandered around the tors to remote Princetown, the highest standard-gauge station in England and home to the notorious Dartmoor Prison. Traffic was never heavy although it was popular with Dartmoor walkers during the summer months. Closure came in 1956 and today much of the route of this remote railway can be walked, on a clear day affording fine, far-reaching views across Dartmoor.

Quarrying for granite on remote Dartmoor and transporting it down to Plymouth for onward shipment was a labour intensive operation. In 1823 the Plymouth & Dartmoor Railway, a 4-ft-6-in-gauge horse-powered tramway, opened between Crabtree, on the River Plym north of Plymouth, and King's Tor Quarry, to the west of Princetown. It was extended southward from Crabtree to Sutton Pool in Plymouth through Leigham Tunnel in 1825 and into Princetown in 1826. The tramway never carried passengers.

Meanwhile, bleak Dartmoor Prison at Princetown had already opened in 1809. Built to house French prisoners of war and later American prisoners of war taken in the War of 1812, it had served its purpose by 1815 and lay empty for thirty-five years until it was reopened as a convict prison in 1850.

The broad-gauge South Devon Railway (SDR) opened its branch line from Plymouth up to Tavistock via Yelverton in 1859. This heavily engineered single-track line wound its way up and across several river valleys and also skirted around the western edge of Dartmoor. A branch from Yelverton to serve the quarries and prison at Princetown was proposed at this time and again in 1874 but neither plan materialized. In 1876 the SDR was absorbed by the Great Western Railway (GWR) and it soon set about obtaining powers to build the branch line through a nominally independent company, the Princetown Railway.

In part the GWR's 10½-mile standard-gauge branch line between Yelverton and Princetown was built along the route of the Plymouth & Dartmoor Railway. With initially only one intermediate station at Dousland, it opened on 11 August 1883 but until Yelverton station was opened two years later trains from Princetown had to continue along the 'main line' to Horrabridge. The line snaked its way up the bleak slopes of Dartmoor around Ingra Tor and King's Tor to end at Princetown terminus; at 1,373 feet above sea level it was the highest standard-gauge station in England.

LEFT: Affording distant views across Dartmoor, the footpath along the course of the old Princetown branch line winds its lonely way up and around Ingra Tor and King's Tor.

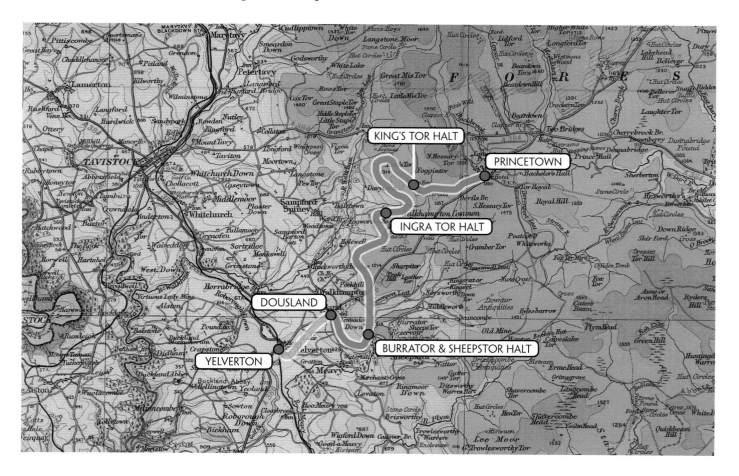

Worked from its opening by the GWR, traffic on the line was never heavy and consisted of five–six passenger trains a day from Mondays–Saturdays. Some trains ran as 'mixed' and these usually consisted of one passenger coach and a few goods wagons. Three simple wooden halts were opened in later years: Burrator & Sheepstor Platform in 1924 for workmen building a nearby reservoir; King's Tor Halt in the same year for local quarry workers; and Ingra Tor Halt in 1936, which was also for quarry workers. The Princetown Railway Company was absorbed by the GWR in 1922 and it passed to the new state-owned British Railways in 1948. Although popular with walkers during the summer months, traffic was dwindling and closure was announced for September 1955. However, the line was reprieved but only for another six months with

closure taking place on 3 March 1956. So many people turned up to travel on the last day that two engines and six coaches were required to haul the last train. Within a year the track was ripped up and the Princetown branch had gone after only seventy-three years of service.

Today much of the route of the Princetown branch can be walked or cycled by mountain bike. Although fine and far-reaching views across Dartmoor can be had on a fine day, visibility can be drastically curtailed when the mist descends – all that is needed is the distant baying of the hounds to conjure up a scene from Arthur Conan Doyle's *Hound of the Baskervilles*!

The trackbed can be followed from Dousland, where the station building and station master's house survive as private residences, as it winds its way up through woodland

and past the car park for Burrator Reservoir. Apart from this access point and at Princetown there is very little contact with civilisation as the trackbed meanders up the slopes, around Ingra Tor and King's Tor and the disused granite quarries. The few granite bridges that remain *in situ* give clues to its railway past but nothing remains of the timber halts erected for quarry workers and walkers. The railway path ends at Princetown although nothing now remains of the station, goods shed and engine shed – the only clues to its railway past here are Station Road and the Railway Inn.

LEFT: High up on Dartmoor, GWR 4400 Class 2-6-2T No. 4403 carries out a spot of shunting at lonely Princetown station in the 1930s.

BELOW: Shrouded in mist and steam, ex-GWR Class 4500 2-6-2T No. 4568 pauses at remote Ingra Tor Halt on 1 March 1956 with the 9.04am train from Yelverton to Princetown – the line closed two days later.

South Devon Railway

Serving the southern edge of Dartmoor, the single-track broad-gauge branch line from Totnes to Ashburton opened in 1872. It was converted to standard-gauge and then absorbed by the GWR in 1897. It was closed to passengers in 1958 and to freight in 1962. Fortunately, the track was not lifted and the line was reopened by Lord Richard Beeching in 1969 as a heritage railway. Unfortunately, the building of the A38 dual carriageway effectively cut the line at Buckfastleigh where today's steam trains terminate. A footpath and bridge over the River Dart links the South Devon Railway's Littlehempston station with Totnes station on the national rail network. Open daily from April to October, selected weekends in February and March, and Christmas and New Year.

East Devon Branch Lines

Sidmouth to Budleigh Salterton and Exmouth

Open to passengers 1874/97/1903–1967 | **Original length** 19¾ miles
Original route operator London & South Western Railway
Length currently open for walkers & cyclists 4 miles | **NCN** 2

Opened between 1874 and 1903, the branch lines to East Devon's seaside resorts had a short life of less than 100 years. During their heyday they carried holidaymakers and day-trippers in their thousands but the post-war years brought dwindling patronage and ultimate closure. Today a 4-mile section of this railway is a popular footpath and cycleway through woodland and rolling Devon countryside.

The first railway to serve the fashionable seaside resort of Sidmouth was a purely local affair and had a very short life. Opening in 1836, this narrow-gauge line was built to aid the construction of a new harbour but the project soon faltered and the railway was closed.

The seaside resort of Exmouth was first reached from Exeter Queen Street (now Exeter Central) by the Exeter & Exmouth Railway along the east shore of the Exe Estuary in 1861. A few miles along the coast the people of Sidmouth had mixed feelings about having their own railway, with many being hostile as they feared the 'riff-raff' would descend on their genteel resort. Nevertheless the Sidmouth Railway received Parliamentary authorization in 1862 to build an 8¼-mile single-track branch line from Sidmouth Junction, on the London & South Western Railway's (LSWR) main line, along the valley of the River Otter to the resort. Progress was very

LEFT: Class 118 diesel multiple unit departs from Littleham station, midway between Exmouth and Budleigh Salterton, in 1960.

slow due to engineering and financial problems but the line finally opened in 1874. It was worked by the LSWR from the start although the Sidmouth Railway remained independent until 1923. Sidmouth station was located nearly 1 mile inland from the coast – some say that this was to deliberately deter day-trippers who would lower the tone of the resort but in reality it was almost certainly due to the geography of the town.

The next piece in this East Devon railway jigsaw came in 1897 when the Budleigh Salterton Railway (BSR) opened the 6½ miles between Tipton St John's, on the Sidmouth line, to Budleigh Salterton. The BSR was also worked by the LSWR from opening and was taken over by the latter in 1912.

The final piece in the jigsaw came as late as 1903 when the LSWR opened its 5-mile line from Exmouth to Budleigh Salterton and for the first time the company's trains could travel on a continuous coastal route between Exeter and Sidmouth Junction.

Once the coastal railway was complete a fairly healthy service of passenger trains was introduced. Trains normally

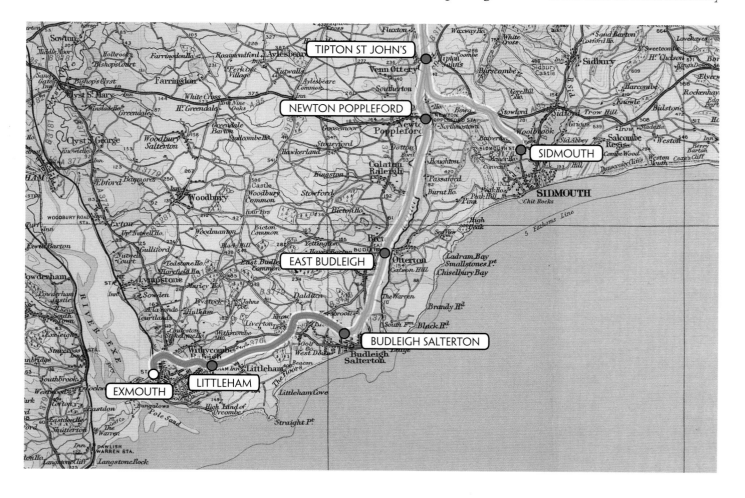

ran from Sidmouth Junction to Sidmouth via Tipton St John's, with a separate service operating from the latter station to Budleigh Salterton and Exmouth where passengers for Exeter had to change trains. Through coaches to Sidmouth and Exmouth from London Waterloo operated on summer Saturdays until 1964, while one of the most interesting workings of a summer Saturday through train from Cleethorpes via the Somerset & Dorset Joint Railway route had ended two years earlier.

However, falling traffic and receipts along with the failure to modernize led all the East Devon branch lines to be recommended for closure in the Beeching Report. In addition to the Exeter to Exmouth line, and the lines from Sidmouth Junction to Sidmouth and Exmouth, other branch lines threatened were Seaton Junction to Seaton, and Axminster to Lyme Regis. Eventually only the Exeter to Exmouth line was reprieved; the Lyme Regis branch closed on 29 November 1965; the Seaton branch closed on 7 March 1966; Sidmouth Junction to Sidmouth

and Exmouth on 6 March 1967. On the main line Sidmouth Junction station also closed but was reopened as Feniton in 1971.

Today there are still some remains of this old railway route. Sidmouth station is reasonably intact with part of the platform, station building and canopies having survived over fifty years since closure. At Tipton St John's the station building is a private residence, while on the Exmouth branch East Budleigh station and canopy is also part of a private residence.

BELOW: Prior to dieselization of this route Ivatt Class 2 2-6-2T No. 41296 arrives at Budleigh Salterton's well-kept station with a train bound for Exmouth.

RIGHT: Following the old railway route, the footpath and cycleway between Exmouth and Budleigh Salterton threads its way through tranquil wooded cuttings away from the hustle and bustle of nearby roads.

Between Budleigh Salterton and Exmouth the trackbed of the railway is now a footpath and cycleway designated as National Cycle Network Route 2. Opened in 1998 and encountering a few railway bridges and cuttings en route, the trail is an important wildlife corridor and pleasant cycle or walk through rolling Devon countryside and mainly deciduous woodland – the section between Bear Lane, northeast of Budleigh, and the roundabout at Knowle is particularly beautiful as the railway path loops round in a tranquil wooded cutting away from all the traffic on the nearby narrow roads. There are cafés at each end of the railway path and at Littleham. Car parks can be found in Exmouth and Budleigh Salterton. Cycle hire is available in Exmouth.

Seaton Tramway

The 4¼-mile branch line from Seaton Junction, on the LSWR's mainline, and the seaside resort of Seaton opened in 1868. After closure in 1966 it was reopened as a 2-ft-9-in-gauge electric tramway and currently operates from a Victorian-style terminus at Seaton then alongside the River Axe estuary to Colyford before completing the journey along the Coly Valley to Colyton. Passengers on this scenic route are carried in miniature replica double-deck electric trams.

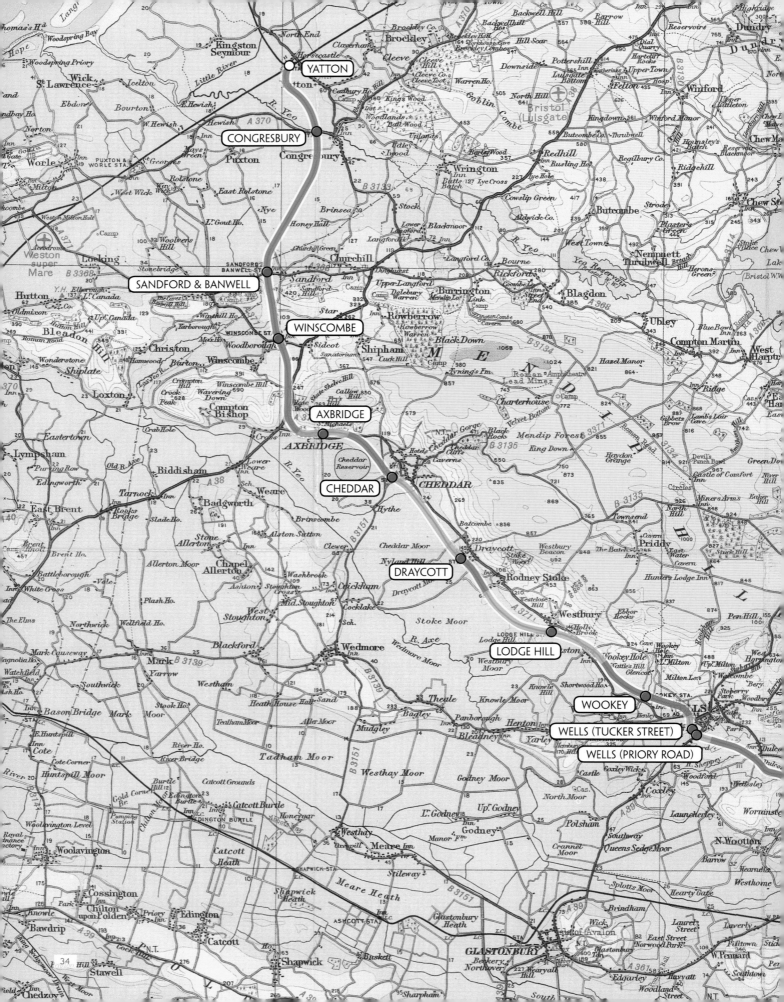

Strawberry Line

Yatton to Witham

Open to passengers 1858/75–1875 | **Original length** 31¾ miles
Original route operator Somerset Central Railway/East Somerset Railway/Cheddar Valley & Yatton Railway
Length currently open for walkers & cyclists 12½ miles | **NCN** 26

Although opened in stages between 1859 and 1870 the railway between
Yatton and Witham via Cheddar and Wells did not become a through route
until 1878 – in that year a little local problem in the latter city involving
running powers over a very short stretch of line was finally resolved.
Transporting milk and seasonal produce such as strawberries were the line's
lifeblood, thus giving it the affectionate nickname of the Strawberry Line.
Since closure to passengers in 1963 the western section of this route has
more recently been reopened as a footpath and cycleway, while the eastern
section is very much alive for stone traffic and a heritage railway.

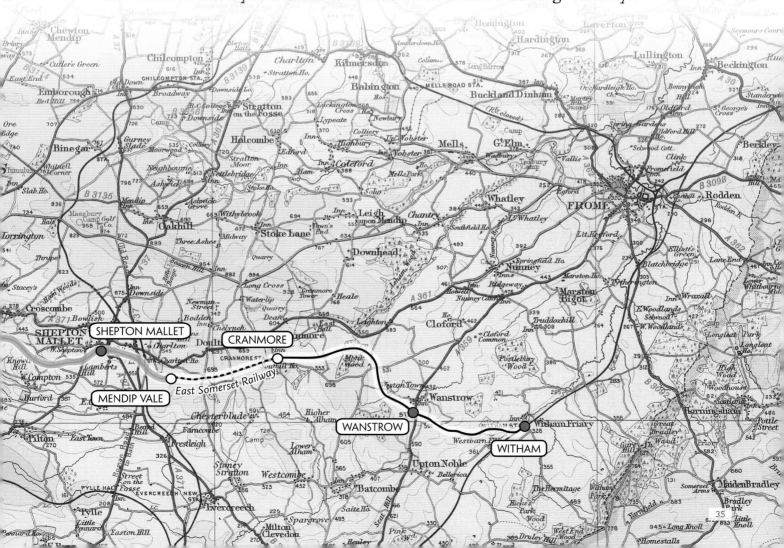

The first railway to serve the small Somerset city of Wells was the Somerset Central Railway's (SCR) 5½-mile line, initially broad-gauge, from Glastonbury, which opened in 1859. Its terminus in the city was at Priory Road. The SCR merged with the Dorset Central Railway in 1862 to form the Somerset & Dorset Railway (S&DR) and its track, including the Wells branch, was also relaid to standard-gauge.

Next on the scene in this part of Somerset was the broad-gauge East Somerset Railway (ESR), which opened throughout from Witham, on the Westbury to Castle Cary line, to Wells in 1862 – its terminus in Wells was just to the east of Priory Road. The next and penultimate stage of what eventually became a through route was the opening of the broad-gauge Cheddar Valley & Yatton Railway (CV&YR), which opened between Yatton, on the Bristol to Taunton main line, to Wells via Cheddar in 1870 – the terminus in Wells of this railway was at Tucker Street.

In 1874 the ESR was absorbed by the Great Western Railway (GWR) and its track converted to standard-gauge. The CV&YR had already been absorbed by the Bristol & Exeter Railway (B&ER) and was also converted to standard-gauge in 1875. A year later the B&ER was amalgamated with the GWR and so the entire route from Yatton to Witham was now owned by one company apart from a very short section (about 550 feet) in Wells, which was owned by the S&DR, thus making through running impossible. This highly unsatisfactory arrangement in Wells was partly resolved when the GWR obtained running powers over the short section and started running through trains in 1878 but that company's trains did not stop at Priory Road until 1934 – until that date passengers travelling, for example, from Cheddar to Glastonbury had to change stations in Wells.

The opening of the line along the Cheddar Valley soon brought day-trippers in their thousands to visit the

famous Cheddar Gorge, Cheddar Caves and nearby Wookey Hole, the latter reached from Wookey station near Wells. The transport of milk in churns and seasonal fruit and vegetables from wayside stations was the staple diet of the railway until its closure. Of note were the special trains laid on during the strawberry season that carried the fruit to distant markets overnight and which give the line its well-deserved nickname of the Strawberry Line.

The immediate years following the Second World War soon brought increased competition from cars, motor buses and lorries. The lifeblood was draining away and closures were soon to follow.

The first railway to disappear was the Glastonbury to Wells branch, which closed on 29 October 1951 and not many people mourned its passing. The Strawberry Line soldiered on but was recommended for closure in the infamous Beeching Report of 1963. The end came soon after as passenger trains were withdrawn from the entire Yatton to Witham line on 9 September of that year.

East Somerset Railway

Founded in 1973 by the artist David Shepherd, the East Somerset Railway currently operates steam trains along the former Yatton to Witham line for about 2½ miles from its headquarters at East Cranmore station to the eastern outskirts of Shepton Mallet. Open weekends from Easter/May to October, on Wednesdays from June to September, and during the Christmas period.

BELOW: A view of deserted Congresbury station on 8 July 1959. The station lost its passenger service on 9 September 1963 when the Yatton to Witham line became an early victim of Dr Beeching's 'axe'.

However, the line did not close entirely as freight traffic continued until 1969 after which it was closed completely west of Cranmore. The section from Witham to Cranmore remained open for bitumen trains until 1985 and for stone traffic from nearby Merehead Quarry, which continues to this day. At Cranmore the artist David Shepherd reopened the station as the headquarters of the newly formed East Somerset Railway in 1973.

Fortunately, much of the remaining route of the Yatton to Witham line has been reopened as a footpath and cycleway known as the Strawberry Line. This well-surfaced traffic-free route is currently composed of three separate sections but plans are afoot to join them up to make a 22-mile continuous route from Yatton to Shepton Mallet. The first and longest section of the Strawberry Line is from Yatton station, still open for business on the Bristol to Taunton line, to Cheddar, a distance of just under 10 miles. A separate 1½-mile section has been reopened between Draycott and Rodney Stoke, as has a 2-mile section from Haybridge to Dulcote via Wells.

There is still much railway infrastructure to see alongside the Strawberry Line between Yatton and Wells. Travelling eastwards from Yatton: traces of the platform at Congresbury (junction for the Wrington Vale Railway until 1931); Sandford & Banwell station has been beautifully restored as a heritage centre complete with track, wagons, a British Railways coach and 1940s Sentinel shunting locomotive; restored platform and brick 'station sculpture' at Winscombe station; Shute Shelve Tunnel, with its solar-powered reflectors; well-preserved Axbridge station building and goods shed (not on the trail but now alongside the busy Axbridge bypass); Cheddar station building (minus overall roof) now used by the stonemasons of Wells Cathedral; Draycott station building is now a private residence; Wells (Tucker Street) goods shed is now a commercial premises.

Sandford & Banwell station, which closed in 1963, has been incorporated into a sheltered housing complex known as Sandford Station Care Village. A short length of track with a 1940s Sentinel shunting locomotive, two goods wagons and a British Railways Mark 1 coach complete the railway scene. The restored station, accessed from the Strawberry Line footpath and National Cycle Route 26, is open for refreshments from April to October.

Somerset Central Railway

Evercreech Junction to Burnham-on-Sea

Open to passengers 1854–1966 | **Original length** 22½ miles
Original route operator Somerset Central Railway
Length currently open for walkers & cyclists 4½ miles

Opened between 1854 and 1862, the western half of this railway closely followed the course of the moribund Glastonbury Canal. The line was relegated to branch line status once the company's main line to Bath opened in 1874 and both were later to become part of the Somerset & Dorset Joint Railway. The railway's Locomotive, Carriage and Wagon Workshops at Highbridge were closed in 1930 with the branch lines to Wells, Burnham-on-Sea, and Bridgwater following in the early 1950s. Steam-worked until the end, the remaining railway soldiered on from Evercreech Junction to Highbridge but with ever-decreasing traffic closure was inevitable and it finally succumbed in 1966. Today the section from Glastonbury to Shapwick is a popular footpath and cycleway that bisects important nature reserves.

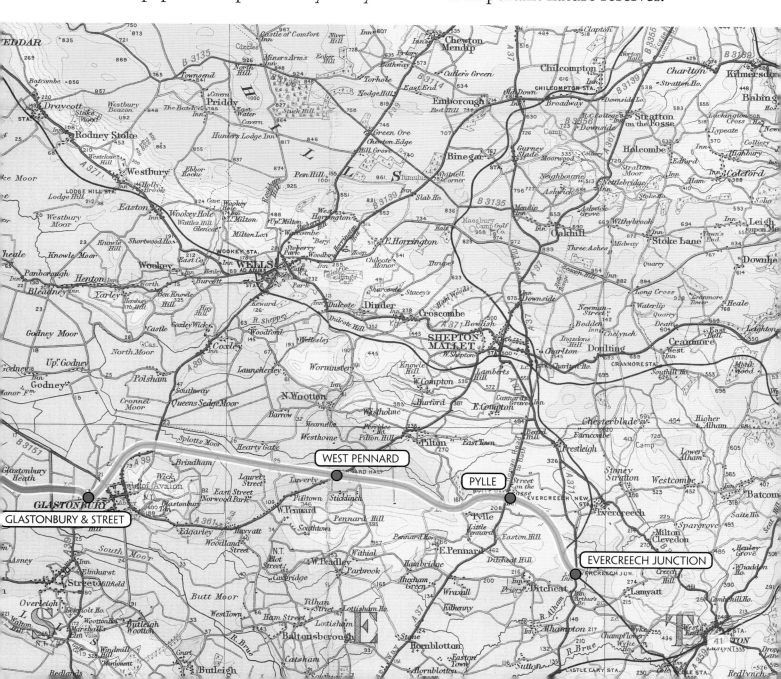

After the completion of broad-gauge Bristol & Exeter Railway via Highbridge in Somerset in 1844 the company sought to purchase a rival canal, the Glastonbury Canal, to stop it being used by other railway companies. Although the deal was completed in 1848 the canal was transferred into the ownership of the fledgling Somerset Central Railway (SCR), which was authorized to build a broad-gauge line from Highbridge and across the Somerset Levels to Glastonbury, a distance of 12 miles, in 1852. The new railway was built closely alongside the canal, in effect making the canal redundant. The canal closed on 1 July 1854 and the railway opened on 17 August.

With its headquarters in Glastonbury the railway company extended the line westwards by 1¾ miles from Highbridge to the coast at Burnham-on-Sea in 1858 and then followed this by opening a 5½-mile branch line to the small city of Wells in the following year. With a dream of linking the Bristol Channel to the English Channel in mind, the main line of the railway was extended from Glastonbury to Cole in 1862, where it met the standard-gauge Dorset Central Railway (DCR) – the latter was worked by the London & South Western Railway (LSWR). In the same year the SCR and the DCR amalgamated to form the Somerset & Dorset Railway (S&DR) and the former SCR routes were converted to standard-gauge.

In 1874 the S&DR opened its 26½-mile main line over the Mendip Hills from Evercreech Junction, south of Cole on the Highbridge line, to Bath (see pages 50–55) and the original main line to Highbridge was relegated to secondary status. The potential of the Channel-Channel through route was never realized, even though the company owned coastal ships that used the port at Burnham-on-Sea for a while. In 1890 the Bridgwater Railway opened a 7¼-mile line from Edington Junction, on the Highbridge branch, to Bridgwater, where it competed with the Great Western Railway for business at the riverside wharves. The line was worked from opening by the S&DR. The following year the Midland Railway (MR) and the LSWR completed their purchase of the S&DR to save it from financial disaster and thereafter it became known as the Somerset & Dorset Joint Railway.

The workshops of the railway were established at Highbridge but after joint ownership took place all locomotive building and heavy overhauls were carried out by the MR at Derby Works. Highbridge Works closed altogether in 1930 with the loss of about 300 jobs. After the opening of the Bath extension the Highbridge branch led a fairly sleepy existence that was occasionally punctuated by excursion traffic to Burnham-on-Sea on summer weekends. Outgoing goods traffic consisted of

The tranquil setting of the River Brue as viewed from the old railway girder bridge to the west of Glastonbury. The railway across the Somerset Levels between Highbridge and Glastonbury opened in 1854 and closed in 1966.

peat extracted by the Eclipse Peat Company from the extensive workings alongside the railway near Ashcott, milk in the form of churns from wayside stations and a creamery at Bason Bridge, and shoes from the Clarks Shoes factories in Street. Britain's railways were nationalized in 1948 and the newly-formed British Railways lost no time in closing loss-making branch lines. Of the S&DJR lines the first to close was the Glastonbury to Wells branch, which ceased operations on 29 October 1951. The short line to Burnham-on-Sea from Highbridge followed and was closed to passenger traffic on 29 October 1952, although it remained open for excursion trains until 8 September 1962 and to goods traffic until 20 May 1963. The Bridgwater branch fared no better and on 1 December 1952 it was closed, although access to the wharves on the River Parrett remained open for goods via the GWR line until 1967.

The whole of the remaining S&DJR network including the Highbridge branch was recommended for closure in the Beeching Report (1963). By now the railway was under the control of British Railways' Western Region and they were keen to rid themselves of this anachronism – most of the goods and passenger traffic on the Highbridge branch had been lost to road competition and passenger trains,

still steam-hauled, usually consisted of just one coach. In that year the poet laureate Sir John Betjeman made a memorable black-and-white documentary film about the line for the BBC's series *Branch Line Railway* in which he mourned not only the imminent passing of the railway but also the end of the livelihoods of the railway workers.

Closure was finally confirmed in 1965, with the date set for 3 January 1966. Railway lovers descended on the railway in their thousands to make a last pilgrimage but at the last minute a local replacement bus operator pulled out of the deal. For the next two months the railway remained open, but with a skeleton service of only two return trains on weekdays and Saturdays on the Highbridge branch. The end finally came on Monday 7 March 1966 – as there were no timetabled services on Sundays the last trains to run were steam-hauled specials that traversed the entire S&DJR network on the previous day. Track on the Highbridge branch was soon lifted apart from the section from Highbridge to Bason Bridge, which was kept open for milk traffic until the line was cut on 3 October 1972 by construction of the new M5 motorway.

Today there is still much to discover along the route of the Highbridge branch. At the site of Evercreech

Junction there is now an industrial estate although some of the station buildings have survived as residential homes. At the next station, which is Pylle, the goods shed has survived, as have the station buildings and goods shed at West Pennard. Part of the trackbed east of Glastonbury can still be discerned as it crosses farmland but on the town's outskirts it has been swallowed up by a bypass. In Glastonbury one of the station's canopies has found a new home in St John's car park, and a thoughtful person has erected a pair of replica level crossing gates close to the former station site. The station itself is no more but the original headquarters of the Somerset Central Railway has survived and is now the offices of a building supplies company.

Just west of Glastonbury a footpath and cycleway now follows the trackbed for much of the next 4½ miles alongside what is left of the moribund Glastonbury Canal. The flooded former peat workings in the Avalon Marshes along this stretch to Ashcott and Shapwick have been turned into nature reserves providing safe havens for some rare nesting birds – information points, hides, footpaths and car parks have been added by the Somerset Wildlife Trust and the RSPB. Refreshments are available at the appropriately named Railway Inn near to the site of Ashcott station. The footpath and cycleway then continues on to end at the site of Shapwick station.

On the Bridgwater branch the section of trackbed from Bawdrip to Cossington is now a footpath and cycleway, forming part of National Cycle Network Route 3.

West Somerset Railway

Opened as a broad-gauge line between Norton Fitzwarren and Watchet in 1862 and extended to Minehead in 1874. It was converted to standard-gauge in 1882 when it became part of the Great Western Railway. Listed for closure in the Beeching Report, the line was used as a location during the filming of the The Beatles' film *A Hard Day's Night* before being closed in 1971. The trackbed was purchased by Somerset County Council in 1973 and it was partially reopened as a steam heritage railway between 1976 and 1979. Although the line now extends to Norton Fitzwarren, where there is a turning triangle, normal services operate between Bishops Lydeard and Minehead. Open weekends and selected days in February, March and December; daily in April, May and October, apart from some Mondays and Fridays; and daily from June to September.

LEFT: 6 March 1966 – on the very last day before closure a special final train was run along the Somerset & Dorset Joint Railway by the Locomotive Club of Great Britain. With a slight sprinkling of snow on the ground, Ivatt Class 2 2-6-2Ts Nos 41307 and 41249 depart from Glastonbury for the last time.

BELOW: The scene today as the old railway trackbed, now a footpath and cycleway, closely follows the moribund Glastonbury Canal between Ashcott and Shapwick.

Colliers Way

Bristol to Frome via Radstock

Open to passengers 1854/73–1959 | **Original length** 24¼ miles
Original route operator Great Western Railway
Length currently open for walkers & cyclists 5¼ miles | **NCN** 24

Starting life as a colliery railway, the Bristol to Frome line was opened throughout in 1873. Its lifeblood was always coal, mined in the North Somerset coalfield, but the route also had a fairly regular passenger service until it was drastically cut in the late 1950s. Although closing to passengers in 1959, parts of the line continued to carry coal until the last colliery closed in 1973. Today the section from Radstock to Great Elm, on the western outskirts of Frome, is a footpath and cycleway that forms part of Colliers Way.

BRISTOL TEMPLE MEADS

BRISLINGTON

WHITCHURCH HALT

PENSFORD

CLUTTON

HALLATROW

FARRINGTON GURNEY HALT

MIDSOMER NORTON & WELTON

RADSTOCK WEST

MELLS ROAD

FROME

47

The 24¼-mile single-track railway across the Mendip Hills between Bristol and Frome was built in two distinct stages but in both cases was designed to tap into the coalfields of North Somerset. The first part to be built was an 8-mile broad-gauge colliery line from Frome to Radstock, which opened on 14 November 1854. At Frome there was a triangular junction with the Wilts, Somerset & Weymouth Railway.

The northern section of the steeply-graded route between Bristol and Radstock was built by the Bristol & North Somerset Railway (B&NSR), which was authorized in 1863. The company faced difficulties in raising capital at a time of dire national financial crisis and it took until 3 September 1873 before the standard-gauge line was open for business. The major engineering feature on the line was the sixteen-arch, 995-ft-long and 95-ft-high Pensford Viaduct over the Chew Valley, which had to be partially rebuilt even before the line was opened. Today this fine viaduct has survived as a Grade II listed structure.

The B&NSR was worked from the outset by the GWR and was absorbed by that company in 1884. At Radstock there was a break of gauge until June 1874 when the colliery line to Frome was converted to standard-gauge, allowing for the first time a direct passenger service between Bristol and Frome. Although primarily a coal-carrying line for the whole of its life, the railway also operated a reasonably frequent passenger service serving intermediate stations at Brislington, Whitchurch, Pensford, Clutton, Hallatrow, Farrington Gurney, Midsomer Norton & Welton, Radstock West, and Mells Road. In 1950 there were eight return journeys on weekdays and three on Sundays but by 1958, with improved local bus services luring customers away, the Sunday service had ceased to operate and the weekday service had been halved, although there were also several other Saturdays-only trains. This loss-making service was nearly at an end and closure to passengers came on 31 October 1959.

The GWR also opened a branch line from Hallatrow to serve collieries at Camerton and this was later extended to Limpley Stoke, on the Bath to Bradford-on-Avon line. Passenger services on this quaint rural backwater first ended in 1915 but were restored in 1923 only to finally cease in 1925. The final goods train from Limpley Stoke to Camerton ran on 14 February 1951 but the line came back to life in 1952 for the filming of the famous Ealing Studios' comedy *The Titfield Thunderbolt*. The track was finally lifted in 1958.

With the closure of many North Somerset collieries an ever-reducing number of coal trains continued to run between Radstock and Bristol until an embankment collapsed at Pensford on 11 July 1968. After that date coal traffic travelled via Frome following the reopening of the section between Radstock and Mells Road, which had been closed completely in 1966. Of course we must not forget the Somerset & Dorset Joint Railway, which crossed this route at Radstock where it served Radstock North station. Following the closure of the S&DJR on 7 March 1966 a short spur was opened between the two lines to serve Writhlington Colliery, which had previously been served by the S&DJR. This traffic lasted until 28 September 1973 and all coal traffic ceased in November 1973 following the closure of the last North Somerset pit at Kilmersdon.

Despite the end of the coal traffic the section from Frome to Radstock was kept open to serve a wagon repair facility in Radstock for several more years and in 1974 a new connection was built between Mells Road and Frome to serve ARC's enormous Whatley Quarry. Today Mendip Rail's US-built Class 59 diesels haul around 2.5 million tonnes of limestone each year from Whatley Quarry for distribution around Britain via

Frome North Junction and Clink Road Junction on the West of England Main Line.

Since closure much of the disused Radstock to Frome railway has been reopened as a footpath and cycleway, forming part of the Colliers Way, which starts at Dundas Aqueduct on the Kennet & Avon Canal near Limpley Stoke and meets the Two Tunnels Greenway (see pages 50–55) at Midford. From Midford the Colliers Way follows the course of the Somerset & Dorset Joint Railway to the outskirts of Wellow then reaches Radstock along a mixture of steep country lanes and the old railway route. Easily recognised by its pit head wheel, Radstock Museum tells the story of the North Somerset coalfields. Following the Colliers Way signs from here the level railway route to Frome is soon regained, continuing southwards to Kilmersdon, then past the site of Mells Road station to Great Elm. En route the disused track of the line remains *in situ*, lost in the undergrowth, while a series of etched and enamelled copperplate signs set into boulders highlight the planting of a linear orchard of Old English apples and pears. From Great Elm the Colliers Way leaves the railway route to avoid the working Whatley Quarry branch line and reaches Frome along country lanes.

Somerset & Dorset Railway Heritage Trust

The Somerset & Dorset Joint Railway closed on 7 March 1966. In more recent years the Trust has restored Midsomer Norton station and goods shed and built a replica signal box (the original was destroyed in a mystery fire when the line closed). About 2 miles of track has been relaid towards Chilcompton. Passenger trains operate under a Light Railway Order and are hauled by one of two operational diesel shunters. Open Sundays, also Mondays for viewing only.

PREVIOUS SPREAD: Surprisingly, the track has never been taken up along the section between Great Elm, near Frome, and the outskirts of Radstock. Here it can be seen under a road bridge not far from the village of Kilmersdon.

LEFT: The old railway line still lies hidden in the undergrowth alongside much of the Colliers Way between Great Elm and the outskirts of Radstock.

BELOW: A Class 120 diesel multiple unit carrying a group of railway enthusiasts visited Radstock West on 30 March 1968. The line was still open for coal traffic, which eventually ceased in 1973.

Somerset & Dorset Joint Railway

Bath Green Park to Templecombe

Open to passengers 1862/74–1966 | **Original length** 37 miles
Original route operators Dorset Central Railway/Somerset Central Railway/Somerset & Dorset Railway
Length currently open for walkers & cyclists 6 miles | **NCN** 244 & 24

Building its heavily-engineered 'Bath Extension' over the Mendip Hills in the 1870s left the Somerset & Dorset Railway virtually bankrupt. It was saved jointly by the Midland Railway and the London & South Western Railway in 1875 and the Somerset & Dorset Joint Railway was born.
Its lifeblood was through traffic between the Midlands and the North to destinations on the South Coast but withdrawal of these through services in 1962 inevitably led to its closure in 1966 – a notable victim of Dr Beeching's 'axe'. Mourned by its faithful railway workers and by railway lovers across the UK, the northerly section of the railway has more recently been reborn as a footpath and cycleway through Britain's longest walking and cycling tunnel.

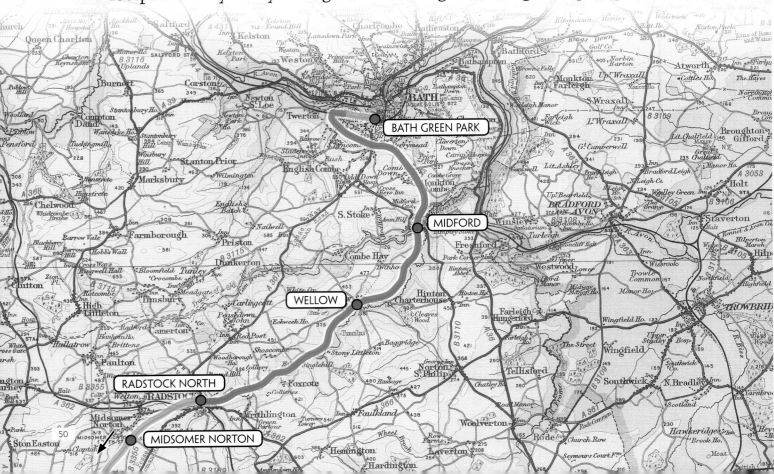

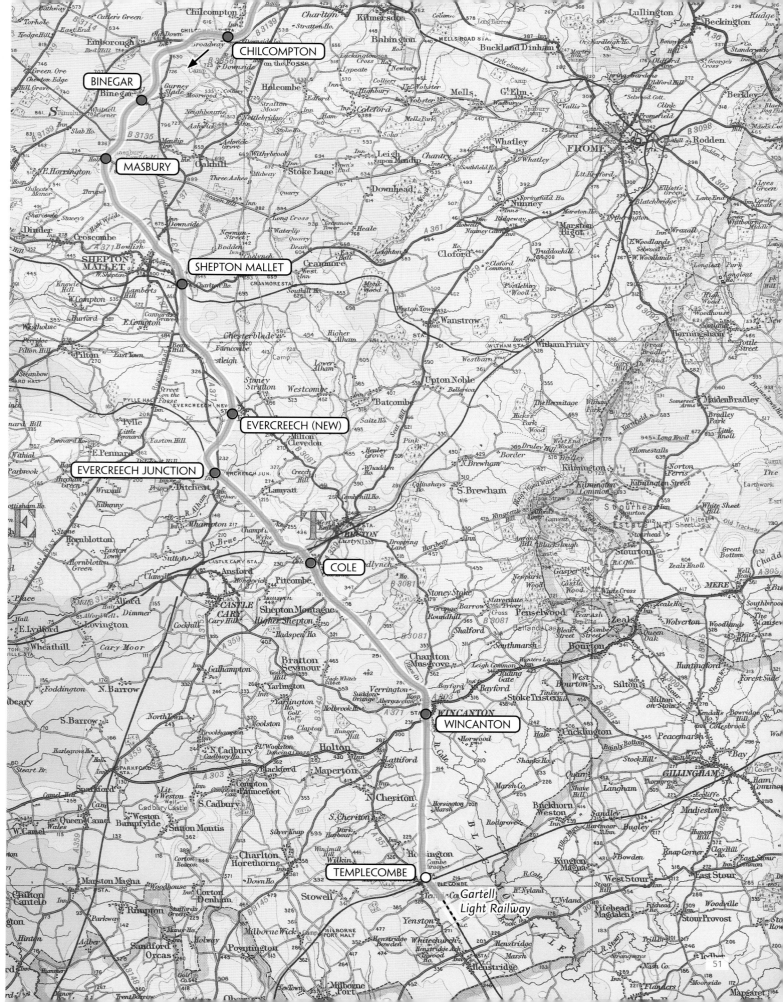

CHILCOMPTON

BINEGAR

MASBURY

SHEPTON MALLET

EVERCREECH (NEW)

EVERCREECH JUNCTION

COLE

WINCANTON

TEMPLECOMBE

Gartell Light Railway

51

As we have seen on pages 40–45, the Somerset & Dorset Railway (S&DR) was formed in 1862 by the merger of the Dorset Central Railway and the Somerset Central Railway. To the north the Midland Railway (MR) had reached Bath in 1869 along its 10-mile branch line from Mangotsfield, on that company's Bristol to Gloucester main line. Trains first terminated at a temporary station but in the following year the line was extended to the new Queen Square terminus, an elegant building on the north bank of the River Avon with a single-span vaulted glass roof. Complete with its original wooden platforms the station was renamed Bath Green Park by British Railways (BR) in 1954.

The S&DR saw great advantages in building a railway to connect with the MR at Bath – it would create a main north-south artery with links to the Midlands and the North of England and in doing so would tap into the North Somerset coalfield. The Bath Extension, as it was called, was a costly project for the railway to take on.

The heavily engineered single-track route from Evercreech Junction to Bath Queen Square took it over the Mendips, to a summit at Masbury of 811 ft above sea level, with gradients as steep as 1-in-50, and involved the building of many tunnels and viaducts. It opened on 20 July 1874 and from the start several trains included through coaches from Birmingham to Bournemouth – at its southern end the S&DR had reached Bournemouth over London & South Western Railway (LSWR) tracks the previous month.

The building of the Bath Extension left the S&DR in dire financial straits. It was left looking for a saviour and in 1875 an agreement was jointly made with the London & South Western Railway and the Midland Railway to purchase the company. Thus was the Somerset & Dorset Joint Railway (SDJR) born with the MR in charge of motive power and the LSWR in charge of rolling stock and infrastructure. To speed up the working of the line several single-line sections and viaducts were doubled but the main obstacle was at Templecombe where the

S&DJR met the LSWR main line – right up to closure trains calling at that station had to reverse out before resuming their journey. Consequently many through trains between the Midlands and the North of England, including the 'Pines Express', introduced in 1927, did not stop there.

The railway was kept very busy during both World Wars and during summer Saturdays handling holiday traffic to and from Bournemouth. Heavy North-South passenger trains all had to be double-headed through smoky single-line tunnels over the Mendips between Bath and Evercreech Junction. This all ended in September 1962 when the through trains ceased to run, a consequence of British Railways' (BR) regional boundary changes in 1958 when the S&DJR north of Templecombe came under Western Region control.

Now devoid of its lifeblood (the through traffic) the S&DJR was recommended for closure in the Beeching Report (1963). Closure, a self-fulfilling prophecy, was confirmed in 1965 and the date was set for 3 January 1966 but a last minute hitch with one of the operators of alternative bus services reprieved the line for two more months, albeit with just a skeleton service. Finally the new date for closure was 7 March that year – railway enthusiasts descended on the railway to pay their last respects and the last service trains ran on Saturday 5 March. The next day a special last train traversed the railway, including the Highbridge branch (see pages 40–45), and then the much-loved S&DJR, steam-operated until the end, was no more.

Despite closure over fifty years ago there is still much to see of the railway. Glorious Bath Green Park station, complete with curved glass roof, has been beautifully restored and is now used by a variety of businesses as well as being a market venue. The Two Tunnels Greenway

LEFT: The Two Tunnels Greenway crosses over Tucking Mill Viaduct, which lies between the northern end of Combe Down Tunnel and Midford.

BELOW: The driver has ex-LMS Class 8F 2-8-0 No. 48309's regulator wide open and full gear as the loco struggles up the 1-in-50 gradient out of Bath towards Devonshire Tunnel with a special to Bournemouth West on 4 April 1965.

opened as a footpath and cycleway between Bath and Midford in 2013. Access to the railway path in Bath is a short distance to the west of Oldfield Park station and from there the 1-in-50 climb out of Bath begins to the 447-yd Devonshire Tunnel, which is soon followed by the 1,829-yd Combe Down Tunnel, the longest walking and cycling tunnel in Britain, if not Europe, which would have taxed drivers of steam locomotives to the limit in its choking confines. Emerging into daylight the railway path continues along Lyncombe Vale and over Tucking Mill Viaduct to reach Midford. Here it becomes the Colliers Way, which continues along the trackbed over Midford Viaduct to Wellow, Radstock and Frome (see pages 46–49). Wellow station building and signal box have survived as a private residence and following closure was once the home of the artist Peter Bake.

Further south Midsomer Norton station has been preserved by the Somerset & Dorset Railway Heritage Trust (see page 49) and the twenty-seven-arch curved Charlton Viaduct in Shepton Mallet now forms the backdrop of Kilver Court Gardens. One mile south of Templecombe the 2-ft-gauge Gartell Light Railway runs along the trackbed – with two working signal boxes it is fully signalled with former BR equipment and operates both steam and diesel-hauled passenger trains on most summer Sundays.

Avon Valley Railway

A heritage railway that operates trains for 3 miles between Oldland and Avon Riverside via Bitton on the ex-Midland Railway route from Mangotsfield to Bath (Green Park). The line closed to passengers in 1966 although coal trains to Bath Gas Works continued until 1973. The headquarters of the railway is at Bitton where the station has been tastefully restored. The line opened in stages between 1987 and 2004 and there are plans to extend it one day to Bath. The railway shares its route with the Bristol & Bath Railway Path, which was the first green traffic-free railway path in Britain, opened by Sustrans in 1984. Open most weekends April to October and selected days during school holidays from February to October, and during the Christmas period.

BELOW & RIGHT: Two modern-day views of Combe Down Tunnel south of Bath, which, at 1,829 yds, is the longest walking and cycling tunnel in Britain. On this page a cyclist heads through the illuminated tunnel, which is closed at night. Opposite is the northern entrance to the single-bore tunnel that must have taxed the steam engine drivers of yesteryear to the limit.

SOUTHERN ENGLAND

New Forest

Brockenhurst to Poole via Ringwood

Open to passengers 1874–1964 | **Original length** 26½ miles
Original route operator London & South Western Railway
Length currently open for walkers 22 miles **& cyclists** 20 miles
NCN 2, 256 & 25

Nicknamed 'Castleman's Corkscrew' after its principal promotor and its subsequent meandering route across the New Forest, the Brockenhurst to Poole railway lost its importance as a through route between Southampton and Weymouth with the opening of a more direct route via Bournemouth in 1893. Despite this it came to life on summer Saturdays when it was used as a diversionary route for holiday trains but this all ended in 1964 with its closure. Today much of its route across the open heathland and woodland of the New Forest National Park can be enjoyed by walkers, cyclists and horse riders.

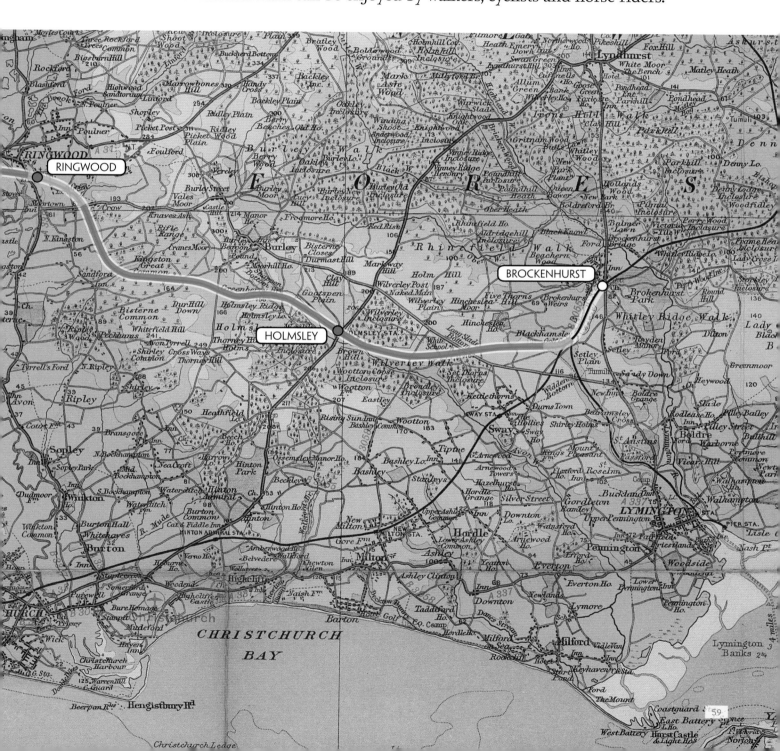

Promoted by Wimborne solicitor Charles Castleman, the Southampton and Dorchester Railway (S&DR) was seen as a first step in opening a railway along the Dorset and East Devon coastline to Exeter. The planned route of the S&DR was far from direct, meandering westward across the New Forest from Southampton through Brockenhurst, Ringwood and Wimborne thence to Hamworthy and Wareham before reaching Dorchester. Much to the horror of the London & South Western Railway (LSWR), which had reached Southampton from London in 1840, Castleman managed to get the Great Western Railway (GWR) to agree to lease and work the planned line. The S&DR received Parliamentary approval in 1845 but not before the GWR had been persuaded by the Chairman of the Railway Board to transfer its lease of the planned line to the LSWR.

This meandering 'corkscrew' railway opened on 1 June 1847 although the collapse of a tunnel at Southampton held up through working for three months while it was rebuilt. At Dorchester the terminus station (later renamed Dorchester South) was built facing west to await the extension along the coast to Exeter that never came. The S&DR was amalgamated with the LSWR in 1848 and Charles Castleman later became Chairman of the latter company from 1873 to 1875.

OPENING SPREAD: The wife of photographer Henry Casserley waits patiently for a train at Golf Links Halt on the Rye & Camber Tramway, 12 July 1931.

BELOW: The Southern Railway concrete platform and station sign have survived alongside the Castleman Trailway at Ashley Heath, to the west of Ringwood.

NEAR RIGHT: Complete with hanging basket, this Southern Railway concrete level crossing post can be seen at Crow, southeast of Ringwood.

FAR RIGHT: The original rails have somehow miraculously survived over fifty-five years since closure at the site of a level crossing at Goatspen Plain in the heart of the New Forest.

The railway completely avoided the south coast of Hampshire – Christchurch, Bournemouth and Poole were just small villages at that time and could only be reached by horse-drawn bus from the nearest station. However their growing popularity led to the Ringwood, Christchurch & Bournemouth Railway being opened from Ringwood to Christchurch via Hurn in 1862 and thence on to Bournemouth in 1870. This roundabout route to the growing resorts was slow and highly unsatisfactory although Poole was reached by the LSWR with a line from Broadstone in 1870. A terminus at Bournemouth (later renamed Bournemouth West) was first reached via the Poole line in 1874 and was used by the Somerset & Dorset Railway (from 1878 the Somerset & Dorset Joint Railway) until its closure in 1965.

The next piece in this complicated railway jigsaw came in 1888 when the LSWR opened a direct double-track line from Brockenhurst to Bournemouth (later renamed Bournemouth Central) via Sway, New Milton and Christchurch. Finally, the missing links between the two stations at Bournemouth and the completion of the Holes Bay to Hamworthy cut-off were completed in 1893 and the direct route along the Hampshire coast and into Dorset to Dorchester was complete. As a result the Ringwood to Christchurch line lost most of its traffic (it closed in 1935) and the 'Corkscrew' line from Brockenhurst to Poole/Hamworthy via Ringwood was relegated to secondary status with push-pull passenger trains, only coming alive on summer Saturdays when London Waterloo to Swanage or Weymouth trains packed with holidaymakers used it as a diversionary route to avoid the choke point of Bournemouth.

The Brockenhurst to Poole/Hamworthy section of the 'corkscrew' was recommended for closure in the Beeching Report (1963). Closure to passenger trains came on 4 May 1964, the same day that the Ringwood to Salisbury line ceased operation – the former Salisbury & Dorset Junction

Railway had originally opened in 1867. The line east of Ringwood closed completely and the track was lifted, however goods traffic continued to serve Wimborne and Ringwood until 7 August 1967. After that the line was cut back to continue to serve the RAOC fuel depot near West Moors until May 1974. Wimborne continued to be served by infrequent goods trains from Poole until May 1977 when the last vestige of 'Castleman's Corkscrew', which was between Brockenhurst and Poole, bit the dust.

Since closure much of the route between Lymington Junction, west of Brockenhurst, and Hamworthy can now be followed on foot while a significant proportion also forms part of the National Cycle Network (NCN). The section between Lymington Junction (south of Brockenhurst on the B3055) to just beyond Holmsley is designated as NCN Route 2 and provides an excellent route for walkers, mountain bikers and horse riders through the open heathland of the New Forest National Park via Long Slade Bottom. Car parks and picnic sites are provided along the route while 1 mile east of Holmsley the straight trackbed has been rebuilt as a minor road. Holmsley station, complete with platforms, is now home to a café and restaurant. One mile beyond Holmsley NCN Route 2 turns south but the railway path and undesignated cycle trail continue on across heathland

to Burbush car park. Here the cycle trail ends although the old railway route can be followed on foot across Kingston Great Common National Nature Reserve to the outskirts of Ringwood.

Although the railway has disappeared in Ringwood, to the west of the town in Bickerley Road the trackbed forms the 16-mile Castleman Trailway (NCN Route 256), a mainly traffic-free waymarked route for walkers and cyclists through heathland and forestry plantations that ends at the Upton Country Park car park near Hamworthy – the concrete platform and nameboard of Ashley Heath station is passed en route. With a few diversions at West Moors, the Castleman Trailway reaches the outskirts of Wimborne where there are more diversions before joining NCN Route 25, which heads south past Broadstone Golf Course to end at Upton Country Park near Hamworthy. From Upton a footpath and cycleway runs along the shore of Holes Bay to Poole railway station.

BELOW: Ex-Southern Railway Q Class 0-6-0 No. 30539 enters Broadstone station with the 4.15 pm train from Brockenhurst to Bournemouth West on 15 July 1960. Built at Eastleigh Works in 1938, this locomotive was withdrawn in January 1963.

Swanage Railway

The branch line from Wareham to the small harbour town of Swanage was opened by the London & South Western Railway in 1885. The coming of the railway transformed the town and it soon became a popular seaside resort with through coaches from London Waterloo on summer Saturdays. Large amounts of clay were also carried from Furzebrook to destinations around the country, notably the Potteries. The branch line was not recommended for closure in the Beeching Report but it was closed anyway despite strong opposition from local people – closure for the branch line came on 1 January 1972, although a short section was retained from Worget Junction to Furzebrook for the clay traffic and to serve the Wytch Farm oil terminal. In 1979 the Swanage Railway started operating steam trains from Swanage and over the following years extended its operations to firstly Corfe Castle, then Norden (for park-and-ride) and finally to Wareham where it connects with the national rail network once again. Open weekends and bank holidays throughout year, daily from the end of February to October, and the Christmas period.

Longmoor Military Railway

Bordon to Liss

Open to passengers 1905/42–1969 | **Original length** c.70 miles
Original route operator Royal Engineers
Length currently open for walkers 3 miles

The Longmoor Military Railway was built by the Royal Engineers between 1905 and 1942 as a railway training facility for soldiers. In its final form it had links at each end to the national rail network at Liss and Bordon. At its peak during the Second World War it had an extent of around 70 miles of running track and sidings, including a 6-mile circular route for continuous operations. It closed in 1969 and efforts to reopen part of it as a heritage railway came to nothing. Today the southern section of this unique railway route can be explored on foot through the heathland

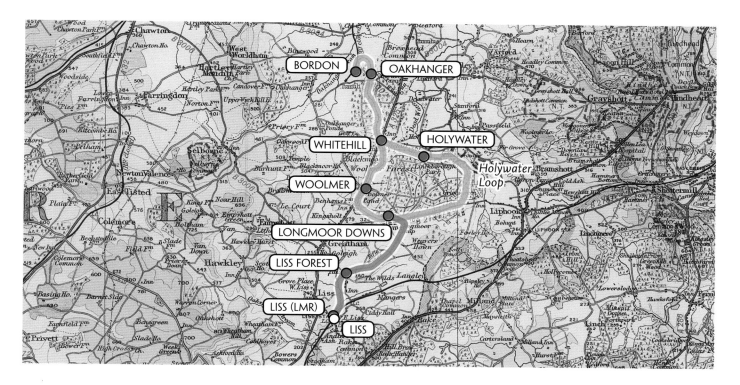

BORDON
OAKHANGER
WHITEHILL
HOLYWATER
Holywater Loop
WOOLMER
LONGMOOR DOWNS
LISS FOREST
LISS (LMR)
LISS

LEFT: Longmoor Military Railway's Austerity Class 0-6-0ST No. AD196 struggles along the wet rails of Holywater Loop near Round Hill with a Railway Correspondence & Travel Society special train on 16 April 1966.

ABOVE: To the north of Liss Forest the trackbed can be followed to Longmoor Camp on days when this section of the route is not closed for Army live firing exercises.

Operating as the Woolmer Instructional Military Railway until 1935, the Longmoor Military Railway (LMR) was built on army land in Hampshire by the Royal Engineers from 1903 onwards as a railway training facility for soldiers. The standard-gauge railway initially ran from the garrison town of Bordon to railway workshops at Longmoor Downs via Oakhanger, Whitehill and Woolmer. In 1933 an extension to Liss via Weavers Down and Liss Forest was opened – at Liss there were sidings and a connection to the Guildford to Portsmouth main line. During the Second World War the railway was further extended with the opening of an eastern loop from Longmoor Downs to a triangular junction at Whitehill via Holywater and Hopkins Bridge, thereby creating a 6-mile circular route for continuous running. The railway was always being modified with sections being built or dismantled by soldiers and at its peak extended to around 70 miles of track and sidings.

At the garrison town of Bordon the LMR connected with the Bordon Light Railway, a 4¾-mile single-track branch to Bentley, on the Aldershot to Alton line. Opening on 11 December 1905, the standard-gauge line was built by the War Department and worked by the London & South Western Railway (LSWR). By the 1950s army traffic had begun to decline as the army's presence at Bordon gradually reduced, and all passenger traffic ceased on 16 September 1957. However, military freight trains continued to operate until 4 April 1966 when the line was closed completely and the track lifted.

A varied collection of locomotives and rolling stock was employed on the LMR including examples from the Midland & Great Northern Joint Railway, Taff Vale Railway, North Staffordshire Railway, Great Western Railway and London, Brighton & South Coast Railway. During the Second World War steam locomotives from the War Department and the US Army Transportation Corps were introduced to train soldiers in the art of driving and firing.

The post-war years brought a reduced role for the LMR – gone were the days when soldiers took over the operations of a foreign railway in the times of war. The Ministry of Defence (MOD) eventually announced the LMR's closure but not before several railway preservation groups expressed an interest in taking over parts of the system. Eventually only the last 1½ miles of the railway, from Liss Forest Road to Liss, was offered by the MOD but planning permission for this fledgling heritage railway was refused. The LMR finally closed on 31 October 1969 although some locomotives (including

BELOW: Built by Hawthorne Leslie in 1922, 0-6-0T *Selborne* waits at Longmoor before departing with a few military top brass on the 3.10 pm train for Liss on 17 May 1934.

two redundant locomotives, 75029 and 92203, which the artist David Shepherd had purchased from British Railways) and rolling stock remained at Longmoor until 1971. Prior to closure the LMR had been used as the location for a number of films including *The Lady Vanishes*, *Bhowani Junction* and *Chitty Chitty Bang Bang* but the most memorable must be the thrilling railway chase in *The Great St Trinian's Train Robbery*.

Today, while the army has a much-reduced presence at Bordon and Longmoor, there is a section of the LMR that can be walked or cycled. At Liss the Liss Riverside Railway Walk, a Local Nature Reserve, runs from Liss railway station along the trackbed of the LMR to Forest Road in Liss Forest, a distance of 1¼ miles. Car parking is provided at each end of the path and there is a picnic site en route. There are still relics of the railway to be seen along this stretch including the old LMR station platform at Liss and three steel and concrete railway bridges. The footpath also extends from Liss Forest to Longmoor Camp along the old railway route when not in use by the army.

The 6-mile circular loop that runs through heathland and woods around Woolmer Forest from Longmoor is only accessible on foot on certain days as this section is normally closed during periods of army activity. Around 60% of the land has international conservation status mainly due to the restricted public access to live firing ranges.

Mid-Hants Railway

The railway over 'The Alps' between Alton and Winchester opened in 1865. It was heavily used during both world wars and was also used as a diversionary route when the main line between Woking and Winchester was closed for engineering work. Since closure in 1973 the 10-mile section between Alton and Alresford has been reopened as a steam-operated heritage railway known as the Watercress Line – so named because it once transported locally grown watercress to markets in London. Open weekends and school holidays January to October, the Christmas period, daily except Mondays and Fridays April to September, daily in August.

BELOW: The platform and rudimentary corrugated shelter of the Longmoor Military Railway's station at Liss have survived for fifty years since closure. Alongside is the Liss Riverside Railway Walk at the start of its route through woodland to Liss Forest.

Golfers' Tramway

Rye to Camber Sands

Open to passengers 1895/1908–1939 | **Original length** 1¾ miles
Original route operator Rye & Camber Tramway
Length currently open for walkers 1½ miles

Originally opened in 1895 to convey golfers to Rye Golf Club, the narrow-gauge Rye & Camber Tramway also proved very popular with day-trippers. The line was extended to Camber Sands in 1908 and remained in operation until the outbreak of the Second World War when it was requisitioned by the Admiralty. It never reopened after the war and was sold for scrap in 1947. Today much of the route of this diminutive railway can be followed on foot.

The townsfolk of Rye, now in East Sussex, were first served by a railway in 1851 when the South Eastern Railway opened its 26-mile line between Ashford and Hastings. Three years later a short branch line was opened along the west bank of the River Rother to Rye Harbour – in medieval times the old hilltop town was a port on the coast but storms and land reclamation have today left it stranded 2 miles inland. Skirting the vast and lonely expanse of Romney Marsh, the Ashford to Hastings line was recommended for closure in the Beeching Report (1963) but was fortunately reprieved and now operates as the Marshlink Line, although the freight-only harbour branch closed in 1962.

Towards the end of the 19th century the game of golf became increasingly popular in the UK with golf clubs being established throughout the country. However, neither Rye nor its near neighbour, Hastings, possessed such a facility until Rye Golf Club opened in the sand dunes of Camber Sands in 1894. The golf club was located

to the east of the River Rother but was difficult to access from Rye due to the poor state of the road from Rye station – often, golfers would arrive at the club with their shoes in a very muddy state.

The problem of accessing the golf course was soon rectified by members of the club and local townsfolk who proposed building a tramway from the east side of Monkbretton Bridge, that crossed the River Rother on the outskirts of Rye, to the golf club. As the tramway was to be built on private land no Act of Parliament was required. The Rye & Camber Tramway was formed in April 1895 and Colonel H. F. Stephens was given the task of supervising its construction. Built to a gauge of 3 ft, the line initially had only two stations: at Rye, next to Monkbretton Bridge, and at Camber, for the golf club. Engineering work was minimal with only one bridge, Broadwater Bridge, which crossed a tributary of the River Rother, and track was spiked directly onto wooden sleepers. The line opened on 15 July 1895 with just one

diminutive 0-4-0T steam locomotive, *Camber*, and one passenger carriage. It was an immediate success, not only with golfers but also with local people riding to the dunes for picnics. A second locomotive, *Victoria*, was purchased in 1897 along with a second carriage.

All continued to go well for the little tramway and in 1908 the line was extended along a low embankment to Camber Sands with the original terminus of Camber being renamed Golf Links Halt. The new terminus proved very popular with day-trippers and during the summer weekends and bank holidays the overflowing trains had to be augmented by two open goods wagons fitted with wooden benches. However, during the winter months trains terminated at Golf Links Halt and the line became dependent on a subsidy from the Rye Golf Club to cover its operating costs. The post-First World War years brought increasing competition from motor vehicles and the tramway was forced to reduce operating costs by purchasing a small petrol tractor in 1925. The steam locomotives were retired but passenger services continued until the outbreak of the Second World War in September 1939 when they ended, never to return. During the war the line was taken over by the Admiralty and used to transport equipment for the PLUTO (Pipeline Under The Ocean) project to a siding serving a new pier close to Golf Links Halt. After the war the worn-out railway's life expired and it was sold for scrap in 1947.

Despite the passage of time since it closed much of the route of the Rye & Camber Tramway can still be followed on foot. At Monkbretton Bridge the wooden terminus station with its corrugated iron roof has long been demolished but the tramway's route across a field from there is now well defined as a footpath. Broadwater Bridge also has gone but the stream can still be crossed

via a footbridge. From here a short detour must be made via the Camber Road as gravel workings have erased the trackbed for a short distance. It is rejoined along a concrete road where the 3-ft-gauge track has been embedded in the concrete as far as Golf Links Halt. Here, in all its glory close to the Rye Lifeboat Station, is the corrugated station building and platform that have miraculously survived adjacent to a siding and run-round loop still embedded in the concrete.

From Golf Links Halt the route of the railway runs along a low embankment that cuts across the middle of the golf course to the site of Camber Sands terminus. Here, among the sand dunes, while nothing now remains of the station's wooden platform and café this is still a pleasant spot to stop and reflect on sunny days gone by when day-trippers descended here in their hundreds.

PREVIOUS SPREAD: An idyllic scene at the Camber Sands terminus on 11 April 1931. The line was extended from Golf Links Halt to the new station in 1908 and the small petrol-engine tractor seen here replaced steam-hauled services in 1925.

TOP RIGHT: The combined total of the Rye & Camber Tramway's steam motive power at Rye station, c.1920.

BOTTOM RIGHT: After closure in 1939 the railway was taken over by the Admiralty for use during the Second World War. Incredibly, the trackwork and corrugated waiting room have survived at Golf Links Halt for over seventy years since the railway was sold for scrap.

Romney, Hythe & Dymchurch Railway

With its headquarters at New Romney, the 15-in-gauge Romney, Hythe & Dymchurch Railway is one of the world's smallest public railways. The brainchild of two wealthy racing drivers, it was opened between Hythe and New Romney by the Duke of York in 1927 and extended to Dungeness lighthouse in 1929. Still operating the original ⅓rd-scale steam locomotives built by Davey Paxman of Colchester, the 13½-mile double-track route along the South Kent coast is fully signalled and features level crossings, a large engine shed and an overall-roofed terminal at Hythe. Open most weekends through the year, and daily from Easter to October.

Cuckoo Trail

Eridge to Polegate

Open to passengers 1849/80–1965/68 | **Original length** 20¼ miles
Original route operator London, Brighton & South Coast Railway
Length currently open for walkers & cyclists 10¾ miles | **NCN** 21

First opened as a 3-mile branch line from Polegate to Hailsham in 1849, the 'Cuckoo Line' was extended north another 17½ miles by the London, Brighton & South Coast Railway to Heathfield and Eridge in 1880. Closure also came in two stages with the northerly section closing in 1965 and the remaining short branch line to Hailsham closing in 1968. Since then the section between Heathfield and Polegate has reopened as a popular footpath and cycleway known as the Cuckoo Trail.

ERIDGE

ROTHERFIELD & MARK CROSS

MAYFIELD

HEATHFIELD

WALDRON & HORAM ROAD

HELLINGLY

HAILSHAM

POLEGATE

The London & Brighton Railway's main line along the south coast of Sussex from Brighton to Hastings via Lewes and Polegate opened on 27 July 1846. Exactly one month later the company was one of three railways that amalgamated to form the London, Brighton & South Coast Railway (LB&SCR). Three years later, on 14 May 1849, the company opened a branch southwards from Polegate to the resort of Eastbourne and northwards from Polegate to the town of Hailsham.

Hailsham remained the terminus of the 3-mile branch line from Polegate for the next thirty-one years. In the intervening years there was a proposal to build a 3-ft-gauge line northwards from Hailsham to Eridge via Heathfield where it would meet the LB&SCR's Tunbridge Wells to Uckfield line, which had opened in 1868. Nothing came of this proposal but the LB&SCR decided that it would like to build a standard-gauge line along the same route. The company obtained Parliamentary authority to build the line in 1876 and opened the 17½-mile single-track line throughout on 1 September 1880. Intermediate stations were located at Hellingly, Waldron & Horeham Road (later known as Horam), Heathfield, Mayfield and Rotherfield & Mark Cross. At Polegate a new junction was built in 1881 facing westwards and the station resited to allow trains from Eridge to travel on to Eastbourne. At the northern end of the line, the line ran parallel to the single-track Uckfield line between Redgate Junction (there was no connection between these two lines) and Eridge until 1894. In that year the Uckfield line was doubled and a physical connection was made at Redgate Junction allowing trains from Polegate to join it there.

The line from Polegate to Eridge was known by railway workers as the 'Cuckoo Line' – apparently the first cuckoo of spring was released by a lady from a basket at Heathfield Fair in April each year. Hailsham was always better served than the rest of the line with up to fourteen trains a day to and from Eastbourne. About half of these trains continued their journey along the 'Cuckoo Line', with three of these continuing on to London Victoria station. Competition from motor cars, buses and lorries was already being felt in the 1930s and with passenger numbers and freight traffic continuing to decline after the Second World War the future for the 'Cuckoo Line' was beginning to look bleak. Despite an improved regular interval timetable being introduced the line was recommended for closure in the Beeching Report (1963) and the end came for passenger trains between Hailsham and Redgate Junction on 14 June 1965 – on the previous day, a Sunday, a special last train, 'The Wealdsman Rail Tour', was run by the Locomotive Club of Great Britain along the line. Goods trains from Polegate continued to serve Heathfield until 26 April 1968. Passenger trains continued to operate on the last section of the 'Cuckoo Line' between Polegate and Hailsham until 9 September 1968. The track was soon lifted and the line reverted slowly back to nature.

Spa Valley Railway

The London, Brighton & South Coast Railway's line between Eridge and Groombridge opened in 1868. At Groombridge it met the company's line from East Grinstead to Tunbridge Wells West, which had opened two years earlier. At Eridge the line from Groombridge continued down to Uckfield and from 1880 it was also served by trains on the 'Cuckoo Line' to Hailsham and Polegate. The railway between East Grinstead and Groombridge was closed early in 1967 but the section from Eridge to Tunbridge Wells West remained open until 1985. The line to Uckfield is still open for business with trains from London Bridge travelling via Oxted.

PREVIOUS SPREAD: Autumn in East Sussex – the Cuckoo Trail near Hellingly.

LEFT: Hellingly station as viewed from the east, 27 April 1972. This section of the Cuckoo Line closed for good in 1968 when goods trains to Heathfield were withdrawn on 26 April. Since then the station has been lovingly restored alongside the Cuckoo Trail.

In 1981 the route of the line from Heathfield southwards to Polegate was purchased jointly by East Sussex County Council and Wealden District Council. Known as the Cuckoo Trail, it was initially reopened as a traffic-free footpath until the early 1990s when Sustrans, the cycling charity organization, resurfaced the route. With an extension southwards from Polegate to Eastbourne (along a non-railway route) the Trail became part of National Cycle Network Route 21 and is currently used by well over 200,000 people annually, nearly three times as many people who used it when it was a railway!

The Trail features sculptures in the form of mileposts and wooden benches carved by a local artist.

The local council had also purchased 11 miles of the trackbed north of Heathfield but with lack of foresight this was sold off in 1986 due to financial cuts. Just north of Heathfield station the 250-yd curving tunnel was reopened to walkers and cyclists in 1997 – following an attack it is now fitted with gates and is currently only open during daylight hours. It is interesting to note here that the UK's first natural gas deposits were found at the entrance to the tunnel in 1895 and lit the station until the 1930s. The street

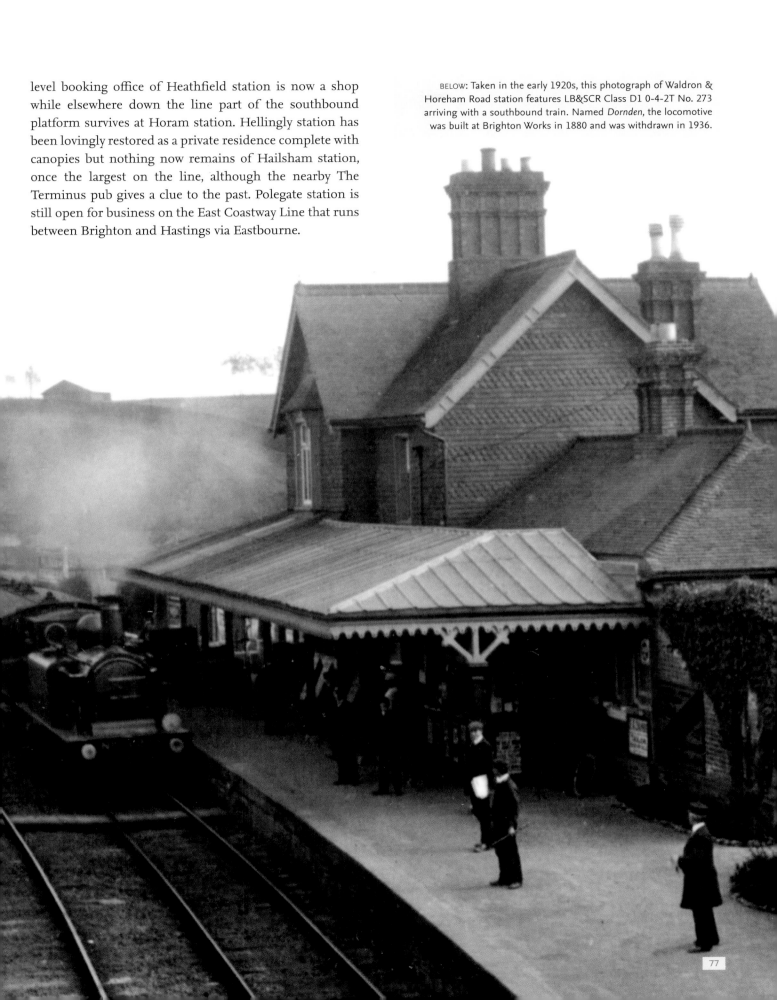

level booking office of Heathfield station is now a shop while elsewhere down the line part of the southbound platform survives at Horam station. Hellingly station has been lovingly restored as a private residence complete with canopies but nothing now remains of Hailsham station, once the largest on the line, although the nearby The Terminus pub gives a clue to the past. Polegate station is still open for business on the East Coastway Line that runs between Brighton and Hastings via Eastbourne.

BELOW: Taken in the early 1920s, this photograph of Waldron & Horeham Road station features LB&SCR Class D1 0-4-2T No. 273 arriving with a southbound train. Named *Dornden*, the locomotive was built at Brighton Works in 1880 and was withdrawn in 1936.

Crab & Winkle Line
Canterbury to Whitstable Harbour

Open to passengers 1830–1931 | **Original length** 11 miles
Original route operator Canterbury & Whitstable Railway
Length currently open for walkers & cyclists 6 miles | **NCN** 1

One of Britain's earliest public railways when it opened in 1830, the Canterbury & Whitstable Railway originally featured three inclined planes and a restricted-height tunnel. It was rebuilt in 1846 to enable steam locomotives to work along the entire line but only specially adapted locomotives with lowered boilers and shorter chimneys could work through the tunnel. Closure for passengers came in 1931 and for goods in 1953. In recent years the Crab & Winkle Line Trust has worked tirelessly to reopen much of the route to walkers and cyclists.

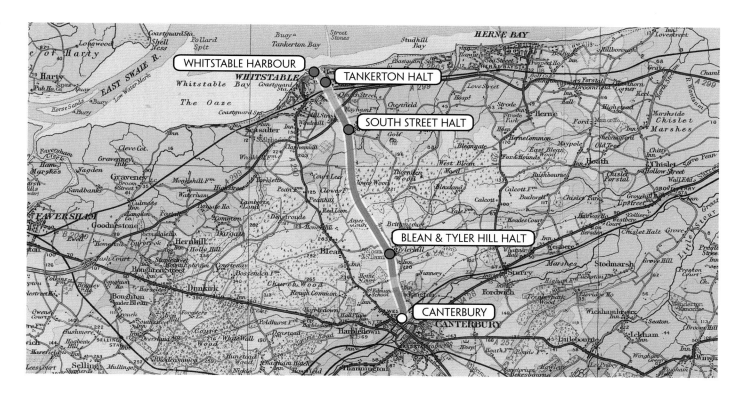

WHITSTABLE HARBOUR

TANKERTON HALT

SOUTH STREET HALT

BLEAN & TYLER HILL HALT

CANTERBURY

LEFT: A group of railwaymen pose for the camera at Whitstable Harbour in 1894. The locomotive is one of the South Eastern Railway's Class R1 0-6-0T locomotives built for the Canterbury & Whitstable Railway with cut-down cab and chimney for working through the restricted height of Tyler Hill Tunnel.

ABOVE: The blocked-up northern portal of Tyler Hill Tunnel today. The restricted height of this tunnel needed specially converted locomotives to operate through it.

For centuries the city of Canterbury in Kent had relied upon the River Stour for its supply of goods and raw materials. It was a time-consuming task as horsedrawn barges often took several days for the meandering 70-mile journey from the coast near Ramsgate along a river that was continually silting up. By the early 19th century the state of the river had reached crisis point and railway pioneer William James put forward a proposal to build a railway from the city to the port of Whitstable, only 11 miles to the north. During 1823 and 1824 he surveyed three possible routes but bankruptcy and illness prevented him from any future involvement. Instead George Stephenson was appointed engineer of the newly formed Canterbury & Whitstable Railway (C&WR), which received Parliamentary approval in 1825.

Stephenson was assisted by Joseph Locke in building the most direct route surveyed by James but this included steep gradients which at that time were not capable of being worked by steam locomotives. Instead stationary steam engines were planned to work trains on the three inclines, with horsepower on the level sections. Construction work commenced in 1828 and the standard-gauge line was opened for passengers and goods on

3 May 1830, just over four months before the opening of the Liverpool & Manchester Railway. At the last moment a decision was taken to use a steam locomotive on the incline out of Whitstable Harbour so the railway ordered one from Robert Stephenson & Company. Named *Invicta*, it was delivered by ship from Newcastle to Whitstable and was at the head of the first train on opening day. Sadly, the locomotive proved incapable of hauling loads on this northerly section of the line and, despite modifications, was soon replaced by a stationary steam engine at Tyler Hill.

Soon facing bankruptcy, the C&WR was taken over by the newly-formed South Eastern Railway in 1844 and two years later the line was rebuilt to allow the use of steam locomotives along its entire length. Despite this only specially adapted locomotives could be used due to the reduced height of the line's only tunnel at Tyler Hill, just to the north of Canterbury. Passenger services were withdrawn on this pioneering railway in 1931 with complete closure following in 1953.

Much of the route of the C&WR was reopened as a footpath and cycleway by the Crab & Winkle Line Trust in 1999; the unfortunate *Invicta* is a static exhibit in

Canterbury Museum. The route features some hills with a 200-ft climb out of Canterbury and there are fine views of Whitstable from the highest point. At Canterbury the original 1845 station in North Lane is now a listed building and from here the signposted route diverts through a housing development that has been built over the trackbed. Now in the grounds of Archbishop's School, the height-restricted Tyler Hill Tunnel has been bricked up though the portals are clearly visible. Following a detour around the tunnel the trackbed is regained near to the site of Blean & Tyler Hill Halt, beyond which is a circular pond built in 1829 that supplied water to the Tyler Hill winding engine. This is halfway along the route and is an ideal spot for a picnic in beautiful wooded glades. Once again following the trackbed, the route continues on a falling gradient, with a diversion or two, to the outskirts of Whitstable. Here a replacement bridge over Teynham Road is awaited to replace the original railway bridge that was unfortunately demolished back in 1969. Glimpses of the railway embankment can be spotted in the town but there are no traces today of the Harbour station or the route of the line along the quays.

Sittingbourne & Kemsley Light Railway

Built in 1905, the Sittingbourne & Kemsley Light Railway is a 2-ft-6-in-gauge former industrial railway that once connected river wharfs to paper mills in Sittingbourne, Kent. Although the mills have now closed, a group of preservationists saved the railway from closure in 1969 and currently operate both steam- and diesel-hauled trains along a 2-mile route between Sittingbourne Viaduct and Kemsley Down. Open on Bank Holiday weekends and Sundays Easter to September, also Wednesdays in August, and weekends in December.

LEFT: Ex-SER Class R1 0-6-0T No. 124 waits to depart from Whitstable station with the 12.10 pm train to Canterbury West on 6 August 1927.

BELOW: Locally-caught oysters destined for London await collection from the Canterbury & Whitstable Railway's old station in Canterbury in the 1890s.

Parkland Walk

Finsbury Park to Alexandra Palace

Open to passengers 1867/73–1954 | **Original length** 4¼ miles
Original route operator Great Northern Railway
Length currently open for walkers 2½ miles

Originally built to serve villages north of London and the Victorian pile of Alexandra Palace, this steeply-graded line eventually lost much of its patronage in 1940 to the extended Northern Line tube service. The remaining Finsbury Park to Alexandra Palace route was starved of electrification, remaining steam-hauled until closure in 1954. Apart from the section through the tunnels on either side of Highgate overground station most of the route has been reopened as a footpath and linear nature reserve known as the Parkland Walk.

Despite the rapid growth of Britain's railway network elsewhere the villages of Edgware, Finchley and Highgate north of London had to wait many years before they, too, were served by a railway. Finally, the Great Northern Railway (GNR), which had operated to York out of King's Cross since 1852, sponsored the Edgware, Highgate & London Railway (EH&LR) to build a steeply-graded branch line from the GNR main line at Finsbury Park to Edgware. Intermediate stations were provided at Stroud Green, Crouch End, Highgate, Finchley and Mill Hill. Powers were also obtained for branch lines from Highgate to Muswell Hill and from Finchley to High Barnet.

The unfinished EH&LR was purchased by the GNR in July 1867 and opened one month later on 22 August. The line was initially single-track but was doubled between Finsbury Park and Finchley in 1870. Highgate station was sandwiched between two tunnels and an extra bore for each of these needed to be constructed when the track was doubled. The branch from Finchley to High Barnet opened on 1 April 1872 while the Muswell Hill branch, constructed by the independent Muswell Hill Railway (MHR), opened between Highgate and Alexandra Palace

via Muswell Hill on 24 May 1873 – also the official opening day of the Palace – with trains being worked by the GNR. Around 125,000 people visited the Palace over the following two weeks but disaster then struck when it was seriously damaged by a fire. The railway from Highgate was subsequently closed, only reopening in May 1875 after the Palace had been rebuilt.

On the Alexandra Palace branch line the intermediate station of Cranley Garden opened in 1902 and the MHR was subsequently purchased by the GNR in 1911. Meanwhile the Charing Cross, Euston & Hampstead Railway (CCE&HR) had opened an electrified underground line to Archway and Golders Green in 1907. The CCE&HR was a founder member of the London Electric Railway in 1910 and remained so until 1933 when all London Underground lines were nationalized, coming under the control of the London Passenger Transport Board (LPTB). Among several recommendations the LPTB proposed was extending the tube line (now known as the Northern Line) from Archway to Finchley via a deep level station at Highgate and then extending the tube services along the existing steam-operated High Barnet and Edgware branches.

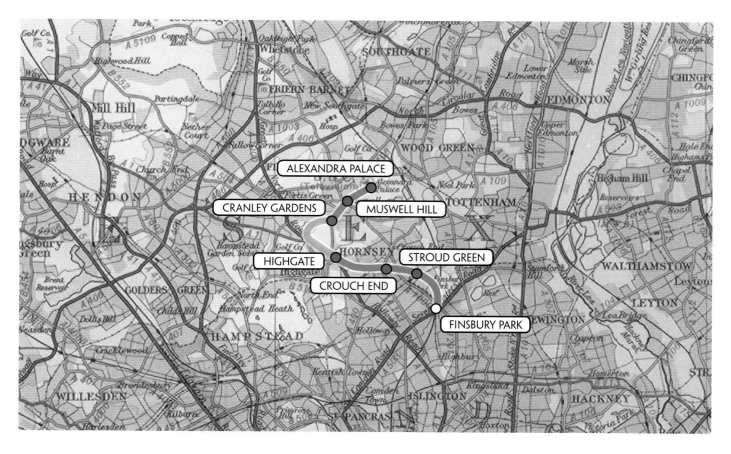

Also proposed was the electrification of the Finsbury Park to Highgate and Alexandra Palace route. In the end the Second World War brought a halt to some of these plans, although the extension of the Northern Line from Archway to East Finchley was completed by July 1939, the electrification of the High Barnet line was completed in April 1940 and the Edgware line electrified as far as Mill Hill East in May 1941 – the section between here and Edgware was closed to passenger traffic.

Although work was started on electrifying the Finsbury Park to Alexandra Palace route this was suspended during the war, never to be revived, and was officially cancelled in 1954. Meanwhile a much-reduced service of steam-hauled passenger trains continued to operate along this route until closure, amidst a national coal shortage and dwindling passenger numbers, on 3 July 1954. Cranley Gardens and Muswell Hill continued to be served by coal trains until 1957, after which the branch from Highgate to Alexandra Palace was completely closed. The Finsbury Park to Edgware line through Highgate continued to be used by goods trains – primarily coal and milk – until

1964 and for the transfer of London Underground stock until September 1970. The track was lifted in 1972 and the route began to revert back to nature.

Following complete closure much of the route of the Finsbury Park to Alexandra Palace railway was reopened as the Parkland Walk in 1984. The only section not accessible is between the twin pairs of tunnels at Highgate and Cranley Gardens. Proposals to allow cyclists and a threat to convert it into a road were both scuppered by extensive local opposition. This dedicated footpath through the North London suburbs was declared a Local Nature Reserve, London's longest, in 1990 and is popular, especially at weekends, with joggers, dog walkers and ramblers.

From Finsbury Park the route follows an embankment to the site of Stroud Green station, which was destroyed by a fire in the 1960s. From here the route enters a cutting and passes under several bridges to Crouch Hill where a former block house that was built in connection with the cancelled electrification project now houses a café, which is accessible from the Parkland Walk. Beyond here Crouch Hill Park lies to the south while at the site of

Crouch End station the overgrown platforms are surprising survivors.

From Crouch End station the Parkland Walk wends its way up through the North London hills and through a cutting before ending at the portals of the first pair of the Highgate tunnels. The tunnels and the site of Highgate station cannot be accessed so a detour must be made via Holmedale Road, Archway Road and Muswell Hill Road to an overbridge at the site of Cranley Garden station (now a school). From here the Parkland Walk rejoins the old railway route as it threads its way through woodland to the seventeen-arch viaduct over St James's Lane, from which there are distant views of the City of London. Beyond here nothing now remains of Muswell Hill station as the Parkland Walk takes a detour under Muswell Hill itself and skirts round a school before entering the landscaped grounds of Alexandra Palace. Here the old railway route ends at a substantial brick overbridge close to the Palace itself, while the small well-proportioned station building at the eastern end survives today as a community centre.

London Transport Museum

Located in the former Flower Market of Covent Garden, this popular and extensive museum houses a large collection of London's public transport and railway vehicles dating from Victorian times to the present day. Of particular interest to railway enthusiasts are early underground trains, the Metropolitan Railway 4-4-0 condensing tank engine dating from 1866 and the Bo-Bo electric locomotive *John Hampden,* which was built in 1922. Open daily throughout the year.

PREVIOUS SPREAD: Cranley Gardens station on 5 June 1937.

LEFT: The exterior of Alexandra Palace station on 3 July 1954, the last day of passenger services from Finsbury Park and Highgate. Note the constable on duty just in case there is a public disturbance!

BELOW: An admirer takes in the colourful modern graffiti that has been daubed on one of the road overbridges on the Parkland Walk.

EASTERN ENGLAND

Blackwater Rail Trail
Witham to Maldon East & Heybridge

Open to passengers 1848–1964 | **Original length** 5¾ miles
Original route operator Eastern Counties Railway
Length currently open for walkers 2 miles

Built to transport grain from Braintree to Maldon Harbour, the line from
Witham to Maldon opened in 1848. The grain traffic never materialized but
the line was kept busy carrying agricultural produce and day-trippers in the
summer months. Although the line worked to capacity during the Second
World War, the post-war years brought decline. The introduction of diesel
railbuses and an improved service failed to arrest this and the line closed
to passengers in 1964. Today much of the route is a footpath known
as the Blackwater Rail Trail.

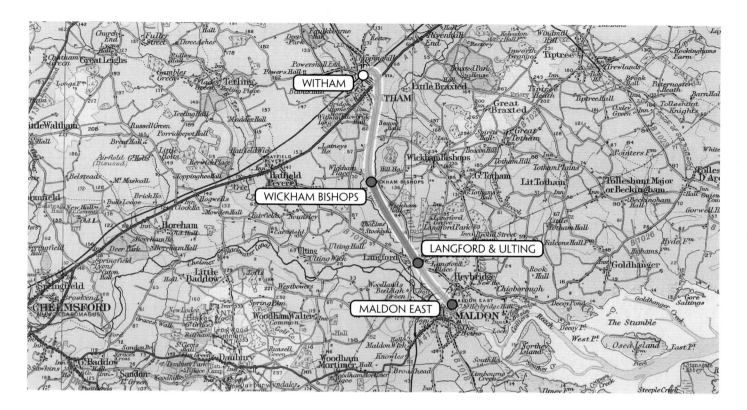

PREVIOUS SPREAD: Seen here from a Maldon to Witham train on 26 May 1956, the simple single platform at Wickam Bishops contrasts greatly with the imposing station building across the track that can be seen in the photograph on this page.

LEFT: A dramatic shot through the timbers underneath the restored bridge between Wickam Bishops and Langford & Ulting stations.

ABOVE: Built by Waggon und Maschinenbau of West Germany, four-wheel railbus E79963 calls at Wickam Bishops station on 14 March 1964, just six months before the Witham to Maldon route closed. The railbus, along with three others of the same class, has been preserved.

Originally built to transport grain from the town of Braintree to the port of Maldon, the Maldon, Witham & Braintree Railway opened in 1848. In fact the company did not survive to see the opening of the line as it had been taken over by the Eastern Counties Railway (ECR) in the previous year – the route from Braintree to Maldon crossed the ECR main line at Witham. However the development of Maldon Harbour for the export of grain never materialized and the line settled down to a fairly quiet existence with around ten passenger trains each weekday. Goods consisted of seasonal fruit and vegetables, agricultural produce, gravel and general merchandise such as coal and timber.

Intermediate stations provided at Wickam Bishops and Langford & Ulting were fairly simple affairs but the terminus at Maldon East was an impressive building built in the Jacobean style and funded by David Waddington, vice-chairman of the ECR and soon to be MP for Maldon. A scandal ensued after it was discovered that Waddington had employed a large number of local men – known locally as 'Waddington's Guinea Pigs' – on the construction of the line in order to secure their votes in the upcoming election. The railway also featured several timber viaducts that precluded the use of heavy locomotives.

The ECR was taken over by the Great Eastern Railway in 1862, which operated it until 1923 when it became part of the newly-formed London & North Eastern Railway. Originally named Maldon, the terminus station was renamed Maldon East in 1889 when a branch line was opened via Maldon West to Woodham Ferrers – this 8¾-mile line saw little traffic and was closed to passengers in 1939 and to freight traffic in 1953. Maldon East was again renamed in 1907 as Maldon East & Heybridge.

After seeing heavy traffic during the Second World War the Witham to Maldon East & Heybridge line faced the same problem as many other rural branch lines across Britain – competition from road transport and bus services. In a bid to halt the decline diesel multiple units and German-built railbuses were introduced in 1958 with a vastly improved service of seventeen return services each weekday. Staff numbers were reduced with tickets being issued on trains but it was all too late as customers had already drifted away. The line was recommended for closure in the Beeching Report (1963) and British Railways

lost no time in implementing this. Closure came on 7 September 1964 although freight in the form of fruit and gravel traffic continued until 15 April 1966. The other section of the original Maldon, Witham & Braintree Railway, from Witham to Braintree, is still open for passenger traffic.

Since closure much of this branch line's route has been reopened as a footpath known as the Blackwater Rail Trail. Designated a Local Wildlife Site, the Trail from near Wickham Bishops to the pretty village of Langford includes views of the River Blackwater. A highlight is the surviving platform at Langford & Ulting station, complete with nameboard, while the virtually inaccessible restored timber trestle bridge near Wickham Bishops, reached via a separate footpath from the B1018, is a Scheduled Monument and the last surviving example of a railway timber trestle bridge in England. However its condition today, some twenty years after restoration, causes some concern, but it is still well worth a visit. The station building at Wickam Bishops is a private residence while the grand terminus station building at Maldon, now housing offices, has survived amidst an industrial estate.

Langford & Beeleigh Railway

This 7¼-in-gauge passenger-carrying railway operates in the 7-acre grounds of the Museum of Power, set each side of the River Blackwater. The railway runs through wooded grounds and meadows from Riverside Halt to the main station at Langford. Trains are normally steam-hauled from a collection of narrow-gauge locomotives and the line features colour light signalling, an engine shed and an overall roofed station at Langford. The railway runs on special events days from March to December.

LEFT: Built in the Jacobean style and opened in 1848, the grand station building at Maldon East has been restored and now houses offices.

BELOW: The restored timber trestle bridge between Wickam Bishops and Langford & Ulting stations is now a scheduled monument and is the only bridge of its kind in England.

Marriott's Way

Norwich City to Aylsham

Open to passengers 1882–1952/59 | **Original length** 24 miles
Original route operator Lynn & Fakenham Railway/Great Eastern Railway
Length currently open for walkers & cyclists 24 miles | **NCN** 1

The Norwich City to Melton Constable and the County School to Wroxham lines in North Norfolk were two completely separate railways that were only physically linked after passenger services ceased in their last years of operation. Since complete closure in 1985, the 24-mile route from Norwich to Aylsham via the famous Themelthorpe Curve has been reopened as a footpath and cycleway known as Marriott's Way.

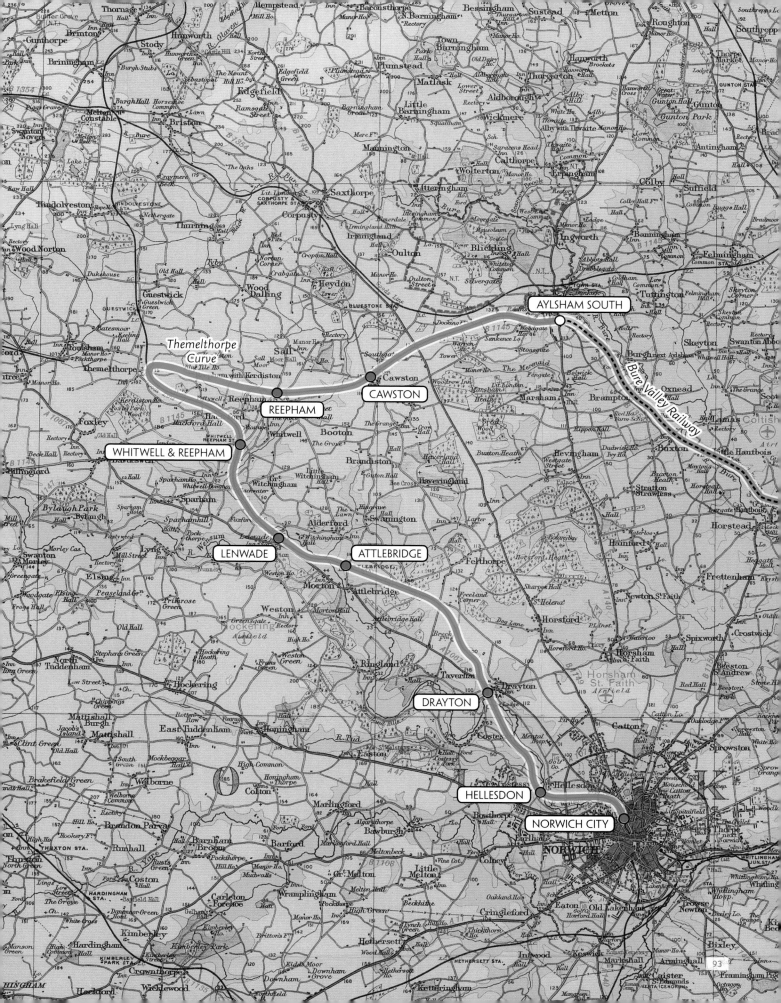

This is the story of two separate railways, both opened in 1882, that had no physical connection even though one crossed over the other until as late as 1960. The full story of one of these lines, the 23¾-mile railway between County School and Wroxham, which opened throughout 1882, is told on pages 98–101. The other railway was the Melton Constable to Norwich City line, which was opened by the Lynn & Fakenham Railway (L&FR) in the same year. In 1883 the L&FR amalgamated with the Yarmouth Union Railway and the Yarmouth & North Norfolk Railway to form the Eastern & Midlands Railway (E&MR), with its headquarters at Melton Constable. The new company opened the line from Melton Constable to Cromer Beach in 1887 and with the takeovers of the Midland & Eastern Railway and the Peterborough, Wisbech & Sutton Bridge Railway soon had a fairly extensive network of lines stretching across North Norfolk with links to the Midlands. For the first time the Great Eastern Railway had a serious rival with many of the two companies' routes being in direct compeitition with each other.

However, the overstretched E&MR soon fell on hard times and was taken over in 1893 by the Great Northern Railway and the Midland Railway. This joint enterprise became the Midland & Great Northern Joint Railway (M&GNJR) and, with a route mileage of 173 miles, allowed the Midland Railway access for the first time to Norwich and the towns, villages and ports of North Norfolk. The M&GNJR was the longest joint railway in Britain, much of it single-track, but during the busy summer months it was stretched to capacity carrying holidaymakers from the Midlands to the seaside resorts of North Norfolk.

In turn, the M&GNJR became jointly owned by the newly formed London & North Eastern Railway and the London, Midland & Scottish Railway in 1923. Melton Constable was the hub of the network, home to its workshops and with lines radiating out to Kings Lynn, Cromer, Yarmouth and Norwich. The works, dubbed as the 'Crewe of North Norfolk' and which once employed over 1,000 people, was closed in 1936. Although the network was kept busy during the Second World War the post-war years brought a rapid decline in traffic, lost to ever-increasing competition from road transport. The 'Muddle & Get Nowhere Railway', as it was by then known, was living on borrowed time and in 1958 British Railways (BR) announced its complete closure. Despite strong local

opposition the end came for passenger services on 2 March 1959 – the Cromer to Melton Constable part of the line was the only section to remain open, only to be closed on 6 April 1964 following publication of the Beeching Report (1963). While most of the former M&GNJR network was closed completely in 1959, the Norwich City to Melton Constable line lingered on for another year handling freight traffic. From that year freight trains to and from Norwich City were diverted onto the County School to Wroxham line via the sharpest radius curve on the entire BR network, which was installed at Themelthorpe, north of Whitwell & Reepham station – the distance from Norwich Thorpe station and Norwich City station (about 1 mile apart) by this circuitous route via Wroxham and Themelthorpe was 40 miles! Freight traffic to Norwich City ended in 1969 when the line was cut back to Lenwade where trains continued until 1983, serving a factory making concrete sections for motorways. By 1985 all track on this remnant of the M&GNJR and the Themelthorpe to Wroxham line had been lifted and the two routes started to revert back to nature.

Since closure the entire route of the railway between Norwich and Aylsham via Themelthorpe has been reopened as a footpath and cycleway known as Marriott's Way – named after the long-serving Chief Engineer and Manager of the M&GNJR, William Marriott. The route starts close to the site of Norwich City station and heads northwest along the wooded valley of the River Wensum, which it crosses on one of three unique A-framed bridges at Hellesdon. Here the remains of the platform walls and signal box foundations lie buried in the undergrowth. The next station along the line was at Drayton but the site is now an industrial estate. At Hellesdon the station survives as a private residence while at Lenwade the station building has been carefully restored, also as a well-screened private residence, and where one of the original level crossing gates miraculously survives in the undergrowth. A number of interlocking concrete sculptures can be seen along the route near here, their forms and material of construction acting as a reminder of the railway's final years of operation.

PREVIOUS SPREAD: Built in Stratford Works for the Great Eastern Railway in 1902, LNER Class D14 4-4-0 No. 8877 gets ready to leave Norwich City station with the 2.55 pm train to Melton Constable on 19 March 1939.

LEFT: Located alongside Marriott's Way, Whitwell & Reepham station has been beautifully restored as a railway museum complete with goods shed, platform, station building and operational track.

BELOW: Among the many restored artefacts at Whitwell & Reepham station are reminders of the railway's illustrious past when it was part of the Midland & Great Northern Joint Railway.

Continuing in a northwesterly direction from Lenwade, the next station was at Whitwell & Reepham, which has been restored as a superb railway museum complete with goods shed, platform, station building, track and operating steam and diesel locomotives. Opened in 2009, the museum holds open days on certain weekends with a variety of events and the operation of trains. Themelthorpe Curve follows as Marriott's Way makes a sharp turn to the east to join the trackbed of the former GER line to Aylsham. The next station was at Reepham, where the carefully restored station building with its platforms is now a welcoming tea room. The last intermediate station before Aylsham was at Cawston and this is now a private residence. Marriott's Way ends at Aylsham, which is the starting point for the 8¾-mile Bure Valley Railway and Bure Valley Footpath & Cycle Trail to Wroxham (see pages 98–101).

North Norfolk Railway

Reopened throughout 1989, this heritage railway operates mainly steam-hauled trains along the 5¼ miles of track of the former Midland & Great Northern Joint Railway between Sheringham and Holt via Weybourne. The stations have all been carefully restored to reflect their past glories and passengers are afforded views of the North Norfolk coastline and heathland. At Sheringham the railway connects with the national rail network's Bittern Line to Cromer, Wroxham and Norwich. Open weekends from March to November, daily from April to October, and during the Christmas period.

A light sprinkling of snow on the ground at Whitwell & Reepham station on 10 January 1959, less than two months before closure. Marriott's Way now passes the restored station along the trackbed on its route from Norwich to Aylsham.

Bure Valley
Footpath & Cycle Trail
County School to Wroxham

Open to passengers 1882–1952 | **Original length** 23¾ miles
Original route operator Great Eastern Railway
Length currently open for walkers & cyclists 8¾ miles (+ 9¼ miles Marriott's Way, see pages 92–97)

A latecomer to the North Norfolk railway scene, the railway between County School and Wroxham was also an early victim of closure to passengers. It was served by a circuitous service of trains running between Norwich and Dereham and was especially busy during the Second World War when several RAF airfields were opened along the line. After closure to passengers in 1952 the eastern half of the line remained open for freight until 1985. The section between Aylsham and Wroxham was reopened in 1990 as the 15-in-gauge Bure Valley Railway with the Bure Valley Footpath & Cycle Trail running alongside it.

The 23¾-mile single-track line between Wroxham and County School was opened in stages by the East Norfolk Railway (ENR) and throughout on 1 May 1882, by which time the company had been absorbed by the Great Eastern Railway (GER). County School station, 1 mile south of the junction between the ENR's line from Wroxham and the GER's Dereham to Wells-next-the-Sea line, did not open until 1886, primarily to serve the nearby Norfolk County School.

The six intermediate stations along the line, of which Aylsham South was the busiest, were served by a passenger service that took a circuitous 38½-mile route between Norwich and Dereham. During the Second World War the line became busy when several RAF airfields were opened near the line – Buxton Lamas station served RAF Coltishall, which was in fact nearer this station than Coltishall station, and Foulsham station was near to the RAF Bomber Command base of the same name. By 1950 there were six passenger services between Norwich and Dereham via Aylsham and County School with five in the opposite direction. By then increased competition from road transport had brought a decline in traffic and the line closed to passengers on 15 September 1952.

Freight trains continued to use the line until 31 October 1964 when it was closed between County School and Themelthorpe. Here a connection had been laid to link with the former Midland & Great Northern (M&GN) Joint Railway freight-only line to Norwich City in 1960 – Themelthorpe Curve was the sharpest radius curve on the British Railways network. This enabled goods trains to run the 40 or so miles from Norwich Thorpe to Norwich City (geographically less than a mile apart!) via Wroxham and Aylsham while the M&GN section north to Melton Constable was completely closed. The goods traffic to Norwich City ceased in 1969 but trains continued to carry concrete products from a factory at Lenwade until 1983 when the entire route from Wroxham was closed completely.

Since closure the trackbed between Wroxham and Aylsham South has been reopened by the 15-in-gauge Bure Valley Railway (BVR, see page 101). Running alongside the railway is the Bure Valley Footpath & Cycle Trail. At Wroxham the BVR and the Trail end close to the national network station, Hoveton & Wroxham, served by diesel trains on the Bittern Line between Norwich and Sheringham, where the impressive signal box has been beautifully restored to its former glory by the Wroxham Signalbox Trust.

At its eastern end the Cycle Trail is 2 miles from the Norfolk Broads Cycling Centre at Bewilderwood in the village of Hoveton. The Trail can be accessed from here via a quiet country lane, joining at a level crossing. With intermediate stations at the picturesque villages of Coltishall, Brampton and Buxton the railway and adjacent traffic-free Trail run through beautiful and peaceful countryside. At Buxton they cross the River Bure on a girder bridge while at Buxton station there is a car park and an adjacent picnic site. The BVR carries cycles on its trains allowing the choice of cycling one way and using the train for the return journey. Westwards from Aylsham the trackbed to Themelthorpe and thence southwards to Norwich is now a footpath and cycleway known as Marriott's Way (see pages 92–97).

Some of the original stations still survive between Wroxham and County School: Coltishall station is a bed and breakfast establishment; Cawston station building is a private residence; Reepham station, with its platforms and goods shed, is now a tea room; Foulsham station is a private residence. At the western end County School station is being restored in readiness for the extension of the 17-mile Mid-Norfolk Railway (see page 97) from Wymondham.

Bure Valley Railway

Operating between Aylsham and Wroxham, the 15-in-gauge Bure Valley Railway (BVR) opened at a cost of £2.5 million in 1990. At Wroxham the BVR connects with the adjacent national network station of Hoveton & Wroxham via a footbridge. The line meanders along the picturesque valley of the River Bure calling at the intermediate stations of Coltishall, Brampton and Buxton. The final approach to Aylsham, through a ¼-mile tunnel, leads to the large overall-roofed terminus, engine shed and workshops. Open weekends from March to December, and daily from April to October.

LEFT: Based on the design of a Leek & Manifold Valley Light Railway locomotive, Bure Valley Railway's 2-6-4T No. 9 *Mark Timothy* is being turned on the turntable at Wroxham station in June 2017.

BELOW: Footpath and railway side by side – a lone walker heads past Buxton station, where there is a picnic site and car park.

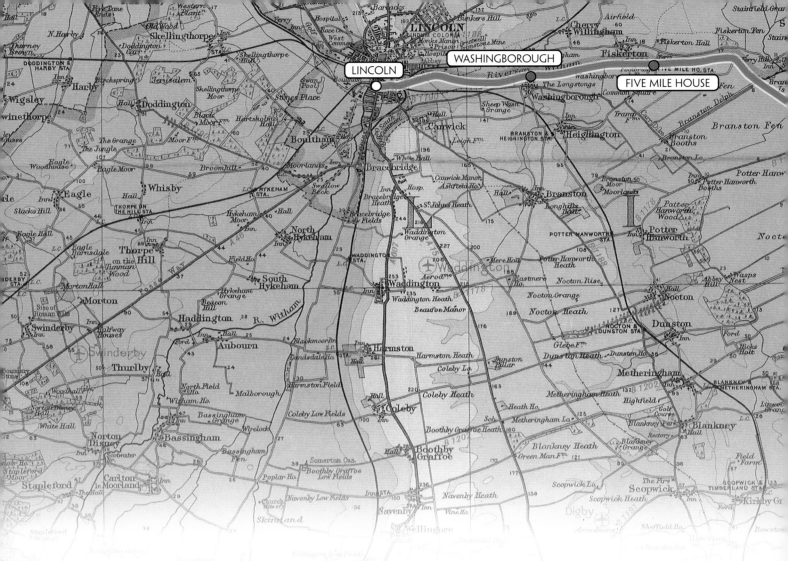

Water Rail Way

Lincoln to Boston

Open to passengers 1848–1963/70 | **Original length** 31 miles
Original route operator Great Northern Railway
Length currently open for walkers & cyclists 17½ miles | **NCN** 1

Opened in 1848, for the first four years of its life the Boston to Lincoln line played an important part in what was eventually to become the East Coast Route. This all ended in 1852 with the completion of the more direct route between Peterborough and Doncaster, after which the line was relegated to secondary status for the rest of its life. Following closure between 1963 and 1981 the route between Lincoln and Woodhall Junction and the section from Langrick to Boston has reopened as a footpath and cycleway known as the Water Rail Way.

In 1846 the Great Northern Railway was authorized by Parliament to build a main line from London to York via Grantham, Retford and Doncaster, with a loop from Peterborough to Lincoln via Spalding and Boston. Construction of the Peterborough to Lincoln loop line was rapid across a flat landscape with the section between Boston and Lincoln closely following the navigable River Witham. This opened in 1848 but it took until 1852 before the main line between London and Doncaster and thence to York with running powers over the York & North Midland Railway was completed.

The Lincolnshire Loop had a short life as a main line and it was soon relegated to secondary status following the opening of a more direct line to Lincoln via Honington in 1867. Intermediate stations on the Loop were provided at Langrick, Dogdyke, Tattershall, Kirkstead, Stixwould, Southrey, Bardney, Five Mile House and Washingboro – in 1855 Kirkstead was renamed Woodhall Junction when the short branch line to Horncastle was opened. The station nameboard at Woodhall Junction was one of the longest in Britain reading 'Woodhall Junction. Change here for Woodhall Spa & Horncastle & for Coningsby & Midville Line'. Bardney became a junction with the opening of the steeply-graded line across the Lincolnshire Wolds to Louth in 1876. The opening of the New Line, or Kirkstead & Little Steeping Line, in 1913 between a junction just south of Woodhall Junction to Bellwater Junction on the

Boston to Louth line provided a much shorter route for trains between Lincoln and the resort of Skegness, providing the Loop with much additional excursion traffic during the summer months although during the winter months it was little used apart from seasonal potato trains that originated at Tumby Woodside.

Traffic went into decline following the Second World War and the railways of Eastern England were particularly badly hit by closures – the Bardney to Louth line closed to passengers in 1951, remaining open for goods traffic until 1971, and the Horncastle branch similarly in 1954. The Beeching Report (1963) spelt the end for most of Lincolnshire's railways and the Lincoln to Boston line was closed in two stages – first to go was the section between Woodhall Junction and Boston, which closed on 17 June 1963. The northern section and the New Line to Skegness held on until 5 October 1970 when they too closed despite strong local opposition. All that remained were freight trains from Lincoln to Bardney and Horncastle via Woodhall Junction – those to Horncastle ceased on 5 April 1971 while those to a sugar beet factory at Bardney ended in January 1981.

In recent years much of the Lincoln Loop has been reopened by Sustrans and the Lincolnshire Waterways Partnership as a footpath and cycleway known as

North Ings Farm Museum Railway

Opened in 1990, the North Ings Farm Museum at Dorrington contains an interesting collection of farm machinery and associated commercial vehicles. A 600-yd-long 2-ft-gauge railway, used on the farm since 1972, operates around the site with passenger trains being hauled by a selection of small diesels and a steam tram. Passengers are carried in carriages that originally ran on the Abbey Light Railway in Leeds. The signal box at Pear Tree Junction was originally in use at Lincoln. Open on the first Sunday of each month from April to October.

LEFT: A railway scene full of 1960s period detail at Bardney as a Skegness to Sheffield (via Lincoln) two-car diesel multiple unit awaits departure. The station site is now a heritage centre alongside the Water Rail Way.

BELOW: The Water Rail Way parallels the Witham Navigation for much of its route between Lincoln and Boston. The station buildings, platforms and signal boxes at Stixwould have all survived for nearly fifty years since closure.

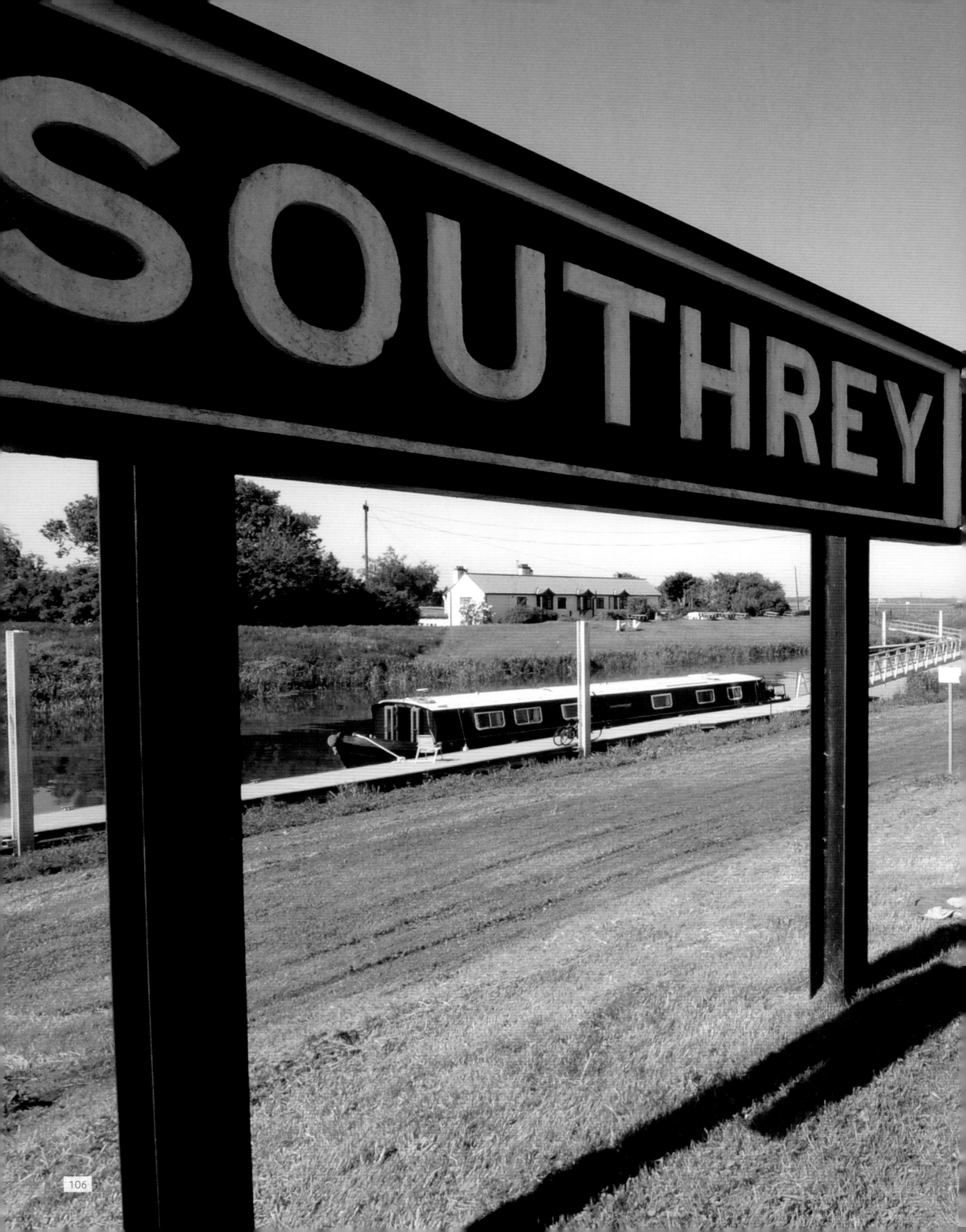
SOUTHREY

the Water Rail Way. Featuring fourteen specially commissioned sculptures – including life-sized sheep made from scrap metal – by local artists, the Way starts near Lincoln station and joins the railway trackbed at Washingboro where the station building is now a private residence. There is much of railway interest along the northern section of the Way as it closely follows the River Witham: Bardney station is now a cycle hire centre and a heritage centre tracing the histories of the Witham Navigation, the railway, a canning factory and a sugar beet factory; station buildings, platforms and signal boxes at Southrey and Stixwould; and Woodhall Junction, now a private residence, with its station building, platforms and level crossing gates. South of here the Way temporarily leaves the trackbed to follow quiet roads to Langrick, and en route a short detour can be made to the station building at Tattershall, which is now an art gallery. Another detour can be made to Dogdyke where a railway bridge and the station master's house still survive – the station was immortalised in the song *Slow Train* by Flanders and Swann in 1964. The Way rejoins the railway trackbed at Langrick, where a café now stands on the site of the station, closely following the River Witham through Anton's Gowt to the outskirts of Boston.

With boats gliding slowly along the Witham Navigation, Southrey station platform, complete with nameboard, is a glorious spot to stop and picnic on the Water Rail Way.

Bedford to Sandy Country Way

Cambridge to Bedford

Open to passengers 1857/62–1968 | **Original length** 29¾ miles
Original route operators Sandy & Potton Railway/Bedford & Cambridge Railway
Length currently open for walkers & cyclists 8½ miles | **NCN** 12 & 51

The Cambridge to Bedford railway once formed the eastern part of the long cross-country Varsity Line between Cambridge and Oxford. Much of the railway closed at the beginning of 1968 although two short unconnected sections – Oxford to Bicester and Bedford St Johns to Bletchley – currently see a passenger service. Since closure much of the 8½-mile section between Sandy and Bedford has been reopened as the Bedford to Sandy Country Way.

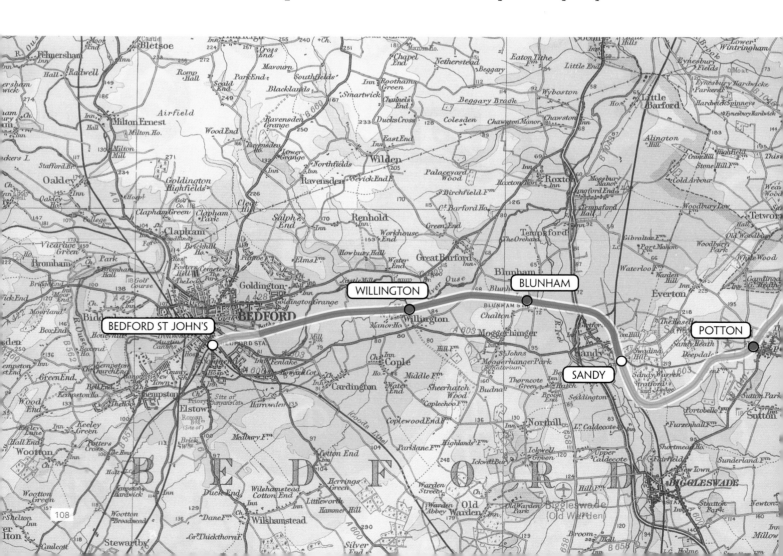

The Bedford to Cambridge railway formed part of the 77-mile cross-country route between Oxford and Cambridge, which was opened in stages over a period of sixteen years. First was the Bedford Railway, which opened the 16-mile line from Bedford to Bletchley in 1846. It was built and operated by the London & Birmingham Railway, and became part of the newly-formed London & North Western Railway (LNWR) in the same year. The second part of this long route was authorized in 1846 – known as the Oxford & Bletchley Junction Railway, it joined forces with the Buckingham & Brackley Junction Railway to form the Buckinghamshire Railway in 1847. This company opened the line from Bletchley to Banbury via Verney Junction in 1850 (the 9½ miles from Bletchley to Verney Junction eventually forming part of the main cross-country route) and the 21¾ miles from Oxford to Verney Junction in 1851. The railway was leased and worked by the LNWR and taken over by that company in 1879.

To the east, the 3½-mile Sandy & Potton Railway was built without an Act of Parliament because it was on private land owned by the son of the then prime minister,

William Peel. It opened in 1857 and was purchased by the Bedford & Cambridge Railway (B&CR) in 1862. The final links in the chain between Oxford and Cambridge, the sections from Bedford to Sandy and from Potton to Cambridge, were opened by the B&CR in 1862. The B&CR was absorbed by the LNWR in 1865.

Until 1951 trains from Cambridge terminated at the LNWR terminus in Oxford – Rewley Road was then closed with trains diverted into the former GWR station. Although the Oxford to Cambridge line was an important cross-country freight route, the withdrawal of passenger services had been threatened as early as 1959. Surviving this threat, the line – dubbed the Varsity Line because it linked two major university cities – continued to function with four through services each weekday plus others where a change at Bletchley was required.

Although the route was not recommended for closure in the Beeching Report (1963), the end came, despite much opposition from rail users, universities and local councils, on 1 January 1968 – that is apart from the Bedford St John's to Bletchley section, which retained a local passenger service, and Bletchley to Oxford, which was kept open for

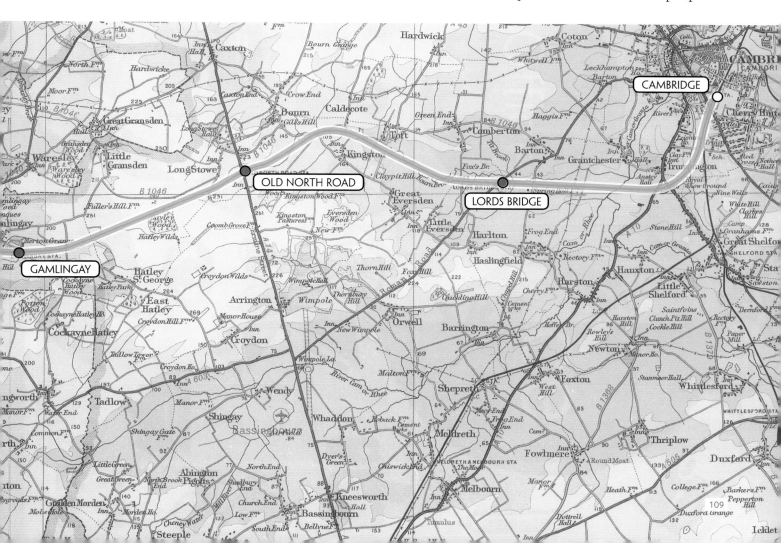

freight movements including access to the large MoD Depot at Bicester. The Oxford to Bicester section was reopened to passenger services in 1987 and there are plans to reopen the currently mothballed section from Bicester to Claydon Junction and then south to Aylesbury to provide a through route between Oxford and London Marylebone.

Between Cambridge and Sandy much of the old railway route has disappeared since closure. The first section from the old junction at Cambridge to Trumpington Park & Ride is now a concrete guided busway (progress indeed!). Lords Bridge station, with its well-preserved buildings, is owned by Cambridge University and is now home to the Mullard Radio Astronomy Observatory, while the 3 miles of trackbed eastwards is now occupied by tracks used by

the Ryle Telescope. Old North Road station buildings, signal box and goods shed have survived into private ownership while at Gamlingay the station building has survived as a private residence. Both the goods shed and station building at Potton have been restored, the latter as a private residence.

Much of the 8½-mile section between Sandy and Bedford St Johns follows the Great Ouse River and has been reopened as a footpath and cycleway known as the Bedford to Sandy Country Way. With a few diversions it also forms part of National Cycle Network Routes 12 and 51. Walking or cycling north from Sandy town centre, the trackbed of the railway is accessed from the end of St Neots Road and thence across the A1 dual carriageway – the site of Girtford Halt has long disappeared beneath a roundabout. The first station along this section of the Varsity Line was at Blunham, 2¼ miles from Sandy, where the original Bedford & Cambridge Railway's stationmaster's

BELOW: This gate at Willington on the Bedford to Sandy Country Way is mounted with a celebration of the railway's history.

house and the station building are now private residences. Part of the platform also survives. Continuing westward along the trackbed the Country Way reaches the site of Willington station, 2¼ miles from Blunham. Here a platelayers' hut and the remains of the station platform, which also served a Bryant & May plantation, lie alongside the trackbed close to a cycle hire shop and café. The church and the National Trust's 16th-century dovecote and stables at Willington are but a short distance from here and are well worth a visit.

After a further detour around the A421 dual carriageway, the Country Way crosses the Great Ouse on a bridge before reaching Priory Country Park on the eastern outskirts of Bedford. Opened in 1986, this 300-acre park alongside the Great Ouse was established on the site of former gravel workings and includes lakes, grassland, woodland and a marina. Several well-known refreshment facilities are conveniently located at the park's entrance. The Country Way continues past the country park to end on Cardington Road in Bedford. Bedford St John's station – for the surviving local service to Bletchley – is but a 10-minute walk west from here.

Rushden Historical Transport Museum

The museum is located at the restored Rushden station in Northamptonshire on the former Midland Railway branch line from Wellingborough to Higham Ferrers. Following closure of the line to passengers in 1959 and to freight in 1969, the Rushden Historical Transport Society took over the building in 1984. The museum collection includes rolling stock, steam and diesel locomotives, railway ephemera and several vintage buses. A real ale bar is housed in a former waiting room. Passenger trains run along a ½-mile of track that has been laid towards Higham Ferrers. Special events, usually at weekends and Bank Holidays, are held at the station throughout the year.

BELOW: A Class 108 diesel multiple unit on an Oxford to Cambridge service departs from Willington station in April 1960. The scene today is very different with just the remains of a platform alongside the Bedford to Sandy Country Way.

CENTRAL ENGLAND

Wye Valley Walk

Chepstow to Ross-on-Wye

Open to passengers 1817/76–1959 | **Original length** 27½ miles
Original route operator Great Western Railway
Length currently open for walkers 14¼ miles **& cyclists** 5½ miles | **NCN** 423 (Monmouth to Symonds Yat)

Opening between 1873 and 1876, the two separate railways along the picturesque Wye Valley between Chepstow and Ross-on-Wye met at Monmouth Troy station. Although there were never any through services, both lines were operated from opening by the Great Western Railway. Both passenger and goods traffic went into decline after the Second World War and both routes were closed to passengers in 1959. Since closure several sections have been reopened as footpaths and the section from Monmouth to Symonds Yat is also a cycle path.

ROSS-ON-WYE

KERNE BRIDGE

LYDBROOK JUNCTION

SYMONDS YAT

MONMOUTH MAY HILL

MONMOUTH TROY

REDBROOK

WHITEBROOK HALT

ST BRIAVELS

TINTERN

NETHERHOPE HALT

TIDENHAM

CHEPSTOW

Devoid of rail transport for the past sixty years, Monmouth was once the junction for three sleepy branch lines radiating out westwards to Pontypool Road, northwards to Ross-on-Wye and southwards to Chepstow. Predating these three railways was the Monmouth Tramroad, a 3-ft-6-in-gauge horse-drawn tramway, or plateway, which opened between a wharf on the east bank of the River Wye at Monmouth to Coleford in 1812. Primarily carrying coal, iron ore, lime and clay from the Forest of Dean, the tramway's wagons had flangeless wheels that ran on L-section flanged cast iron rails. Closure came in the 1870s following the opening of the standard-gauge lines along the Wye Valley.

The first standard-gauge railway to reach Monmouth was the 16-mile Coleford, Monmouth, Usk & Pontypool Railway (CMU&PR), which opened between Pontypool Road and Monmouth in 1857. Passenger services terminated at Monmouth Troy station but the line continued on over the River Wye via Monmouth Viaduct, completed in 1861, where it met the Monmouth Tramroad at Wyesham Wharf. The railway was leased to the West Midlands Railway (itself leased to the Great Western Railway) in 1861 but the planned extension to Coleford along the route of the tramway was abandoned. Finally, in 1881, the CMU&PR was transferred to the Great Western Railway (GWR) by Act of Parliament. The line from Pontypool Road to Monmouth Troy closed on 30 May 1955 amidst a national rail strike.

The second standard-gauge line to open to Monmouth was the Ross & Monmouth Railway, which opened its

12½-mile route down the Wye Valley between Ross-on-Wye and Monmouth May Hill in 1873. It was worked from opening by the GWR but remained an independent company until 1921 when it was amalgamated with that company. With intermediate stations at Kerne Bridge, Lydbrook Junction (where it met the Severn & Wye Railway, see pages 120–125) and Symonds Yat, it crossed the River Wye twice and had two tunnels, at Lydbrook and Symonds Yat. Walford Halt near Ross opened in 1931 and Hadnock Halt near Monmouth opened in 1951. An extension over the Wye by way of a girder bridge linking Monmouth May Hill and Troy stations opened in 1874. Closure to passengers came on 5 January 1959 although the section from Ross to Lydbrook remained open for freight until 1965.

OPENING SPREAD: A lone cyclist crosses the impressive Fledborough Viaduct on what is now National Cycle Network Route 647. Crossing the River Trent on the former Chesterfield to Lincoln railway, the viaduct is 890-yds long and has fifty-nine arches and four trussed steel spans.

PREVIOUS SPREAD: It's rush hour at Netherhope Halt on the Wye Valley Line on 11 April 1955. Beyond the halt is the entrance to the 1,190-yd-long Tidenham Tunnel, beyond which is Tintern Quarry and Tintern station.

BELOW: Monmouth Troy station on 11 April 1955. Ex-GWR Class 1400 0-4-2T No. 1445 has just arrived after propelling the 11am auto-train from Ross-on-Wye.

The third standard-gauge railway to reach Monmouth was the 14-mile Wye Valley Railway, which opened in 1876 between Wye Valley Junction near Chepstow and Monmouth Troy. Closely following the picturesque Wye Valley for its entire route, it crossed the river three times and had two tunnels, at Tidenham and Tintern. Operated from opening by the GWR, the line initially had intermediate stations at Tidenham, Tintern, St Briavels and Redbrook but halts were later opened at Netherhope (1932), Brockweir (1929), Llandogo (1927), Whitebrook (1927), Penallt (1931) and Wyesham (1931). Primarily a tourist line, the railway also served stone quarries at

Tidenham and Tintern. Increasing competition from road transport after the Second World War brought a decline in traffic and passenger services were withdrawn on 5 January 1959 – the same day as the passenger service between Monmouth and Ross-on-Wye. Goods traffic continued until 6 January 1964 when the railway was closed completely between Monmouth and Tintern Quarry. The latter continued to be served by stone trains until 1981 and thereafter the line was cut back to the quarry at Tidenham until it closed in 1991.

The 5-mile Coleford Railway from Wyesham Junction on the Wye Valley line to Coleford opened in 1883. Built along the course of the Monmouth Tramroad for much of its length, it physically met the Severn & Wye Railway at Coleford, although the two railways had separate stations in the town. The GWR soon took control but the line had a very brief life, closing in 1917, although the short section from Coleford to Whitecliff Quarry remained open for stone traffic until 1976.

Since closure several sections of the railway up the Wye Valley have been reopened as footpaths while the section from Monmouth to Symonds Yat is also a cycleway. Starting at the southern end of the line the trackbed from Wye Valley Junction, near Chepstow, to Tintern is owned by the cycling charity Sustrans. They propose reopening this as a cycleway through Tidenham and Tintern Tunnels. The section between these two tunnels is currently a footpath reached across the River Wye from Tintern via the bridge that once carried the short branch line to the Abbey Tinplate Works. The beautifully restored station at Tintern is now a café, picnic site and railway museum (see right). The Wye Valley Walk Long Distance Path passes through the site and continues along the trackbed to Brockweir. From Llandogo the trackbed alongside the Wye is rejoined for much of the next 4 miles to Redbrook where it crosses the river via Penallt Viaduct. Here there is a car park and shops, while on the opposite bank of the river is the charming Boat Inn.

Currently the trackbed between Redbrook and Monmouth is not a footpath but at Monmouth the 1861-built twenty-arch red sandstone Monmouth Viaduct has survived (although the iron central section has been removed). Close to the viaduct the Ross & Monmouth Railway's 1874-built three-span girder bridge over the Wye that connected Monmouth Troy station with Monmouth May Hill station has survived intact and is crossed by a footpath. Monmouth Troy station building has found a new home on the Gloucestershire-Warwickshire Railway where it was re-erected at Winchcombe station. The 5 miles of trackbed along the east bank of the River Wye between the outskirts of Monmouth is now a footpath and cycleway forming part of the Wye Valley Walk and National Cycle Network Route 423. Of interest to lovers of lost railways on this section are the platforms at the sites of Monmouth May Hill station and Hadnock Halt, while at Symonds Yat the platforms have survived in a hotel car park. Beyond the station is the bricked-up entrance to Symonds Yat Tunnel. Beyond the tunnel is the site of Lydbrook Junction and the bricked-up entrance to the second tunnel on the line, under Coppett Hill, which can be accessed via a footpath. At Kerne Bridge the station building is now a private residence. At Ross-on-Wye the goods shed and engine shed are both lucky survivors.

LEFT: Penallt Viaduct over the River Wye at Redbrook has survived for almost sixty years since the closure of the railway. A footbridge attached to the side of the viaduct provides access for walkers and cyclists to the Boat Inn, on the west bank of the Wye.

BELOW: At restored Tintern station there is car parking, a café, a picnic site and a museum.

Locally restored stations
Tintern

Reopened in 1975, the restored station building with its platform and signal box at Tintern is now an information centre and café with a display of local railway history. Two restored passenger carriages stand on a short length of track while a 5-in-gauge miniature railway operates through the site on selected weekends. Adjacent is a wooded car park. Open daily from Easter to October.

Coleford

Founded in 1988, the Coleford Great Western Railway Museum is located in the former GWR goods shed at Coleford. Tracing the history of local railways, the museum also includes a restored GWR signal box, a 7¼-in-gauge miniature railway and a standard-gauge Peckett 0-4-0 saddle tank and former GWR rolling stock. Open in the afternoon on Fridays, Saturdays and Bank Holidays.

Forest of Dean

Lydney to Coleford and Cinderford

Open to passengers 1810/1900–1929 | **Original length** 17¾ miles
Original route operator Severn & Wye Railway & Canal Company
Length currently open for walkers & cyclists 12¼ miles | **NCN** 42 (part)

The Severn & Wye Railway had a long career transporting minerals from the Forest of Dean. Starting life in 1810 as a horse-drawn tramway and canal, it progressed to broad-gauge before becoming a steam-operated standard-gauge railway. It was saved from bankruptcy by the Midland and Great Western railways in 1885 after joining forces with the Severn Bridge Railway. Passenger traffic ceased in 1929 but mineral traffic continued until 1976. Since closure much of the route has reopened as a circular footpath and cycleway.

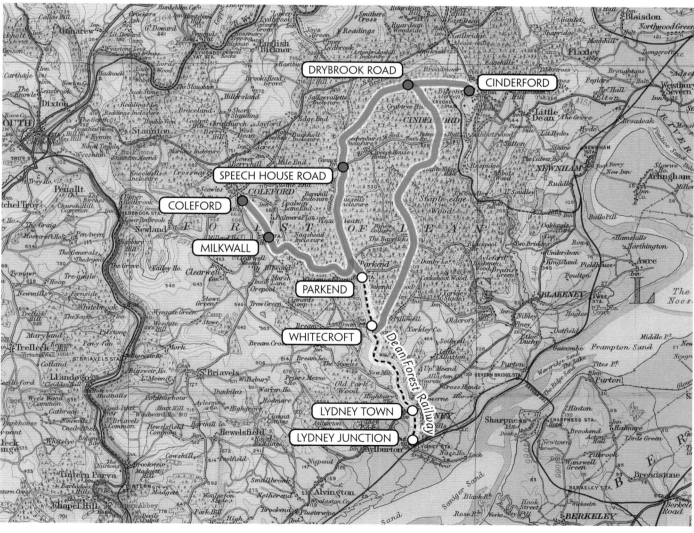

By the early 19th century the Forest of Dean on the west bank of the River Severn in Gloucestershire had become a small, but important, player in the Industrial Revolution. The mining of coal and iron ore were especially important but transporting these raw materials to local ironworks or to the nearest rivers for onward shipment was a slow process. Enter the Severn & Wye Railway & Canal Company (S&WR), which in 1809 began the construction of a tramway through the forest between Lydney and Lydbrook and a 1-mile canal linking Lydney

PREVIOUS SPREAD LEFT: Managed by the Forestry Commission, the Forest of Dean Family Cycle Trail follows old railway routes through the forest for 9½ miles. The footpath and cycleway is seen here near Cannop, where there is a cycle hire centre.

PREVIOUS SPREAD RIGHT: Ex-GWR Class 5400 0-6-0PT No. 5417 has just arrived at Cinderford with the 11.15 am train from Gloucester Central on 12 July 1956. This service ended on 1 November 1958 but the station remained open for goods traffic until 1967.

with the River Severn. The steeply graded 3-ft-6-in-gauge horse-drawn tramway, or plateway, opened in 1810 and the canal in 1813, with both enterprises speeding up the transport of raw materials.

In 1851 the broad-gauge (7 ft 0¼ in) South Wales Railway, engineered by Isambard Kingdom Brunel, opened along the west bank of the River Severn between Gloucester and Chepstow via Lydney. However, the change of gauge between the railway and tramway at Lydney was to become an ever-increasing problem. By the 1860s the tramway was worn out after over fifty years of service and in 1868, after successfully experimenting with steam haulage, a broad-gauge line was laid alongside it between Lydney and Speech House Road. Broad-gauge steam locomotives replaced horsepower but more changes were soon looming when the main line between Gloucester and Chepstow was converted from broad- to standard-gauge (4 ft 8½ in) by the Great Western Railway (GWR). By 1874 both the broad-gauge section of the S&WR and the rest of the

tramway had been rebuilt to standard-gauge. An extension was also built over the impressive Lydbrook Viaduct to Lydbrook Junction where the S&WR met the newly opened Ross & Monmouth Railway (see pages 114–119). In the same year a mineral loop line was opened between Drybrook Road Junction and Tufts Junction, just south of Whitecroft, and a year later a 2¾-mile branch line from Parkend to Coleford was opened. The latter met the Coleford Railway from Wyesham Junction, near Monmouth, when it opened in 1883.

In 1879 the S&WR amalgamated with the Severn Bridge Railway on the day that the bridge opened,

LEFT: Station sites such as Speech House Road and Drybrook Road on the Forest of Dean Family Cycle Trail are marked today by station nameboards mounted on old railway sleepers.

BELOW: The imposing Dicke Bridge carries the B4226 over the Forest of Dean Family Cycle Trail, formerly the Severn & Wye Railway's Mineral Loop, between Speech House and Ruspidge.

17 October. Over a mile in length, the single-track bridge was built primarily to carry coal from the Forest of Dean to Sharpness Docks but also provided a route for a passenger service between Lydney and Berkeley Road station on the Midland Railway's (MR) main line between Gloucester and Bristol. However, the looming opening of the Severn Railway Tunnel and a miners' strike in the Forest was a serious blow to the joint company, which went bankrupt in 1885. The company was sold to the GWR and the MR and the railway became Severn & Wye Joint Railway (S&WJR) in 1894. Along with several short colliery branches and the opening of a short branch line from Drybrook Road to Cinderford in 1900, the S&WJR finally reached its maximum extent of 39 miles.

The years following the First World War brought a decline in passengers using the S&WJR north of Lydney and the services to Coleford, Lydbrook Junction and Cinderford all ceased on 8 July 1929. All that remained was the passenger service over the Severn Bridge between

Lydney Town and Berkeley Road but this ceased on 25 October 1960 following a collision by two barges in thick fog – the damaged bridge was never reopened and was demolished in 1967.

Despite the loss of passenger services the S&WJR was kept busy transporting minerals and freight for many more years. The beginning of the end came when the Serridge Junction to Lydbrook Junction section closed in 1956. With the closure of the last collieries in the area the line northwards from Coleford Junction to Speech House Road and beyond closed completely on 12 August 1963 but the Coleford branch via Parkend remained open for stone traffic from Whitecliff Quarry until 26 March 1976.

At Cinderford a loop line had opened in 1908 allowing GWR trains from Bullo Pill to reach the station – passenger trains via this route continued until

3 November 1958 but the line remained open for freight traffic until 1967.

Since closure much of the old S&WJR north of Lydney has found a new lease of life. The 4¼-mile Dean Forest Railway (see right) now operates passenger trains between Lydney Junction and Parkend. From here the trackbed of the 2¾-mile branch line to Coleford via Milkwall is now a footpath and cycleway – at Coleford the Great Western Railway Museum is located in the former GWR goods shed (see page 119).

The trackbed of the main route of the S&WJR from Parkend to Speech House Road and Drybrook Road and thence back down the route of the Mineral Loop is a 9½-mile circular footpath and cycleway known as the Forest of Dean Family Cycle Trail. Managed by the Forestry Commission, it also forms part of National Cycle

A Stephenson Locomotive Society Special visited Serridge Junction on 13 May 1961. The lead loco is ex-GWR Class 5700 0-6-0PT No. 8701 while near the rear is Class 6400 0-6-0PT No. 6437.

Network Route 42 from Parkend to just beyond Drybrook Road (and thence to Cinderford). Station sites such as Speech House Road and Drybrook Road are marked today by station nameboards mounted on old railway sleepers while remnants of collieries can be seen at Foxes Bridge, Lightmoor and New Fancy. Although accessed from Parkend station, this pleasant and level circular route through woodland is centred on the Cycle Centre at Cannop, the site of Cannop Colliery (closed in 1960), where there is a large car park, café and cycle hire centre.

From the site of Drybrook Road station a narrow footpath follows a wooded embankment that was once the trackbed of the branch line to Cinderford. Not far from here is the restored Ruspidge Halt on the trackbed of the GWR line from Bullo Pill to Cinderford, which is now the Cinderford Linear Park.

Dean Forest Railway

Reopened fully in 2006, the Dean Forest Railway operates steam and diesel trains along the 4¼-mile stretch of the old S&WJR route from Lydney Junction (for the national rail network) to Parkend. The railway's headquarters is at Norchard where there is a two-level station, engine shed and workshop. Originally closed in 1929, Whitecroft station was reopened in 2012 after an eighteen-month restoration programme. A 2½-mile extension to Speech House Road is currently planned with the eventual goal of reaching Cinderford. The old station building from Panteg & Griffithstown near Pontypool has been earmarked for Speech House Road. Open certain weekends in February and weekends in November, Wednesdays and weekends from Easter to October, and during the pre-Christmas period.

Great Malvern to Ashchurch

Open to passengers 1840/64–1952/61 | **Original length** 14 miles
Original route operators Birmingham & Gloucester Railway/Midland Railway
Length currently open for walkers 5 miles **& cyclists** 1½ miles

This cross-country line between Ashchurch and Great Malvern via Tewkesbury opened in two stages between 1840 and 1864. It never lived up to expectations and led a fairly quiet life until the section west of Upton-on-Severn was closed completely in 1952. The eastern section, from Ashchurch to Upton-on-Severn, lost its passenger service in 1961 and closed completely in 1964. Since closure several sections have reopened as footpaths and the section from Tewkesbury to Ashchurch is also a cycleway.

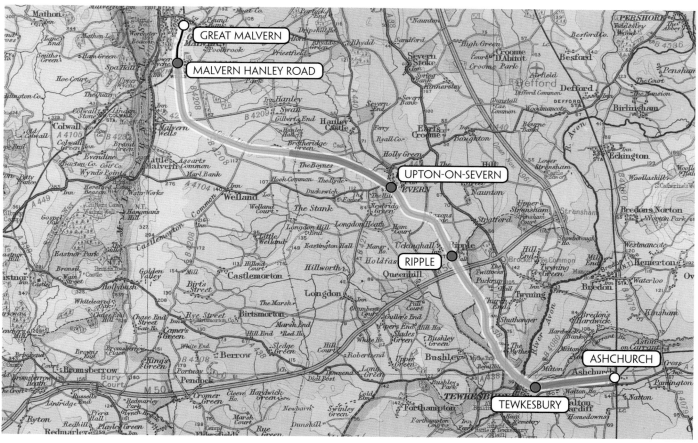

The 14-mile line between Great Malvern, on the Worcester & Hereford Railway, and Ashchurch, on the Birmingham & Gloucester Railway (B&GR), was built in two stages. On 21 July 1840, only one month after the B&GR main line opened between Cheltenham and Bromsgrove, the company opened a 1¾-mile branch line between Ashchurch and Tewkesbury with a short branch to wharves on the River Severn.

The second section of this route was built by the Tewkesbury & Malvern Railway with financial backing from the Midland Railway (MR). Opening throughout on 16 May 1864, it was worked from the outset by the MR, which acquired the line in 1877. The line was initially single-track but doubled later before being partly re-singled in 1913. Major engineering works included a single-span bridge over the River Avon and a five-span bridge over the River Severn, a 420-yd tunnel and a long viaduct and embankment over the Avon/Severn floodplain west of Tewkesbury. The line was linked to the Birmingham & Gloucester Loop (via Redditch) at Ashchurch by way of a spur crossing the main line on the level.

Serving intermediate stations at Malvern Wells (Hanley Road), Upton-on-Severn, Ripple and Tewkesbury, passenger trains consisted of through trains between Great Malvern and Ashchurch along with a shuttle service between Tewkesbury and Ashchurch. In 1950 these amounted to four weekday through return services plus three extra between Tewkesbury and Ashchurch and four in the other direction. Passenger traffic, especially between Great Malvern and Upton-on-Severn, was never heavy and that 6¾-mile section closed completely on 1 December 1952. The Ashchurch to Upton-on-Severn passenger service continued until closure on 14 August 1961 although goods traffic continued to reach Upton until July 1963 and Tewkesbury until November 1964.

PREVIOUS SPREAD LEFT: Midway between Tewkesbury and Upton-on-Severn, Ripple station was located between the 145-yd five-span bridge over the River Severn and the 420-yd-long Mythe Tunnel. It is now a tastefully converted private residence.

PREVIOUS SPREAD RIGHT: Ex-Midland Railway 3F 0-6-0 No. 43645 of Gloucester Barnwood shed (85E) waits to depart from Upton-on-Severn with a short passenger train for Ashchurch on 20 June 1959.

While the stations at Malvern Wells (Hanley Road), Upton-on-Severn, Tewkesbury and Ashchurch have all been demolished, the station building at Ripple, complete with platforms, is now a private residence. Footpaths run along several sections of the railway trackbed from Malvern. Today the site of Malvern (Hanley Road) station is a car park in the Three Counties Showground. The line of trees through the car park and beyond, where it first becomes a high embankment followed by a cutting, are visible clues to the route of the railway. At Brotheridge Green, near Upton-on-Severn, there is a public footpath along a tree-lined cutting followed by an embankment that is now managed by the Worcestershire Wildlife Trust – over thirty species of butterflies have been recorded in this corridor reserve.

An embankment, viaducts and bridges once crossed the floodplain at The Mythe near Tewkesbury. These were demolished in 2013 as part of the Tewkesbury flood prevention scheme and the recycled bricks were used to build the new station at Broadway on the Gloucestershire-Warwickshire Railway (see box).

Although Ashchurch station was closed in 1971 and its buildings demolished, it was rebuilt and reopened in 1997 and is now known as 'Ashchurch for Tewkesbury'. Much of the trackbed to the west of the station from here to Tewkesbury is now a 1½-mile footpath and cycleway.

Gloucestershire-Warwickshire Railway

One of the last main line railways built in Britain, the line between Stratford-upon-Avon and Cheltenham was opened in 1908. Passenger services ceased in 1966 and the line was closed in 1976. Since then the section from Cheltenham Racecourse station to Broadway has been reopened by the Gloucestershire-Warwickshire Railway, with its headquarters at Toddington. With intermediate stations at Gotherington, Winchcombe, Hayles Abbey and Toddington, the railway operates both diesel and steam-hauled trains in the shadow of the Cotswold escarpment. Open weekends and Bank Holidays from April to November, Tuesdays to Thursdays from April to October, and the Christmas period.

LEFT: Now home to a colony of bats, the bricked-up entrance to Mythe Tunnel lies between Tewkesbury and Ripple where there was also once a long embankment and viaduct over the River Avon floodplain.

BELOW: Seen here in 1951, the former Tewkesbury & Malvern Railway's station in Malvern became known as Malvern Hanley Road on 2 March of that year. It closed in 1952 following closure of the line between Upton-on-Severn and Malvern.

WHALEY BRIDGE

SHALCROSS

FERNILEE

HARPUR HILL

HINDLOW

DOWLOW HALT

HURDLOW

PARSLEY HAY

High Peak Trail
Whaley Bridge to High Peak Junction

Open to passengers 1830/1832–77 | **Original length** 33 miles
Original route operator Cromford & High Peak Railway
Length currently open for walkers & cyclists 17 miles | **NCN** 54 & 68

One of the oldest and also one of the highest standard-gauge railways in
Britain, the 33-mile Cromford & High Peak Railway linked two canals,
crossing the exposed Peak District plateau by way of a series of inclines at
each end. The northern half was later rebuilt by the London & North
Western Railway but the southern half, with its inclines, remained in
operation until closure in 1967. Since closure much of the railway trackbed
has been reopened as a footpath and cycleway known as the High Peak Trail.

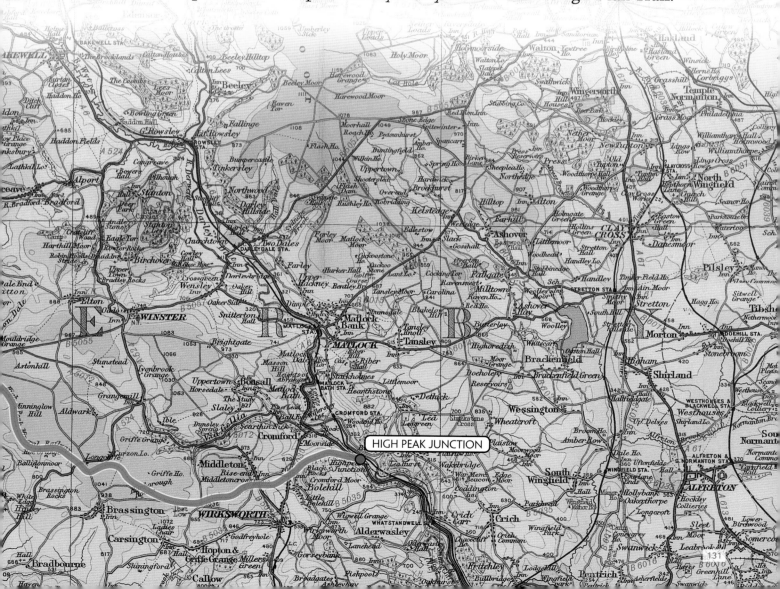

Not only one of the earliest lines built in Britain but also one of the highest, the 33-mile Cromford & High Peak Railway (C&HPR) linked the Peak Forest Canal at Whaley Bridge with the Cromford Canal at Cromford Wharf. Receiving Parliamentary approval in 1825 – the year the Stockton & Darlington Railway opened – its route from Whaley Bridge involved climbing to over 1,000 ft in 5 miles by way of four inclines. Reaching the 1,266-ft summit at Ladmanlow, the railway crossed the Peak District plateau before descending by way of five inclines to Cromford. The gradients of these inclines ranged from 1-in-7 to 1-in-16. A notable engineering feature of this route, even today, are the massive dry stone embankments that were built to carry the railway across valleys.

The standard-gauge (4 ft 8½ in) railway opened from Cromford Wharf to Hurdlow in 1830 – the same year that the Liverpool & Manchester Railway opened – and from there to Whaley Bridge in 1832. Trains were at first hauled on the level sections by horses but these were gradually replaced by steam locomotives from 1841 onwards. The inclines were worked by static steam engines that hauled the trains up and down by means of rope or chain and later by steel cables. The railway also served many limestone quarries along its length and these provided much of its freight traffic until closure.

The inclines slowed down travel times considerably and it could take a couple of days for a mineral train to travel along the full extent of the line. Several inclines were later combined as one and one of these, Hopton Incline, became adhesion-worked when more powerful locomotives were introduced – its 1-in-14 gradient was the steepest adhesion-worked incline in Britain. The railway also had the sharpest curve – with a 55-yd radius – at Gotham. Passengers were carried from 1874 but operating just the one train a day in each direction up and down the inclines was a slow business (it took

5½ hours) and this service was discontinued in 1877 after a passenger was killed.

The C&HPR remained isolated from Britain's fast-expanding rail network until 1853. In that year it was connected via a short spur from Cromford Wharf to the newly-opened Manchester, Buxton, Matlock & Midlands Junction Railway (see pages 140–145) at High Peak Junction. Four years later the northern end was connected with Stockport, Disley & Whaley Bridge Railway. The C&HPR was leased by the London & North Western Railway (L&NWR) in 1862 and finally taken over by that company in 1887. Seeing a potential route for its trains from London Euston to Buxton, the L&NWR rebuilt the section of the C&HPR northwards from Parsley Hay to Hindlow then built a new line from there through Higher Buxton to Buxton, where it connected with that company's line to Manchester. Southwards from Parsley Hay the L&NWR built a new line to Ashbourne (see pages 136–139)

where it connected with the North Staffordshire Railway's (NSR) route from Uttoxeter, which had opened in 1852. The route from Parsley Hay to Buxton opened in 1892 and the original route down the inclines to Whaley Bridge was closed. The Parsley Hay to Ashbourne line opened in 1899 and for a while the L&NWR operated through coaches between London Euston and Buxton via the NSR's line to Uttoxeter.

What remained of the old C&HPR – High Peak Junction to Parsley Hay – was kept busy serving the many limestone quarries along its length. While this traffic held up in the immediate years after the Second World War the same cannot be said for regular passenger

BELOW: The top of the 1-in-8 gradient Middleton Incline on 4 May 1934. On the left wagons wait to be lowered by steel hawsers down the incline while on the right a wagon has nearly completed its upward journey.

services between Ashbourne and Buxton, which ceased on 1 November 1954. By the early 1960s stone traffic on the C&HPR was in decline and the first section to close in 1963 was between Parsley Hay and the bottom of the Middleton Incline. Steam-hauled to the bitter end, the remainder of the line soldiered on until the spring of 1967 when it too closed.

Much of the trackbed and the inclines of the long-abandoned route at the northern end of the P&HPR from between Ladmanlow (the summit of the line) to Whaley Bridge via the Goyt Valley can be followed today. A road now runs down Bunsall Incline towards Fernilee Reservoir.

Following closure of the C&HPR, Derbyshire County Council and the Peak District National Park purchased the majority of the trackbed between High Peak Junction and Dowlow, resurfaced it with crushed limestone, and reopened it as a footpath, cycleway and bridle path. The High Peak Trail, as it is known, is 17 miles long with much of it crossing the exposed Peak District plateau at elevations of over 1,000 ft. Apart from the inclines it is fairly level and forms part of National Cycle Network Routes 54 and 68; it also meets the 13-mile Tissington Trail (see pages 136–139) from Ashbourne at Parsley Hay. Car parks and picnic sites are provided at Hurdlow, Parsley Hay, Friden, Minninglow, Middleton Top and Black Rocks while at High Peak Junction a car park is reached via a footbridge over the River Derwent. At Parsley Hay, Middleton Top and High Peak Junction there are also visitor centres and refreshment facilities.

The massive dry stone embankments that have survived since being completed in 1830 are a feature of this long route – Minninglow Embankment, which is nearly 300 yds long and 50 ft high, has been listed by Historic England for its special architectural and historic interest. Also of interest is the restored engine house at Middleton Top – this Scheduled Ancient Monument houses a working beam engine built by the Butterley Company in 1829, which can be see in action on selected Sundays and Bank Holidays from Easter to October.

Between Parsley Hay and High Peak Junction walkers and cyclists first pass through Newhaven Tunnel then past the sites of goods yards at Friden. Minninglow and

Longcliffe before descending the 1-in-14 Hopton Incline, through Hopton Tunnel to reach Middleton Top. After descending the 1-in-8 Middleton Incline the Trail continues southwards to Steeple House, for the National Stone Centre, Ecclesbourne Valley Railway (see page 139) and the Steeple Grange Light Railway (see box), before descending the 1-in-8 Sheep Pasture Incline to end at Cromford Wharf. Here the C&HPR buildings have all been restored to their original state and form part of the Derwent Valley Mills World Heritage Site, which covers nearly 5 square miles along a 15-mile stretch of the River Derwent from Matlock Bath to Derby.

LEFT: Photographed by famous railway photographer Henry Casserley, his wife Kathleen and young son Richard pose at the bottom of the 1-in-14 Hopton Incline on 16 July 1940 – this was the steepest adhesion-worked standard-gauge incline in Britain.

BELOW: Built in 1829 by the Butterley Company of Ripley, the steam-powered winding house at the top of Middleton Incline has been restored and is occasionally operated for the public.

Steeple Grange Light Railway

This 18-in-gauge railway follows ½-mile of the trackbed of the limestone quarry branch of the Cromford & High Peak Railway from Steeple House on the High Peak Trail to Middleton Quarry. It opened in 1883, closed in 1967, and was reopened in 1985. Passengers are carried in former National Coal Board miners' coaches and trains are hauled by diminutive petrol, diesel and battery locomotives that once worked in quarries and mines. The ½-mile line features a steep 1-in-27 gradient on what was nicknamed the Killer's Branch, so named as it was originally built for the Killer Brothers of Wirksworth, owners of Middleton Quarry, who paid for its construction. An extension to the National Stone Centre is being considered for the future. Open Sundays and Bank Holidays from Easter to the end of September.

Tissington Trail

Ashbourne to Buxton

Open to passengers 1899–1954 | **Original length** 22½ miles
Original route operator London & North Western Railway
Length currently open for walkers & cyclists 13 miles (see also High Peak Trail, pages 130–135) | **NCN** 68

A railway with two distinctive sections, one dating from 1830 and the other a brand new line, that together became a through route in 1899. Serving nothing but a few scattered villages along its route over the exposed Peak District plateau, the southern part came alive at weekends and Bank Holidays bringing ramblers to visit the scenic delights of Dovedale. All this ended in 1963 and within a few years the entire railway, except for a short section that still serves quarries near Buxton, had closed. Since then the southern section from Ashbourne to Parsley Hay has reopened as a footpath and cycleway known as the Tissington Trail.

BUXTON
HIGHER BUXTON
HINDLOW
DOWLOW HALT
HURDLOW
PARSLEY HAY
HARTINGTON
ALSOP-EN-LE-DALE
High Peak Trail
TISSINGTON
THORPE CLOUD
ASHBOURNE

BAKEWELL
WIRKSWORTH

The 22½-mile Ashbourne to Buxton route consisted of two distinct sections – the northern half was a rebuild of one of the earliest railways in Britain, while the southern half was a latecomer to the railway scene. As we read on pages 130–135, the Cromford & High Peak Railway (C&HPR) was opened throughout in 1832. It was taken over by the London & North Western Railway (L&NWR) in 1887 and the company set about rebuilding the northern half of the line between Parsley Hay and Hindlow and constructing a new line from there to Buxton. Buxton had already been reached by the L&NWR from Manchester in 1863 and passenger services between the town and Parsley Hay along the rebuilt railway commenced in 1894.

Meanwhile, to the south, the town of Ashbourne had already been reached by the North Staffordshire Railway (NSR) in 1852. The L&NWR had already seen this as a potential route for trains to and from Buxton and had obtained Parliamentary approval in 1890 to build a new 13-mile line between Ashbourne and Parsley Hay, thus creating a new route to the south for its trains from Buxton.

With intermediate stations at Thorpe Cloud, Tissington, Alsop-en-le-Dale and Hartington, the new meandering single-track railway opened in 1899. A new joint station was opened at the same time in Ashbourne by the NSR and the L&NWR. Initially the passenger service consisted of six trains each way during weekdays and three on Sundays. Through coaches to and from London Euston were attached to some of these trains, offering passengers a through service to and from Buxton. This pattern of services continued up to the First World War when the through coaches were discontinued. Passenger traffic along this sparsely populated route was light during the winter – snow often blocked the line for days – but the summer months brought hordes of ramblers heading for the delights of Dovedale. Goods traffic was important, with the line carrying limestone from the quarries at the northern end of the line, along with farm produce and milk that was collected daily in churns and transported to London from the intermediate stations.

The years following the Second World War brought a rapid decline in traffic brought on by increased competition from road transport. Regular passenger services – by then reduced to just three trains each way on weekdays – ceased on 30 October 1954, although special trains for ramblers and excursions to visit floral well

dressings continued until 1963. Freight traffic continued to dwindle and the line between Ashbourne and Hartington closed completely on 7 October 1963, the former NSR route south to Uttoxeter closed in 1964, and the Hartington to Hindlow via Parsley Hay route closed in 1967. All that remained of this route was the section from Buxton to limestone quarries at Hindlow, which is still open for mineral traffic today.

Today the entire length of the line from Ashbourne to Parsley Hay is a footpath and cycleway know as the Tissington Trail. From Parsley Hay the route north to Dowlow forms part of the High Peak Trail from Cromford Wharf (see pages 130–135). Opened in 1971 by Derbyshire County Council and the Peak District National Authority, the traffic-free Tissington Trail, so-named after one of the villages it once served, was one of the first such schemes in Britain. Its fairly level crushed limestone surface makes it ideal for cyclists, wheelchairs and pushchairs while its elevation of over 1,000 ft affords fine views over the surrounding countryside. Car parks and picnic sites are located at all of the former intermediate stations and there are cycle hire shops at Ashbourne and Parsley Hay.

At Ashbourne the Trail first burrows through the 378-yd Church Street Tunnel then dips down and up where a viaduct has been demolished. Heading north the Trail reaches the site of Thorpe Cloud station, once popular with ramblers brought here by excursion trains for visiting nearby Dovedale. At Tissington station one of the platforms has survived (alongside the picnic site) while at Hartington station the restored L&NWR signal box is now a visitor centre. North of here the Trail enters the ¾-mile long and 60-ft-deep Coldeaton Cutting, carved through the limestone by the railway builders at the end of the 19th century. The Trail ends at Parsley Hay junction for the High Peak Trail.

PREVIOUS SPREAD: Once popular with ramblers, Tissington station is viewed from a northbound train on 7 August 1953. The train was the 10.10 am from Uttoxeter to Buxton hauled by ex-LMS 2-6-4T No. 42368. This passenger service ceased just over a year later.

LEFT: The start of the Tissington Trail in Ashbourne is through the 378-yd-long Church Street Tunnel, which opened to rail traffic in 1899. The tunnel is now owned by Sustrans.

RIGHT: Located on the Tissington Trail is the restored signal box at the site of Hartington station. It is now an information centre open at weekends and bank holidays.

Ecclesbourne Valley Railway

The Duffield to Wirksworth branch line in Derbyshire was opened by the Midland Railway in 1867. Passenger services ceased in 1947 but the line remained open for limestone traffic until 1989. It was reopened throughout as a heritage railway by the Ecclesbourne Valley Railway in 2010. The railway also operates trains on the steeply-graded mineral line from Wirksworth to Ravenstor (for the National Stone Centre, the High Peak Trail and the Steeple Grange Light Railway). Services are operated by restored diesel multiple units, with steam haulage on special events days. Open Tuesdays, weekends and Bank Holidays from February to October, also Thursdays and Fridays April, June to September, and on Tuesdays and Saturdays only in November.

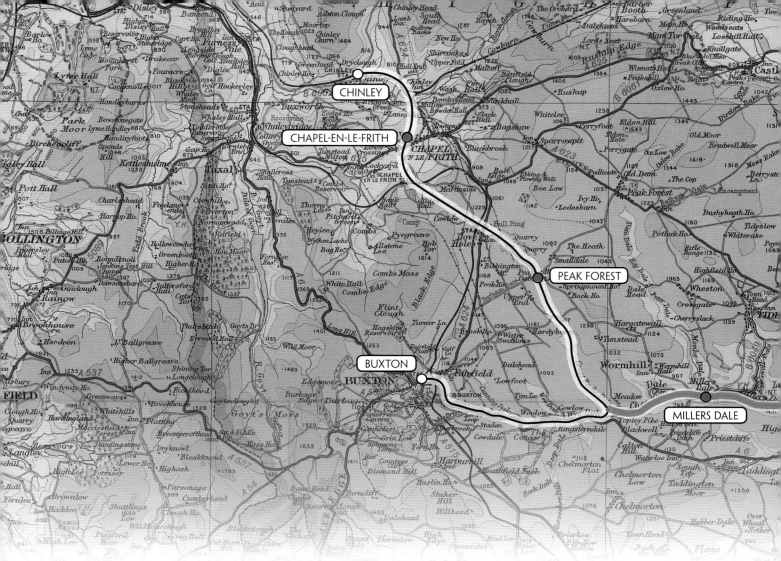

Monsal Trail

Matlock to Buxton and Chinley

Open to passengers 1849/63–1968 | **Original length** 20 miles
Original route operator Midland Railway
Length currently open for walkers & cyclists 8½ miles | **NCN** 680

Completed by the Midland Railway in 1867, this highly
engineered line through the Derbyshire Dales featured numerous tunnels
and viaducts and was dubbed by the company's publicity department as
'Little Switzerland'. It was used by through trains between London
St Pancras and Manchester for 101 years until complete closure in 1968.
Despite closure, sections of the route are very much alive today in the form
of a national rail network branch line, a heritage railway, a magnificent
footpath and cycleway and a freight-only line.

MONSAL DALE

GREAT LONGSTONE

HASSOP

BAKEWELL

ROWSLEY SOUTH

DARLEY DALE

Peak Rail

MATLOCK

What was to eventually become a highly scenic main line through the heart of the Derbyshire Dales started life in 1849 as a branch line from Ambergate, on the Midland Railway's (MR) main line between Derby and Sheffield, to Rowsley. Built by the Manchester, Buxton, Matlock & Midlands Junction Railway (MBM&MJR), the company never achieved its goals due to the high cost of building the first section of line – this had no less than six bridges over the meandering River Derwent and seven tunnels. The line was leased jointly by the MR and the London & North Western Railway for nineteen years and worked by the former.

Seeking to open a through route to Buxton and Manchester, the Midland Railway obtained Parliamentary approval to extend the MBM&MJR's line from Rowsley to Buxton in 1860. Although only 15 miles long, building this extension through the heart of the Derbyshire Dales would prove to be a major challenge for the MR as it involved building two large viaducts (Monsal Dale and Millers Dale) and seven tunnels – one of these was a cut-and-cover tunnel built to hide the railway from the view of the Duke of Rutland where it passed his stately home at Haddon Hall.

The railway to Buxton was completed in 1863, by which time the MR had already agreed with the Manchester, Sheffield & Lincolnshire Railway (later to become the Great Central Railway) to join its new line from Marple at New Mills, thus achieving its goal of reaching Manchester. To reach New Mills the MR built a new line from a junction west of Millers Dale and through the 2,984-yd-long Dove Holes Tunnel before descending to Chapel-en-le-Frith and Chinley. The line opened in 1867 and for the first time the MR could run through trains between London St Pancras and Manchester London Road. The Millers Dale to Buxton section became a branch line although through trains to and from London continued to serve the town.

Many of the stations along the line were built in a Swiss chalet style with wide overhanging eves and this, along with the magnificent scenery, led the MR to give

the line the title of 'Little Switzerland' in their publicity material. With the route to Manchester open the steeply-graded line was kept busy with through expresses and heavy freight trains, the latter requiring banking assistance from Rowsley up to Peak Forest. In later years 'The Palatine' and 'The Peak Express' were the principal express trains between London St Pancras and Manchester Central. Discontinued during the Second World War, only the former returned, in 1957, continuing until 1964. Introduced in 1960, 'The Midland Pullman' – a streamlined six-car diesel train finished in blue – speeded up services between the two cities, whilst the West Coast Main Line was being electrified. Once the latter was completed the Blue Pullmans were withdrawn in 1967.

Meanwhile the notorious Beeching Report had been published in 1963. Despite spelling the end for around 4,000 miles of railway, the line through the Derbyshire Dales was not recommended for complete closure – instead the Hope Valley route between Manchester and Sheffield was to be sacrificed. In the end the former was closed and the latter reprieved. All intermediate stations north of Matlock and the Millers Dale to Buxton branch

line were closed on 6 March 1967, leaving just a local service from Derby to Matlock and a number of through express trains to and from Manchester. The latter ceased on 1 July 1968 and the line between Matlock and Peak Forest Junction closed completely.

Despite this closure fifty years ago, almost the entire route is very much alive today, in one form or another. The 6¾-mile section from Ambergate to Matlock (Derwent Valley Line), with intermediate stations at Whatstandwell, Cromford and Matlock Bath, is served by local diesel trains from Derby. The 4-mile section from Matlock to Rowsley South is now a heritage railway worked by Peak Rail (see page 145).

LEFT: Ex-LMS 4F 0-6-0 No. 44026 crosses Monsal Dale on Headstone Viaduct with a southbound freight on 15 May 1953. Despite not being recommended for closure in the Beeching Report (1963), the line between Matlock and Peak Forest Junction closed in 1968.

BELOW: Set in the beautiful Derbyshire Dales, Headstone Viaduct is now used by walkers and cyclists using the Monsal Trail. The 100-yd-long five-arch viaduct carried the railway over the River Wye in Monsal Dale.

Pride of place must go to the 8½-mile section from Coombs Road Viaduct, just south of Bakewell, to Topley Pike Junction, west of Millers Dale, which is now a glorious footpath and cycleway known as the Monsal Trail. Opened in 1981 by the Peak District National Park, the Trail passes through six tunnels although for many years walkers and cyclists had to divert around four of these – cut through solid limestone, Chee Tor No. 1, Litton, Cressbrook and Headstone tunnels were finally reopened in May 2011. The Monsal Trail also crosses three viaducts – Millers Dale, Headstone and Coombs Road. The most famous of these is the 72-ft-high, five-arch Headstone Viaduct, which soars above the Wye Valley in Monsal Dale. Also of interest to lovers of lost railways are the former station buildings that have survived along the Trail – Millers Dale (with platforms and car park), Monsal Dale (platform only), Great Longstone (Grade II listed with platforms), Hassop (with car park and café) and Bakewell (Grade II listed with platforms, now used as a warehouse).

At the northern end the railway route through Dove Holes Tunnel to Chinley remains open for mineral traffic from limestone quarries at Dowlow south of Buxton – this line still has semaphore signals operated from manual signal boxes.

BELOW: Ex-LMS 5MT 4-6-0 No. 45073 makes a fine sight as it heads through Millers Dale station with a train of empty coal wagons on 1 November 1963. Built in 1935 at Crewe Works, this locomotive was withdrawn in August 1968, the date of the end of standard-gauge steam haulage on British Railways.

Peak Rail

Reopened throughout in 1996, Peak Rail operates heritage diesel and steam trains on the 4-mile route between Matlock, Darley Dale and Rowsley South. A connection to the national rail network at Matlock was completed in 2011. An extension to the site of Rowsley station followed by an extension through the closed Haddon Tunnel to Bakewell are planned for the future. The Heritage Shunters Trust has a large collection of ex-British Railways diesel shunters at its base in Rowsley. The railway is open at weekends and on Bank Holidays from April to October, and on certain weekdays during the summer and school holidays.

Chesterfield to Lincoln

Open to passengers 1897–1951/55 | **Original length** 39½ miles
Original route operator Lancashire, Derbyshire & East Coast Railway
Length currently open for walkers & cyclists 11 miles | **NCN** 647 & 64

One of the longest railways planned in Britain at the end of the
19th century, the heavily engineered Lancashire, Derbyshire & East Coast
Railway failed miserably to achieve its goal. In the east the major
engineering feature is the fifty-nine-arch Fledborough Viaduct but in the
west the notorious 1½-mile Bolsover Tunnel was dogged by subsidence and
flooding. The tunnel closed in 1951 leaving the rest of the railway with
a skeleton passenger service until closure in 1959. Collieries kept
much of the line open until the last, Thoresby, closed in 2015.
Today a Network Rail test track makes use of the mid-section
while 11 miles at the eastern end is a footpath and cycleway.

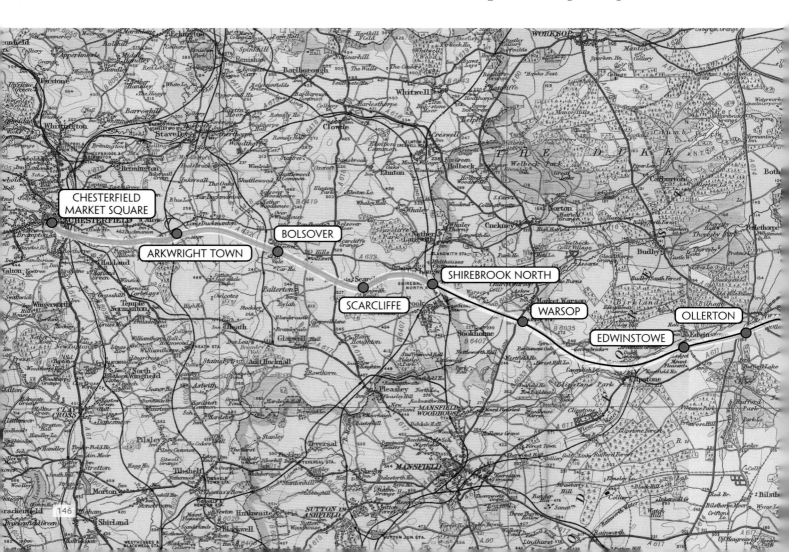

If completed as authorized by Parliament in 1891, the 170-mile east-west proposed network of the Lancashire, Derbyshire & East Coast Railway (LD&ECR) would have been the largest railway project to be built in Britain at the end of the 19th century. Its main purpose was to carry coal from the Derbyshire and Nottinghamshire coalfield to proposed new docks at Warrington on the Manchester Ship Canal in the northwest and Sutton-on-Sea on the Lincolnshire coast in the east. However, due to lack of funds, only the 39½-mile section from Chesterfield to Lincoln along with a 12-mile branch from Langwith Junction to Beighton Junction near Worksop were ever built. The main line involved major civil engineering work including Boythorpe Viaduct at Chesterfield, the 370-ft-long Doe Lea Viaduct, two tunnels (including the troublesome 2,624-yd-long Bolsover Tunnel), several long rock cuttings and the 890-yd-long, fifty-nine-arch plus four trussed steel spans, Fledborough Viaduct over the River Trent. Supported financially by the Great Eastern Railway, which also wanted access to the coalfields, the fledgling LD&ECR opened between Chesterfield Market

Place and Pyewipe Junction near Lincoln on 8 March 1897. The Beighton branch was completely opened on 30 May 1900. The headquarters of the railway was at Chesterfield Market Square station, a grand building with four curved platforms. The Great Central Railway purchased the unfinished LD&ECR at the beginning of 1907 with the ambitious project never completed.

The Achilles' heel of the Chesterfield to Lincoln route was always the notorious double-track Bolsover Tunnel. At nearly 1½ miles long it had always suffered badly from mining subsidence and the constant threat of flooding, although much of the water was piped to supply the town of Bolsover. Concerns over its poor condition and also the nearby Doe Lea Viaduct led to the premature closure of the line between Chesterfield Market Place and Shirebrook North on 3 December 1951. By then Market Place station was little used with just a skeleton service of two or three trains to and from Lincoln on weekdays plus a couple more to and from Shirebrook North. It was also slow, with trains taking up to 1¾ hours for the 39½-mile journey. The Beighton branch had already lost its Sheffield

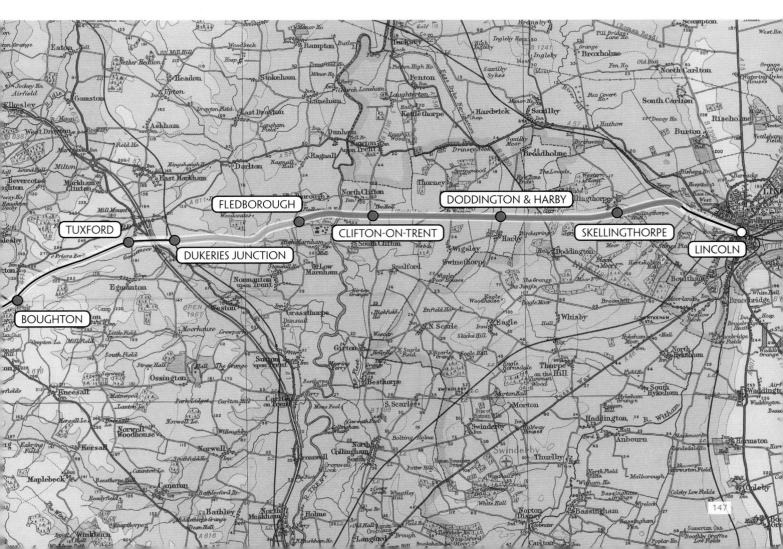

to Mansfield passenger service on 10 September 1939 although summer weekend excursions to Skegness from stations along the line continued until 1964.

The remaining passenger service between Shirebrook North and Lincoln Central continued until 19 September 1955 when it ceased, although summer excursion trains to Skegness continued to use the route until 1964. The route's lifeblood, coal, gradually declined with the closure of pits and today there are none left – the last, Thoresby Colliery, closed in 2015 bringing an end to deep coal mining in Britain. The trackbed of the Beighton branch was lifted in stages following the closure of collieries between 1967 and 1984 and the line west of High Marnham Power Station across Fledborough Viaduct to Pyewipe Junction was lifted in the early 1980s. Coal trains to the power station ceased on 29 October 2003 and all that remains of the LD&ECR today is the

BELOW: The manually operated signal box at Edwinstowe on 10 August 1963. Just to the west was Clipstone Junction where the lines for Mansfield and Chesterfield diverged.

10½-mile section from Shirebrook, on the Robin Hood Line, to High Marnham, which is used as a Network Rail test track known as the Rail Innovation & Development Centre (Tuxford). Three miles of this route is double track while the 4-mile branch line towards the former Bevercotes Colliery via Boughton Brake Tunnel is also included in the facility.

Chesterfield's grand Market Place station was sadly demolished in 1973 but the impressive Fledborough Viaduct has survived. The trackbed from the site of Fledborough station and across the viaduct to Pyewipe Junction is now a level traffic-free footpath and cycleway forming part of National Cycle Network Routes 647 (Fledborough to Doddington & Harby) and 64 (Doddington & Harby to Pyewipe Junction). Apart from the impressive viaduct little remains of the railway but a replica station nameboard has been erected on the surviving platforms at Fledborough and a replica distant signal has been erected close to the viaduct. At Doddington there is a café and cycle shop.

Barrow Hill Roundhouse

The last surviving operational roundhouse in the UK, Barrow Hill, was opened by the Midland Railway in 1870. With twenty-four roads radiating out from a central turntable, the roundhouse was in use by British Rail until 1991. After complete restoration it was reopened in 1998 and is now home to a large number of preserved working steam and diesel locomotives. It also has a physical link with the national rail network and is often visited by railtours. Open during weekends throughout the year.

BELOW: A footpath and National Cycle Network Route 647 now pass through the site of Clifton-on-Trent station. Opened by the Lancashire, Derbyshire & East Coast Railway in 1897, the station lost its passenger service in 1955 but coal trains continued pass through en route to High Marnham Power Station until 1980.

Wirral Way

Hooton to West Kirby

Open to passengers 1866/86–1956 | **Original length** 12 miles
Original route operator Great Western & London & North Western Joint Railway
Length currently open for walkers & cyclists 11½ miles | **NCN** 56 & 89

Opened in two stages between 1866 and 1886, much of this railway ran close to the western coast of the Wirral Peninsula. Operated by Great Western Railway auto-trains, the intensive passenger service of the 1930s gave way to a decline in passenger traffic after the Second World War. Closure to passengers came in 1956, after which the line was used by freight trains and for training drivers of new diesel multiple units. Complete closure came in 1962 and since then nearly all of the trackbed has been reopened as a footpath and cycleway.

This is the story of the 12-mile single-track line between Hooton, on the Chester to Birkenhead main line, and the town of West Kirby, which was opened in two stages on the Wirral Peninsula by the Great Western Railway (GWR) and the London & North Western Railway (L&NWR) Joint Railway (GW&L&NWJR). The main line had already been opened in 1840 by the Chester & Birkenhead Railway, which then went on to merge with the Birkenhead, Lancashire & Cheshire Railway in 1859 to become the Birkenhead Railway. It was taken over by the GW&L&NWJR in 1860.

On 1 October 1866 the joint company opened a 4¾-mile branch from Hooton to Parkgate. Intermediate stations were provided at Hadlow Road and Neston, where a moribund colliery was reopened. The branch was later extended 7¼ miles up the Wirral coastline from Parkgate to West Kirby in 1886 – the latter station had already been served by Wirral Railway trains from Birkenhead since 1878. The new extension served intermediate stations at Heswall, Thurstaston, Caldy and Kirby Park and the whole route was well-served by a frequent number of passenger trains up until the outbreak of the Second World War. Although Neston Colliery closed in 1927 passenger traffic peaked on the line in the 1930s with up to twenty return services on weekdays.

Passenger traffic went into decline in the post-war years with many customers being wooed away by bus operators. Train services were reduced and the only bright spot was schoolchildren who still travelled by train on weekdays during term time to and from West Kirby. Sadly even this wasn't enough to save the line, which closed to passengers on 17 September 1956. Goods traffic and diesel multiple unit learner drivers continued to use the route until its complete closure on 7 May 1962.

Since closure almost the entire route from Willaston, near Hooton, and along the coast of the Dee Estuary to West Kirby has been reopened as the Wirral Way footpath and cycleway through a linear park known as

the Wirral Country Park. National Cycle Network Route 56 follows the route between Hooton and Neston and Route 89 between Neston and West Kirby. The first of its kind in Britain, Wirral Country Park was opened in 1973 and today supports numerous species of butterflies and birds, especially along the coastal stretch between West Kirby and Parkgate. Popular with ramblers and cyclists alike, it has useful connections with the national rail network at West Kirby and Neston (with its colourfully-decorated underpass this station lies on the Borderlands Line between Wrexham Central and Bidston), while Hooton station is a short walk away from its eastern end. There are two visitor centres along this old railway path with the one at Hadlow Road station near Willaston (just west of Hooton) being of great interest to lovers of lost railways. Here the 1866-built station building (the only survivor along this route) and platform have been beautifully restored to reflect the 1950s period, complete with signal box, signal and a length of track. The other visitor centre is at Thurstaston station, south of West Kirby, where the two platforms have survived – located close to the coast, the station here closed to passengers in 1954, two years before others on this route. A proposal to reopen 4 miles of track between Hooton and Neston as a heritage railway seems to have been quietly forgotten.

Eaton Hall Railway

Extending to 4½ miles, the 15-in-gauge Eaton Hall Railway was built in 1896 for the 1st Duke of Westminster by Sir Arthur Heywood. The railway provided transport for coal and stores around the Duke's country estate near Eccleston in Cheshire and had branch lines to a brickyard, the estate works and a trans-shipment siding on the GWR main line at Balderton. The railway was closed in 1947 but reopened in 1996, using a replica of one of the original engines. Open during Garden Open Days in the summer months (four per year).

PREVIOUS SPREAD: Ex-GWR Class 1400 0-4-2T No. 1457 propels an afternoon auto-train for Hooton out of West Kirby station on 20 April 1954. Closure of this route came on 17 September 1956.

LEFT: The restored station at Hadlow Road is one of the highlights for users of the Wirral Way today. Opened in 1866 and closed in 1956, the station is now an information centre and home to a wonderful collection of railway artefacts, a restored signal box and a length of track.

BELOW: Overseen by a group of nuns, a children's church outing is about to enjoy the delights of West Kirby on 20 April 1954. Their auto-train has just arrived with the 2.50 pm service from Hooton with ex-GWR Class 1400 0-4-2T No. 1457 in charge.

WALES

Swansea Bikepath Network
Swansea to Mumbles Head and Gowerton

Open to passengers 1806/98–1959/64 | **Original length** 5½ miles (tramway), 12½ miles (railway)
Original route operator Oystermouth Railway/Llanelly Railway
Length currently open for walkers & cyclists 10 miles | **NCN** 4 (Swansea to Gowerton)

Opened along the shoreline of Swansea Bay in 1806, the Oystermouth
Railway was the first railway in the world to carry fare-paying passengers.
It was later electrified but was closed by its new bus operator owner in 1959.
Running alongside it for part of the way was the railway line to
Pontarddulais, which opened in 1867 and formed part of the London &
North Western Railway's route through Central Wales to Shrewsbury.
This closed in 1964 and today both the tramway and railway
routes are a footpath and cycleway.

This is the story of an early pre-Victorian tramway and a later Victorian railway. The first was opened in 1806 as a 4-ft-gauge horse-drawn tramway, or plateway, which ran from the Swansea Canal and along the sweeping shoreline of Swansea Bay to Oystermouth. The Oystermouth Railway, as it was known, was built to transport coal, iron ore and limestone from quarries around Mumbles and in 1807 it started carrying fare-paying passengers from The Mount terminus in Swansea – it was the first railway in the world to do so, and The Mount was the world's first railway station. The tramway closed in 1827 following the opening of a new, parallel turnpike road.

In 1855 the derelict tramway was relaid to the conventional standard-gauge and a horse-drawn passenger service was reintroduced between Swansea and Oystermouth. Steam-haulage was introduced in 1877 and the line was extended to a new pier at Mumbles Head in 1898, by which time the railway was known as the Swansea

& Mumbles Railway (S&MR). Steam-haulage continued until 1929 when electric trams took over operations – built by Brush, the double-deck tramcars were the largest of their kind in Britain and could each seat 106 passengers. Power was supplied using overhead wires operating at 650V DC and journey time between Swansea Rutland Street and Mumbles Pier was 19 minutes.

PREVIOUS SPREAD: For users of the Mawddach Trail to Dolgellau a toll footpath and cycleway parallels the Cambrian Coast Line across Barmouth Bridge from Barmouth to Morfa Mawddach. Opened in 1867, the 764-yd-long bridge is a Grade II* listed wooden railway viaduct with 113 wooden trestles and a lifting section.

LEFT: The approach to Swansea Bay station on 10 September 1951. On the left is the Swansea & Mumbles Railway with its overhead 650V DC electric wires. On the right is the double-track of the line from Swansea Victoria to Pontarddulais. In the middle distance is the pedestrian bridge with its stone staircases (see page 159).

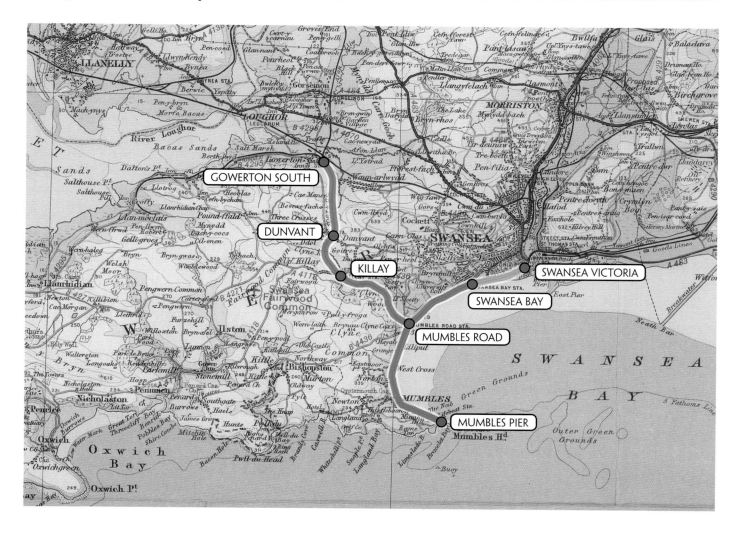

The S&MR met its end when it was purchased by South Wales Transport, the operator of bus services in Swansea, in 1958. Without much ado the new owner sought to abandon the tramway and it closed completely on 11 October 1959. In its haste to rid itself of the tramway the new owners immediately ripped up the track and scrapped the tramcars – one of these was saved for preservation but was sadly later destroyed in a fire.

The second part of this story is the 12½-mile standard-gauge railway that was built between Swansea Victoria and Pontarddulais. Partly running parallel with the tramway along the coast of Swansea Bay, the Llanelly Railway (later to become the Swansea & Carmarthen Railway), opened across the Gower Peninsula in 1867. The railway ran alongside the tramway, before crossing it and heading north between the tram stops at Ashleigh Road and Blackpill. Intermediate stations were provided at Swansea Bay, Mumbles Road, Killay, Dunvant, Gowerton South, Gorseinon and Groves End. This line later formed the southern part of what was to become the London & North Western Railway's (L&NWR) Central Wales Line from Craven Arms. The entire 95¼-mile route through sparsely populated country and serving small intermediate spa towns and villages was completed in 1868. Apart from the section between Llandeilo and Pontarddulais, which was operated jointly with the Great Western Railway (GWR), the long single-track route had been taken over by the L&NWR by 1891. With their entry into GWR territory the L&NWR were able to operate through coaches to Swansea Victoria station from as far afield as London Euston, Manchester and the Midlands.

Although the Central Wales Line was recommended for closure in the Beeching Report (1963), only the section northwards from Swansea Victoria to Pontarddulais became a victim – from 15 June 1964 Central Wales Line trains were diverted from Pontarddulais to Llanelli and the line from Swansea Victoria closed.

Today the entire length of the Swansea & Mumbles Railway to Mumbles Pier and the former L&NWR line as far as Gowerton are a footpath and cycleway that forms part of the Swansea Bikepath Network. The section of the old tramway from Swansea Marina to Blackpill and thence northwards along the old railway route to

Gowerton via the Clyne Valley Country Park also forms part of National Cycle Network Route 4. Of interest to lovers of lost railways are the stone abutments either side of the A4067 dual carriageway that skirts Swansea Bay – although the bridge has been removed the fenced-off massive stone steps form a stunning backdrop to the sandy beach at Brymill – and, nearby, a restored bowstring girder bridge has been incorporated into the cycleway and footpath.

Nothing now remains of any of the stations on the two routes apart from the remains of platforms at Killay and Dunvant while the cutting at Gowerton South station is a small park. Beyond here several sections of the trackbed to Pontarddulais are now footpaths – the longest is the 2½-mile stretch between Gorseinon and Waungron, which forms part of the Gower Way Long Distance Path. There are currently plans to reopen the entire section from Gowerton to Pontarddulais as a cycleway. Pontarddulais station is still served by trains on the Heart of Wales Line.

LEFT: Two double-deck tramcars of the Swansea & Mumbles Railway halt to pick up some passengers at Mumbles on 27 August 1948. The tramway was closed in 1959.

BELOW: The impressive stone staircases to nowhere are all that remain today of a pedestrian footbridge that once crossed the railway, electric tramway and a main road alongside the coast at Swansea Bay.

Swiss Valley Cycle Route
Llanelli to Cross Hands

Open to passengers 1883 – no passenger service | **Original length** 13 miles
Original route operator Llanelly & Mynydd Mawr Railway
Length currently open for walkers & cyclists 11 miles | **NCN** 47

Opened in 1803, the Llanelly & Mynydd Mawr Railway was one of the earliest publicly authorized railways in Britain. After serving numerous collieries in the hills above Llanelli it had fallen into disuse by the 1840s but was reborn forty years later as a standard-gauge line, with part of it remaining in operation until 1989. Since closure almost the entire length of the line's trackbed has been reopened as the Swiss Valley Cycle Route.

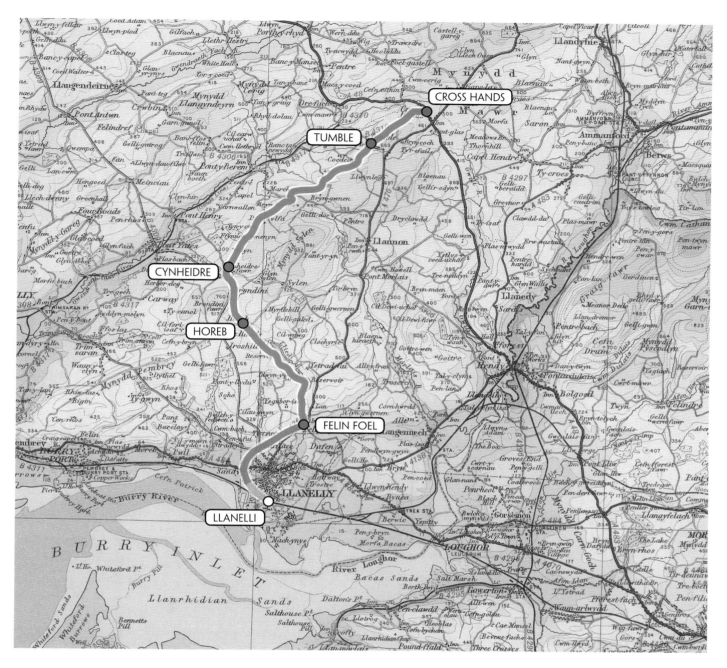

By the late 18th century a number of short canals had been built to carry coal from collieries, located inland from Llanelli, to the coast. Primitive wooden horse-drawn tramways connected the collieries to the canals. This was all a very slow and time-consuming operation and, with more coal deposits being discovered in the hills north of Llanelli, a more efficient method of transporting the coal was required. To this end the 4-ft-gauge Carmarthenshire Railway (CR) – actually a horse-drawn plateway with L-shaped rails – received Parliamentary authorization in 1802.

The heavily engineered CR opened for business up the valley of the River Lliedi between Llanelli and Cynheidre in 1803 and was extended into the hills at Cross Hands in 1805. It was an immediate success, not only carrying coal and anthracite but also serving an ironworks and lime kilns. However, an alternative route for the anthracite from Cross Hands to new docks at Llanelli via Tirydail and Pontarddulais was opened by the Llanelly Railway & Dock Company in 1835 – this standard-gauge railway first used horsepower but locomotives were introduced in 1840.

Consequently, much of the CR had fallen into disuse within a few years.

Fast forward to 1872 when the Llanelly & Mynydd Mawr Railway (L&MMR) was authorized to build a railway from Llanelli to Cross Hands, with much of its route following the course of the abandoned tramway. Raising capital for this project was difficult and work only started on its construction in 1880. Abounding in sharp curves, the steeply graded 13-mile line eventually opened in 1883 using steam locomotives and was worked by the contractor who built it. It never operated a regular passenger service, although workmen's trains were operated, but had goods depots at Llanelli Queen Victoria Road, Felin Foel, Horeb, Cynheidre, Cwmblawd, Tumble, and Cross Hands. In 1903 the L&MMR was connected to the new North Dock at Llanelli, thus giving the railway much-improved access to ships for its mineral traffic.

Serving numerous collieries along its length, the L&MMR was taken over by the Great Western Railway in the 'Big Four Grouping' of 1923. With miners being carried to work in former Metropolitan Railway coaches,

the workmen's trains ceased in 1928. Anthracite production had been falling for some years and traffic on the line went into decline. In 1948 the line passed into the ownership of British Railways (BR) and it would probably have been closed had it not been for a major expansion of Cynheidre Colliery. Realignment of track to iron out the sharp curves, a new passing loop at Magpie Grove, and new signal boxes and signalling between Llanelli and Cynheidre allowed longer coal trains to be hauled by more powerful steam locomotives. The work was completed by 1962 but traffic failed to live up to expectations. Steam locomotives were replaced by diesels in 1965 and the signal boxes closed in 1968, by which time the northern section of the line had already closed. Cynheidre Colliery finally closed in 1989 and the railway route started to revert back to nature.

In 1999 an attempt was made by local preservationists – the Llanelli & Mynydd Mawr Railway – to purchase the line and reopen it as a heritage railway. They failed to achieve this, the track was lifted and 11 miles of the route between Llanelli and Cross Hands was purchased by local

authorities and reopened as a footpath and cycleway known as the Swiss Valley Cycle Route. Forming part of National Cycle Network Route 47, it climbs gently along the route of the former railway from the Millennium Coastal Park into the hills above Llanelli, past the Lliedi Reservoirs to Tumble and Cross Hands. Although there were no passenger stations along this route there are plenty of reminders of its railway past in the shape of numerous over- and under-bridges.

The traffic-free route has a tarmac surface and starts at Sandy Water Park in Llanelli. After passing the Felinfoel Brewery, the tranquil Lliedi Reservoirs are reached, offering magnificent views of the Gwendraeth Valley. At Horeb there is a picnic site conveniently located a short distance from the Waun Wyllt Inn. Although it failed to achieve its goal of reopening the railway, the recently-formed Llanelli & Mynydd Mawr Railway has established a heritage centre on the site of Cynheidre Colliery, alongside the Swiss Valley Cycle Route. Track has been laid within the site and the eventual aim is to provide a 1-mile stretch of line to allow the running of trains. A locomotive shed has already been built and several

steam and diesel locomotives, along with rolling stock, are awaiting restoration. Sadly, a visit by the author in 2017 found the site padlocked with rusting track and neglected rolling stock – its future may be in some doubt.

Continuing north through the former mining village of Tumble, with its working men's club, the cycle path passes close to the Mynydd Mawr Woodland Park, a regenerated former colliery owned by the Woodland Trust, before terminating at Cross Hands.

PREVIOUS SPREAD: BR-built Class 1643 0-6-0PT No. 1643 departs from Cross Hands on its return journey to Llanelli with an enthusiasts', special on 26 June 1965. No mod cons here as the day-trippers had to travel in open wooden goods wagons in the rain!

LEFT: No. 1643 heads up the old Llanelly & Mynydd Mawr Railway past the modern signal box at Magpie Grove with an enthusiasts special for Cross Hands on 26 June 1965. Plastic macs, caps and duffle bags to the fore in the pouring rain! Those were the days my friend.

BELOW: Following the course of the old Llanelly & Mynydd Mawr Railway, the 11-mile Swiss Cycle Route (National Cycle Network Route 47) heads into the hills affording users stunning views of the Gwendraeth Valley.

Heads of the Valleys Line

Abergavenny to Merthyr Tydfil

Open to passengers 1879–1958 | **Original length** 24½ miles
Original route operator Merthyr, Tredegar & Abergavenny Railway
Length currently open for walkers & cyclists 7 miles | **NCN** 46

The heavily engineered and steeply-graded Heads of the Valleys railway between Abergavenny and Merthyr Tydfil was both costly to build and operate. It provided the London & North Western Railway with a back-door route to Cardiff and Newport Docks but by the 1950s traffic was in decline. Following closure in 1958 a section of this highly scenic line through the Clydach Gorge has reopened as a footpath and cycleway.

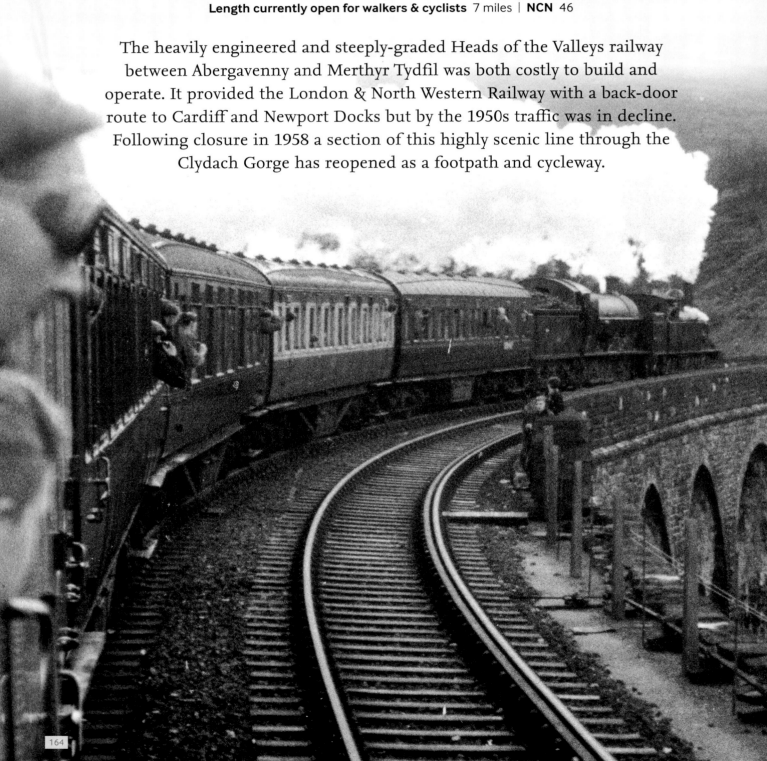

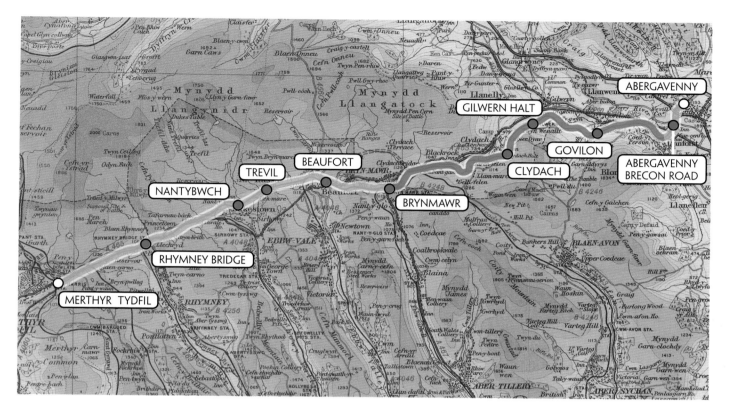

When it was completed in 1879 the 24½-mile double-track Heads of the Valleys Line between Abergavenny and Merthyr Tydfil was undoubtedly one of the most scenic switchback railways in Britain. By the early 19th century a network of horse-drawn tramroads had been opened in the South Wales Valleys linking the then world's largest group of ironworks with collieries and canals. One of these early railways was Bailey's Tramroad that linked ironworks at Nantyglo with the Monmouthshire Canal at Govilon. Opening in 1822 to a gauge of 4 ft 4 in, the tramroad was sold to the newly incorporated Merthyr, Tredegar & Abergavenny Railway (MT&AR) in 1859 by its wealthy owner, industrialist and ironmaster Crawshay Bailey (who just happened to be chairman of the MT&AR).

The steeply-graded and initially single-track MT&AR was opened between Abergavenny and Brynmawr on 29 September 1862 but by then the London & North Western Railway (L&NWR) had already seen a golden opportunity to tap into the industrial riches of South Wales by leasing the MT&AR in November 1861 for 1,000 years. Construction continued westwards from Brynmawr with the section to Beaufort and Trevil being opened in 1864.

The unfinished MT&AR was absorbed by the L&NWR in 1866 but construction westwards from Trevil was slow, with the next section to Nantybwch and Rhymney Bridge being opened in 1871 – southwards from Nantybwch the L&NWR's branch to Tredegar and Nine Mile Point gave the company running powers to Newport. The line between Nantybwch and Rhymney Bridge was jointly built and worked with the Rhymney Railway and offered the L&NWR a back-door route through to Cardiff. The next section to open, in 1873, was from Rhymney Bridge to Penywern Junction, from where a connection was made via Ivor Junction and Brecon & Merthyr Railway (B&MR) metals to Dowlais Central. Westwards from Penywern Junction the final looping entry to Merthyr Tydfil High Street was completed in 1879 via Morlais Tunnel, Morlais Junction and the B&M&L&NW Joint Railway.

Meanwhile, to cope with increased freight traffic the entire route had been doubled in 1877, necessitating the boring of two new tunnels and widening numerous viaducts. During the First World War the route became very busy handling coal trains – known as 'Jellicoe Specials' – destined for northern Scotland to fuel Britain's Grand Fleet in Scapa Flow. Through coaches from other parts of the L&NWR system found their way to Merthyr and even a Travelling Post Office coach from Euston reached the town via Stafford and Shrewsbury. The years following the Second World War brought ever-increasing

PREVIOUS SPREAD: Last train – two ex-L&NWR locomotives, 7F 0-8-0 No. 49121 and Webb 0-6-2 Coal Tank No. 58926 (now preserved), double-head a Stephenson Locomotive Society special train over Clydach Viaduct on the climb towards Clydach Tunnel on 5 January 1958. The line between Abergavenny Brecon Road and Brynmawr closed completely the next day.

BELOW: Opening in 1863 and approached from the east via a viaduct, Clydach station was a short distance from the twin-bore Clydach Tunnels. The station is seen here from an Abergavenny-bound train on 13 September 1951.

competition from road transport and a subsequent decline in traffic. By 1950 there were only five trains running each weekday between Abergavenny and Merthyr, with trains taking a leisurely 1 hr 33 mins for the 24½-mile journey. The steeply-graded double-track line was also costly to maintain and operate and closure, when it was announced, came as no surprise. The last regular passenger trains ran on 4 January 1958 although a Stephenson Locomotive Society special was run over the entire route on the next day, a Sunday. The 1¼-mile section at the eastern end from Abergavenny Junction to Brecon Road station remained open for goods traffic until 1971.

Since closure several sections of the Heads of the Valleys Line have been obliterated by new roads. However, the highly scenic section of the trackbed through the Clydach Gorge between Llanfoist, on the southwestern outskirts of Abergavenny, and Brynmawr has been reopened as a footpath and cycleway. Forming part of National Cycle Network Route 46, it takes in stunning views of the Clydach Gorge Area of Outstanding Natural Beauty, the Brecon Beacons and Skirrid and Sugar Loaf mountains. In the gorge are reminders of its industrial heritage including the remains of the late-18th-century Clydach Ironworks, limestone quarries and several pairs of lime kilns. Of interest to lovers of lost railways are the

bricked-up tunnel mouths at Clydach and Brynmawr – the trail takes an alternative route to avoid these – and the curving Nant Dyar viaduct. This section can also be reached via steep and narrow lanes to the village of Clydach and a small car park close to the closed Llanelli Quarry. The station building at Govilon survives as a private residence alongside the cycleway, as do the platforms at Gilwern Halt and Clydach and the platform shelters at Gelli Felen Halt.

LEFT: Clydach station building is today a private residence, complete with platforms. The bricked-up Clydach Tunnels lie beyond in the shadows.

BELOW: Looking east along the top of Clydach Viaduct on the highly scenic section of the Heads of the Valleys footpath and cycleway. The viaduct is 104 yds long and 75 ft high and offers fine views of the Clydach Gorge below.

Pontypool & Blaenavon Railway

The London & North Western Railway branch line between Pontypool and Blaenavon closed to passengers as early as 1941. Coal traffic kept it open until 1980 when the Big Pit Colliery closed. Since then the line has been reopened as a heritage railway by the Pontypool & Blaenavon Railway and trains – steam and diesel – currently operate the 2½ miles between Whistle Inn, Blaenavon High Level and Coed Avon, with a branch line to the Big Pit Mining Museum. The eventual aim of the railway is to operate trains the 8 miles between Brynmawr and Abersychan. Open most weekends from Easter to early September, and selected Wednesdays in July and August.

Ystwyth Trail
Aberystwyth to Pencader

Open to passengers 1867–1964 | **Original length** 41¼ miles
Original route operator Manchester & Milford Railway
Length currently open for walkers & cyclists 15¼ miles | **NCN** 81

The Manchester & Milford Railway was a grandiose scheme to link the North of England with Pembrokeshire by rail. In this respect it was an utter failure with the meandering single-track route that was eventually built serving only scattered farming communities, villages and a couple of small towns in West Wales. It became a victim of Dr Beeching's 'axe' in 1964/5 and closed completely in 1973. In recent years much of the trackbed between Aberystwyth and Tregaron has been reopened as the Ystwyth Trail.

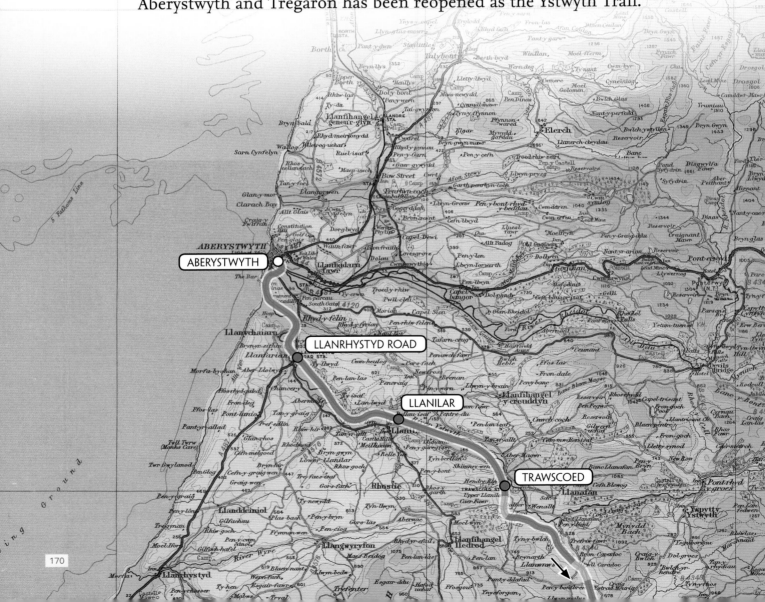

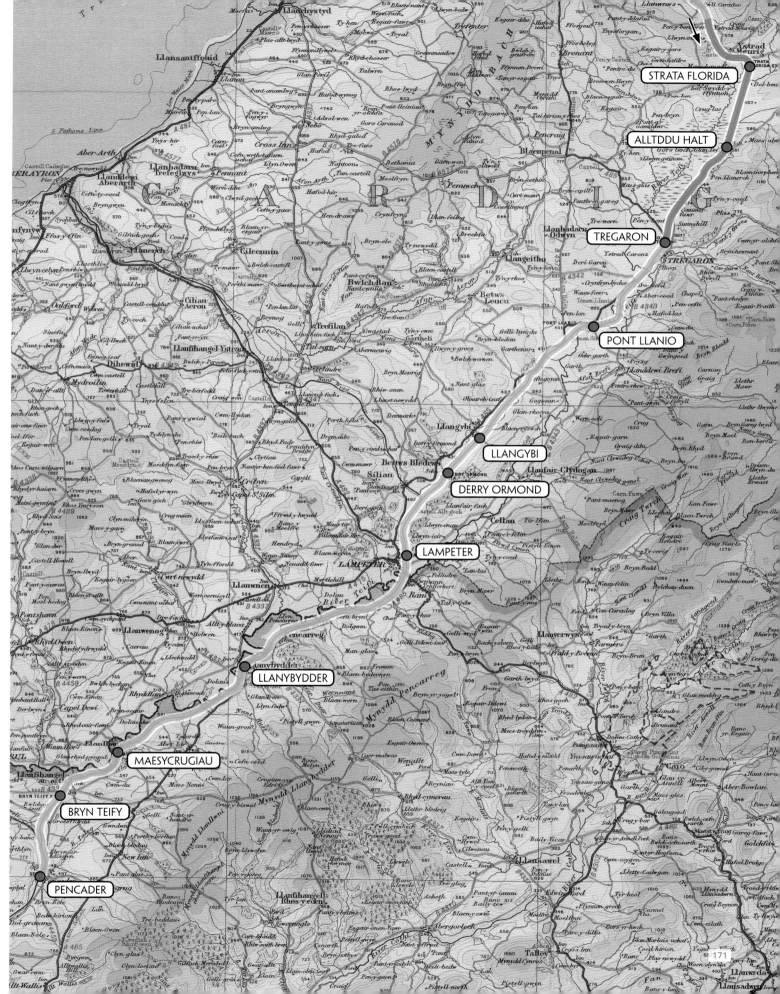

STRATA FLORIDA

ALLTDDU HALT

TREGARON

PONT LLANIO

LLANGYBI

DERRY ORMOND

LAMPETER

LLANYBYDDER

MAESYCRUGIAU

BRYN TEIFY

PENCADER

What was to become a 56¼-mile single-track line serving a few small towns, farming communities and villages in West Wales started life as a grand and ambitious scheme to link Manchester with the port of Milford Haven. The planned route would have involved building a line across the Cambrian Mountains from Llanidloes on the Mid-Wales Railway to Pencader. Here it would link up with the bankrupt Carmarthen & Cardigan Railway (C&CR), which had opened from Carmarthen in 1864. Although construction started at Llanidloes this was soon shelved, instead the Manchester & Milford Railway (M&MR) chose the cheaper alternative of building a single-track line from Aberystwyth to Pencader – one can only imagine how long the journey would have taken between Manchester and Milford Haven via this route!

The M&MR opened between Pencader and Lampeter in 1866 and throughout to Aberystwyth in 1867, a distance of 41¼ miles. Never achieving its goal of providing a through route between the North of England and Pembrokeshire, the railway was never a financial success and was leased to the Great Western Railway (GWR) in 1906 before being taken over by that company in 1911. Meanwhile, in the south, the C&CR had been kept operational by an Official Receiver until it was taken over by the GWR in 1881.

The entire route between Aberystwyth and Carmarthen was now in the ownership of the GWR and the company opened a 12½-mile branch line – in effect a Light Railway – from Aberayron Junction, north of Lampeter, to Aberayron (for New Quay) in 1911. With the 'main line' taking a meandering inland route, the coastal villages of Cardiganshire never developed into destinations for holidaymakers and consequently traffic on the line was relatively light, although through coaches to Aberystwyth were provided from South Wales during the summer holiday period. In the late 1950s and early 1960s through trains were also run along the route on summer Saturdays between Swansea and Butlin's Holiday Camp at Pwllheli. Goods traffic mainly consisted of outgoing agricultural produce, especially milk, and incoming merchandise such as fertilizer and coal.

The Aberayron branch lost its passenger service on 10 February 1951 and by the end of that decade traffic on the 'main line' was in serious decline. The three passenger trains each way (weekdays only) took about 2 hrs and 30 min to cover the 56¼ miles – they could not compete with cars and buses and closure was on the cards. The line was recommended for closure in the Beeching Report (1963) and the date set for the 'axe' to fall was 22 February 1965. However, severe flooding at Llanilar, south of Aberystwyth, on 14 December 1964 severed the line and it immediately closed completely north of Strata Florida station. The formal closure for the rest of the route went ahead, leaving just goods traffic to Lampeter and milk traffic from a creamery on the Aberayron branch. The latter ceased on 1 October 1973 when the railway south to Carmarthen closed completely and the remaining track was lifted in 1975.

Since closure much of the trackbed of the line between Aberystwyth and Tregaron has been reopened as a footpath and cycleway known as the Ystwyth Trail, forming part of National Cycle Network Route 81. Two short sections of this route are diverted onto roads because of problems encountered with local landowners: they are south of Trawscoed on the B4575 (1.2 miles) and on the B4340 through Tyn Y Graig (1.8 miles). Aberystwyth station is served by trains on the national rail network and also by the Vale of Rheidol Railway.

LEFT: Located between Strata Florida and Tregaron stations, the little-used Alltddu Halt is seen here on 17 June 1963. BR-built Manor Class 4-6-0 No. 7826 *Longworth Manor* is approaching with the 11.55 am train from Aberystwyth to Carmarthen.

BELOW: Dappled sunlight and a road overbridge on the Ystwyth Trail near the site of Trawscoed station.

With a bit of searching but obviously with respect for private property, lost railway sleuths will have a field day along this route. From north to south: platforms at Llanilar station; platform and remains of station at Trawscoed; restored signal box at Strata Florida; water tower at Pont Llanio; station building and platform at Derry Ormond; goods shed and the bridge over the River Teifi at Lampeter; the station building and goods shed at Llanybydder; the Railway Inn at Maesycrugiau; tunnel and platform at Bryn Teifi.

South of Pencader the Gwili Railway now operates a 4½-mile heritage railway between Danycoed Halt, Bronwydd Arms and Abergwili Junction (see box).

LEFT: Ex-GWR Manor Class 4-6-0 No. 7814 *Fringford Manor* of Machynlleth shed hauling an Aberystwyth to Carmarthen train in the early 1960s. Built at Swindon Works in 1939, this locomotive was withdrawn in September 1965.

BELOW: The Ystwyth Trail, seen here below the hill of Pen Dinas, near Aberystwyth. The earthworks of an important Iron Age, Celtic hillfort can be found on the hill, which is topped by the more recent Wellington Monument.

Gwili Railway

The Carmarthen & Cardigan Railway opened its single-line railway along the valley of the River Gwili between Carmarthen and Pencader in 1864. Eventually becoming part of the Great Western Railway's meandering route between Aberystwyth and Carmarthen, the railway closed to passengers in 1965. Milk trains continued until 1973, when the line closed completely. Founded in 1978, the Gwili Railway now operates steam and diesel trains north from its headquarters at Bronwydd Arms to Llwyfan Cerrig and Danycoed Halt and south to Abergwili Junction, on the outskirts of Carmarthen, a total distance of 4½ miles. Future plans include an extension northward to Llanpumpsaint but this will involve rebuilding seven railway bridges that crisscross the River Gwili. Open school holidays, bank holidays and most weekends from February to December, and daily except some Mondays, Tuesdays and Fridays from April to October, daily in July and August.

Mawddach Trail

Morfa Mawddach (Barmouth Junction) to Dolgellau

Open to passengers 1865/69–1965 | **Original length** 7½ miles
Original route operators Cambrian Railways/Great Western Railway
Length currently open for walkers & cyclists 7 miles | **NCN** 8

For nearly 100 years the long cross-country railway between Ruabon and Barmouth was an important route for trains of holidaymakers seeking to escape the industrial Midlands. Serving only small towns and villages along its length it became a victim of Dr Beeching's 'axe' in 1965, since when two sections have been reopened by preservationists. At its western end the Mawddach Trail footpath and cycleway follows the trackbed alongside the highly scenic Mawddach Estuary.

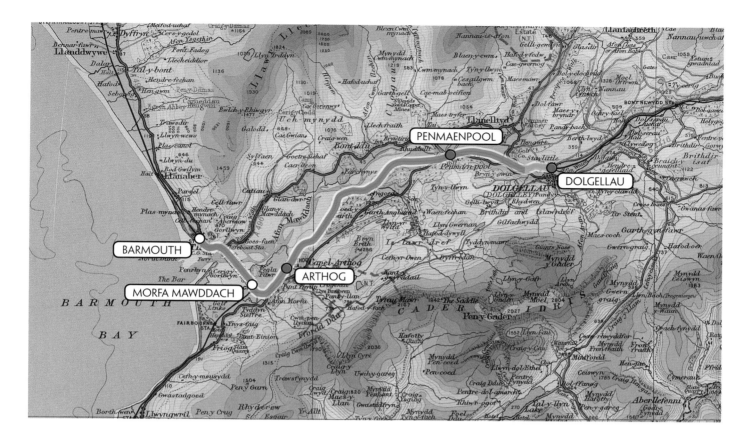

What was to become a 52¾-mile single-track through route from Ruabon to Barmouth Junction started life as a series of independent railway companies that were worked and eventually taken over by the Great Western Railway (GWR). In the east the first line to open was the Vale of Llangollen Railway, which opened along the valley of the River Dee between Ruabon and Llangollen in 1862. Continuing along the scenic Dee Valley, the Llangollen & Corwen Railway opened through the 689-yd Berwyn Tunnel in 1865. This was followed by the Corwen & Bala Railway and the Bala & Dolgelly Railway, both of which opened in 1868. All four railways were worked from opening by the GWR and by 1896 all had been taken over by that company.

At the western end Cambrian Railways (CR) had already opened a 5½-mile branch line along the south shore of the Mawddach Estuary from Barmouth Junction, on the coastal route between Machynlleth and Pwllheli, to Penmaenpool in 1865. But here it stopped, with the missing 2½ miles to Dolgellau remaining unfinished due to lack of funds. Eventually, following pressure from GWR, the CR completed the link and opened it in 1869 – the cross-country route was finally open. Barmouth was

reached from Barmouth Junction via the 764-yd Barmouth Bridge over the Mawddach Estuary, which had been opened by the CR as part of its coastal route in 1867. The CR eventually amalgamated with the GWR in 1922.

The opening of the Ruabon to Barmouth Junction route soon led to the growth of Barmouth as a popular resort. During the summer months through carriages from London Paddington, Birkenhead, Birmingham and Manchester brought holidaymakers anxious to escape the industrial toil and grime for a week or two. Apart from the two world wars this traffic continued until the 1950s but by then competition from cars and buses was beginning to be felt. Closure of associated branch lines started in 1953 when the Corwen to Denbigh line (opened 1865) lost its passenger service. Next to go was the Bala Junction to Blaenau Ffestiniog line (opened 1883), which closed to passengers in 1960. The entire route between Ruabon and Barmouth Junction was recommended for closure in the Beeching Report (1963), through goods trains ceased in 1964, and a closure date of 18 January 1965 was set for passenger services. In the event serious flooding severed the line between Llangollen and Bala Junction on 12 December 1964, leaving just the two extremities – Ruabon to Llangollen and Bala Junction to Barmouth Junction – to continue until the appointed closure date.

Since closure three sections of this long cross-country route have come back to life. The standard-gauge Llangollen Railway now operates trains between Llangollen and Corwen East, while the narrow-gauge Bala Lake Railway (see box) runs trains between Bala and Llanuwchllyn. At the western end of the route the 7-mile section alongside the Mawddach Estuary between Morfa Mawddach station (formerly Barmouth Junction) and Dolgellau has been reopened as a footpath and cycleway known as the Mawddach Trail. Also forming part of National Cycle Network Route 8, the Trail continues from Morfa Mawddach to Barmouth via Barmouth Bridge, over which a small toll is payable. Both Morfa Mawddach

and Barmouth stations are served by trains on the national rail network's Cambrian Coast route. Car parking for Trail users can be found at Morfa Mawddach, Penmaenpool and Dolgellau.

Set below the slopes of Cadair Idris, the Mawddach Trail runs alongside the wide tidal Mawddach Estuary for much of its length. With stunning views of Snowdonia and the surrounding hills, the Trail is highly popular with naturalists visiting the Arthog Bog and Mawddach Valley RSPB Reserves that are found along the route. These are some of the finest places for wildlife in Britain where a profusion of plants, insects and birds can be found throughout the year. At Penmaenpool a GWR signal still guards the former station site where the signal box has been restored as a hide for birdwatchers. Overlooking the wooden toll bridge across the river, the

superbly located George III hotel is an ideal spot to stop for refreshments. From the car park the Trail continues eastwards to the outskirts of Dolgellau where the trackbed of the line has long disappeared beneath the A470 bypass.

PREVIOUS SPREAD: Looking in pristine ex-works condition BR Standard Class 2 2-6-0 No. 78000 halts at Barmouth Junction (Morfa Mawddach) station on 27 May 1961 while a delivery of milk is unloaded from the luggage van. The locomotive was built at Darlington Works in 1952 and withdrawn in 1965.

LEFT: One of Britain's finest lost railway walks, the Mawddach Trail closely hugs the shoreline of the beautiful Mawddach Estuary between Morfa Mawddach and Penmaenpool.

BELOW: Ex-GWR 2251 Class 0-6-0 No. 3204 hurries through Penmaenpool station on 14 July 1962 at the head of a breakdown train bound for Barmouth. This locomotive was built at Swindon Works in October 1946 and withdrawn in March 1963.

Bala Lake Railway

This 2-ft-gauge railway operates steam and diesel trains along the route of the Bala & Dolgelly Railway (opened in 1868 and closed in 1965). The 4½-mile route runs alongside the eastern shore of Lake Bala between Bala (Penybont) and Llanuwchllyn, the headquarters of the railway and where the original station buildings, goods shed and signal box have been restored. The steam locomotives on the line include examples built by Hunslet that once worked at the Dinorwig Slate Quarry in North Wales. Open daily except Mondays and Fridays from April to September, daily in July and August, and during half-term school holidays in February and October.

Lon Eifion

Caernarfon to Afon Wen

Open to passengers 1867–1964 | **Original length** 18¾ miles
Original route operator Carnarvonshire Railway
Length currently open for walkers & cyclists 12 miles | **NCN** 8

Partly built along the route of a horse-drawn, narrow-gauge, slate-carrying tramway, the 18¾-mile standard-gauge railway between Caernarfon and Afon Wen opened in 1867. It was used on summer Saturdays by through trains from Liverpool, Manchester and London Euston but declining traffic led to its closure in 1964. Since then the trackbed between Caernarfon and Bryncir has been reopened as a footpath and cycleway.

CAERNARVON

CAERNARFON

BONTNEWYDD

DINAS JUNCTION

LLANWNDA

GROESLON

PENYGROES

PANT GLAS

BRYNCIR

YNYS

LLANGYBI

CHWILOG

AFON WEN

Welsh Highland Railway

The 9-mile, 3-ft-6-in-gauge Nantlle Railway was the first railway to reach Caernarfon. Opening in 1828, the line was built by Robert Stephenson between slate quarries in the Nantlle Valley and Caernarfon Harbour via Penygroes. Although known to carry passengers, it was in reality a horse-drawn tramway built to carry slate for onward shipment from the harbour. The first standard-gauge line was opened between Menai Bridge station and Caernarfon by the Bangor & Carnarvon Railway (B&CR) in 1852. In 1865 the Nantlle Railway was taken over by the newly-formed Carnarvonshire Railway (CR), which had been authorized in 1862 to build a standard-gauge line from Caernarfon to Afon Wen – the narrow-gauge line was rebuilt as a single-track standard-gauge line between Caernarfon and Penygroes in 1866 and the extension southwards to the Cambrian line at Afon Wen opened the following year. By 1870 the London & North Western

Railway had taken over both the B&CR and the CR (including what remained of the Nantlle Railway) and had opened a branch line from Caernarfon to Llanberis.

A latecomer to North Wales was the 1-ft-11½-in-gauge North Wales Narrow Gauge Railway, which opened between Dinas Junction, south of Caernarfon, and Bryngwyn in 1877. It later became the Welsh Highland Railway (WHR) and was finally completed to Porthmadog via Beddgelert in 1923. It closed in 1937 following a period when it was leased by the Ffestiniog Railway.

By the 1930s the Caernarfon to Afon Wen line had become busy during summer Saturdays with passenger trains from as far afield as Manchester, Liverpool and London Euston carrying happy bands of holidaymakers to destinations in North Wales – excursion trains also ran to Llanberis (for Snowdon), reached via a branch line from Caernarfon. These trains returned after the Second

PREVIOUS SPREAD: Desolation Row! Six years after closure of the Caernarfon to Afon Wen line this was the sad scene at Llangybi station in 1970.

LEFT: Looking north at Dinas Junction in 1909. On the left two L&NWR trains pass on the Caernarfon to Afon Wen line, while on the right is the North Wales Narrow-Gauge Railways' northern terminus of its line from Bryngwyn and South Snowdon. Today the Lon Eifion path and cycleway follows the old standard-gauge route while the reborn narrow-gauge Welsh Highland Railway has been reopened between Caernarfon and Porthmadog.

World War when the Butlins Holiday Camp at Penychain, near Afon Wen, opened for business in 1947. During the summer season through trains to Pwlheli and Porthmadog from as far afield as London Euston – of which 'The Welshman' was the premier service – would operate via the North Wales Coast Line to Bangor and then along the railway via Caernarfon and Afon Wen. 'The Welshman' ran until 1962 and took 7 hrs 23 mins to complete the journey from Euston to Porthmadog! The summer timetable for that year shows eleven southbound and northbound trains operating on Saturdays although from Mondays to Fridays this dropped to nine and ten respectively. There were no trains on Sundays.

Diesel multiple units replaced steam haulage on most local trains in 1958 but this cost-saving measure was to no avail. Recommended for closure in the Beeching Report (1963), the Caernarfon to Afon Wen section closed on 7 December 1964, although the track was not lifted immediately. The line from Menai Bridge to Caernarfon lasted longer, no doubt to cater for special trains arriving for the investiture of Prince Charles on 1 July 1969.

Closure came on 5 January 1970 but a fire on the Britannia Tubular Bridge on the Chester to Holyhead main line that year reprieved the line to cater for freightliner services. Once the bridge had been rebuilt these trains ceased and the line finally closed on 5 February 1972.

Since closure of the Caernarfon to Afon Wen line, 12 miles of the trackbed between Caernarfon and Bryncir has reopened as a footpath and cycleway known as Lon Eifion, although road 'improvements' have obliterated most of the old stations. Lon Eifion was joined between Caernarfon and Dinas in 2000 by the reborn Welsh Highland Railway (see box) which, since 2011, operates narrow-gauge trains to Porthmadog along the reopened and highly scenic line via Beddgelert. Lon Eifion and the railway are separated by a fence as far as Dinas – served by a WHR halt at Bontnewydd at the midway point. At Dinas, Lon Eifion parts company with the railway and continues southward to reach the site of Groeslon station where there is a café and the Inigo Jones Slate Works. Further south the well-surfaced path continues through Penygroes

(once the junction for the Nantlle Railway) and Pant Glas (where the brick-built railway shelter still stands) to end at Bryncir, where there is a car park alongside the surviving platforms, and a water tank.

Although Lon Eifion terminates at Bryncir, there are still some remains of the stations to the south: the crossing keeper's cottage at Ynys is now a private residence; the station building at Llangybi is also a private residence; part of the platform has survived at Chwilog; the station master's house at Afon Wen is a private residence. Trains on the Cambrian Line between Porthmadog and Pwllheli still pass through Afon Wen but nothing remains of the station with its refreshment room.

LEFT: The Lon Eifion footpath and cycleway to Bryncir starts at the northern terminus of the reborn Welsh Highland Railway, close to historic Caernarfon Castle.

BELOW: The site of Bryncir station lies at the southern end of the Lon Eifion footpath and cycleway from Caernarfon. The platform and a water tower are the only reminders of the railway, which closed in 1964.

Welsh Highland Railway

With much of it following the course of the original Welsh Highland Railway, which closed in 1937, this 25-mile 1-ft-11-in-gauge railway was reopened in stages between 1997 and 2011. It is one of Britain's longest heritage railways and undoubtably the most scenic. Trains operate through Snowdonia between Caernarfon and Porthmadog Harbour where they connect with the Ffestiniog Railway — intermediate stations are provided at Bontnewydd, Dinas, Tryfan Junction, Waunfawr, Rhyd Ddu, Beddgelert, Nantmor, and Pont Croesor. Between Caernarfon and Dinas the railway runs along the trackbed of the old standard-gauge line to Afon Wen, which closed in 1964. Trains are normally hauled by restored articulated Beyer-Garratt steam locomotives that once worked in South Africa. Open half-term week in February, daily except Mondays, Tuesdays and Fridays in March, daily except certain Mondays and Fridays from April to June and October, daily from July to September.

NORTHERN ENGLAND
and the
ISLE OF MAN

Isle of Man Steam Heritage Trail

Douglas to Peel

Open to passengers 1873–1965/68 | **Original length** 11½ miles
Original route operator Isle of Man Railway
Length currently open for walkers 10 miles

Opened in 1873, the 11½-mile narrow-gauge railway between Douglas and Peel was the first of what eventually became a 46-mile network of steam railways serving the Isle of Man. After falling on hard times in the 1960s it was briefly rescued by the Marquess of Ailsa before finally closing in 1968. Since then much of the route has been reopened as a footpath known as the Steam Heritage Trail.

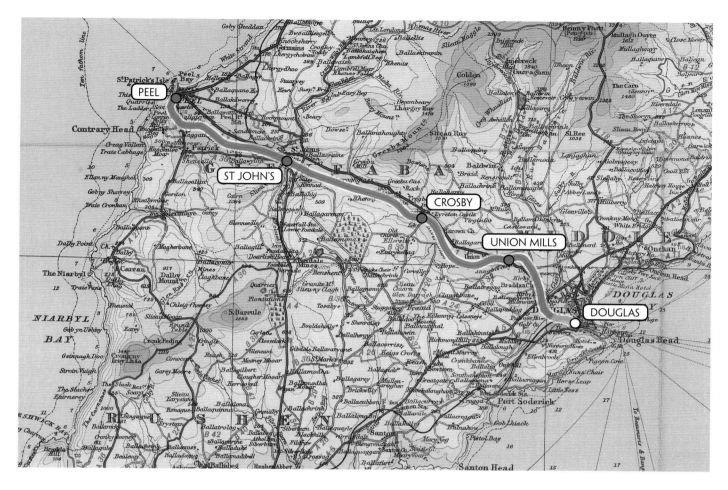

By the mid-19th century the Isle of Man was becoming an increasingly popular destination for holidaymakers from the industrialised North of England. Ferry services from Liverpool enabled thousands of workers and their families to escape the toil and grime for their week of annual holiday each summer. In 1863 the Manx people were given autonomy by the British Crown, enabling them to spend locally raised taxes on improving agriculture, education and transport. Seizing their opportunity, Victorian investors poured into the island, building hotels and railways.

The first railway to be built on the island was the Isle of Man Railway's (IOMR) 11½-mile single-track line from the east coast capital, Douglas, to the west coast port of Peel. A narrow-gauge of 3 ft was chosen due to the mountainous nature of the island and this gauge became the standard for all the Isle of Man railways with the exception of one – the 3-ft-6-in-gauge Snaefell Mountain Railway, which opened in 1895. Crossing the centre of the island from east to west, the Douglas to Peel line opened on 1 July 1873 with motive power provided by three 2-4-0 locomotives supplied by Beyer, Peacock & Co. Ltd. of Gorton, Manchester.

The IOMR had also planned to build lines from Douglas to Castletown and from St John's, on the Peel line, to Ramsey but lack of financial support led to the latter route being dropped. However, the line to Castletown was built along with an extension to Port Erin, where a deep-water harbour was planned. Although the latter never saw the light of day, the 15½-mile single-track line opened on 1 August 1874, just in time for the annual deluge of holidaymakers (see page 193).

PREVIOUS SPREAD: The Bowes Railway near Gateshead is arguably the closest you can experience in the 21st century to the 'real thing' as far as British industrial railways are concerned, with the correct locomotive and wagons on home ground. Andrew Barclay 0-4-0 saddle tank 'N.C.B. No. 22' (built in 1949) negotiates the Pelaw Curve near Blackham's Hill heading a demonstration coal train on 31 August 1998.

LEFT: Ex-County Donegal Railway Walker Brothers' Railcars Nos 19 and 20 depart from St John's with a service for Peel on 28 August 1967. These former Irish railcars are currently stored at Douglas awaiting full restoration.

Built by Beyer, Peacock in 1894, Isle of Man Railway 2-4-0T No. 8 *Fenella* waits to depart from St John's station with a Peel to Douglas train on 28 August 1967. This line finally closed one year later but it has since been reopened as a footpath known as the Steam Heritage Trail.

Meanwhile, the townsfolk and businessmen of Ramsey were regretting the decision by the IOMR not to build a railway to serve their community. Eventually a completely separate company, the Manx Northern Railway (MNR), opened the 16½-mile single-track line between St John's and the town in 1879 (for the full story see pages 194–199). A 2½-mile branch line from St John's to Foxdale was opened by the Foxdale Railway in 1886 (see pages 200–201). The latter was taken over by the MNR in 1891 which, in turn, was absorbed by the IOMR in 1905, giving the enlarged company a total of 46 route miles. The final railway to be built was a short branch line southwards from Peel to an alien internment camp at Knockaloe, which opened in 1915. The branch line outlived its purpose at the end of the First World War and it closed in 1920.

The immediate inter-war years saw increasing numbers of holidaymakers heading for the island from the North of England and the railway network boomed – in 1920 over 1.5 million passengers were carried. But economic recession coupled with increased competition from motor buses led to this figure being nearly halved by the 1930s. All this ended in 1939 with the outbreak of the Second World War but, despite the loss of holidaymakers, the railways of the island were kept busy transporting prisoners of war and service personnel until 1945.

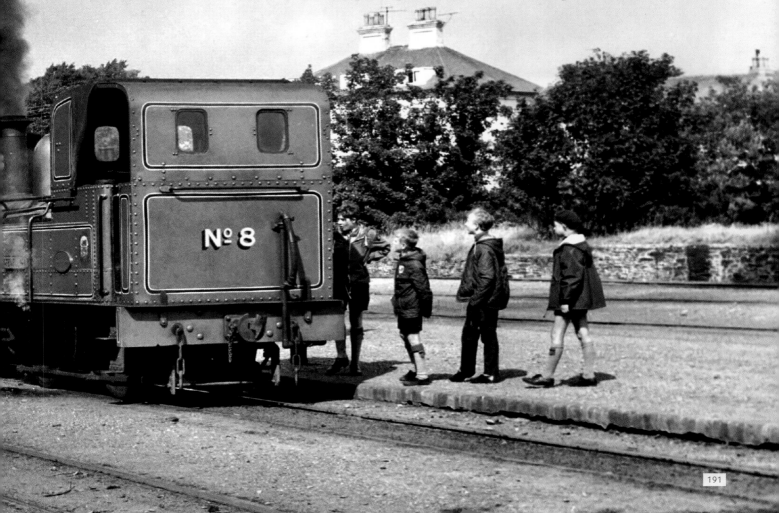

By 1947 holidaymakers had returned and the railways were busy once again but before long the worn-out system, with its vintage locomotives and old rolling stock, was struggling to survive. By 1961 passenger numbers had declined again and the passenger service between St John's and Ramsey was withdrawn for the winter months. The railways struggled on until November 1965 when they were abruptly closed. A saviour in the form of the Marquess of Ailsa then leased all three routes, which were reopened for the summer months in 1967. However, this optimism was short-lived as the Douglas to Peel and the St John's to Ramsey lines closed for good in September 1968. The Douglas to Port Erin line remained open until it was nationalized by the Manx Government in 1978 (see box).

The track on the Douglas to Peel section was eventually lifted in 1975 and the trackbed purchased by the Manx Government. Since then the 10-mile section from Quarter Bridge, on the western outskirts of Douglas, to Peel has been reopened as a footpath known as the Steam Heritage Trail – at St John's it links up with railway footpaths to Sulby (12 miles) and Foxdale (2 miles). Despite the passage of fifty years since the railway closed there is still much to interest lovers of lost railways along this route. At Union Mills station one platform survives alongside a rail-mounted crane and a short section of 3-ft-gauge track while the crossing keeper's cottages at Crosby and Ballacraine Halt have been restored as shelters for walkers. The station building at St John's is now a private residence and the station site a car park.

The station building at Peel has also survived and now forms part of the House of Manannan heritage centre. Nearby is a display of old narrow-gauge railway features including a water tower, signal, lamp standard, level crossing gate, a short section of track and part of a grounded railway carriage.

LEFT: Union Mills station today with its platform and small rail-mounted crane seen through the arch of the road bridge at the western end of the station. The Steam Heritage Trail footpath passes through on its route from Douglas to Peel.

BELOW: A water tower, signal, platform end and a coach body mark the site today of Peel station. Nearby is the Manx Transport Museum.

Isle of Man Steam Railway

Opened in 1874, this 15½-mile 3-ft-gauge railway from Douglas to Port Erin narrowly escaped closure when it was nationalized by the Manx Government in 1978. Since then it has enchanted visitors to the Isle of Man with its Victorian atmosphere, coastal scenery, restored stations and vintage locomotives and rolling stock. Trains are hauled by the original Beyer, Peacock 2-4-0 steam locomotives, the oldest of which dates from 1874. The Isle of Man Railway Museum is located at Port Erin station. Open daily from mid-March to early November.

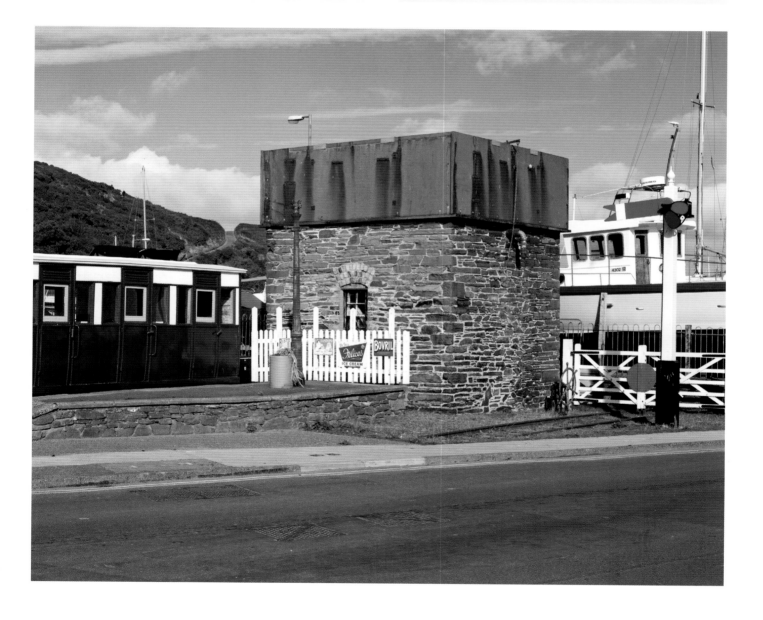

Manx Northern Railway

St John's to Ramsey

Open to passengers 1879–1965/68 | **Original length** 16½ miles
Original route operator Manx Northern Railway
Length currently open for walkers 12 miles

After several years of disappointment, the townsfolk and businessmen
of Ramsey in the Isle of Man finally got their own railway in 1879.
Its meandering route involved the construction of two viaducts and an
exposed section high above the island's rugged west coast. Run down
and neglected, the railway closed in 1965 only to be reopened for the
summers of 1967 and 1968, after which it closed completely.
Since then much of its route has been reopened as a footpath.

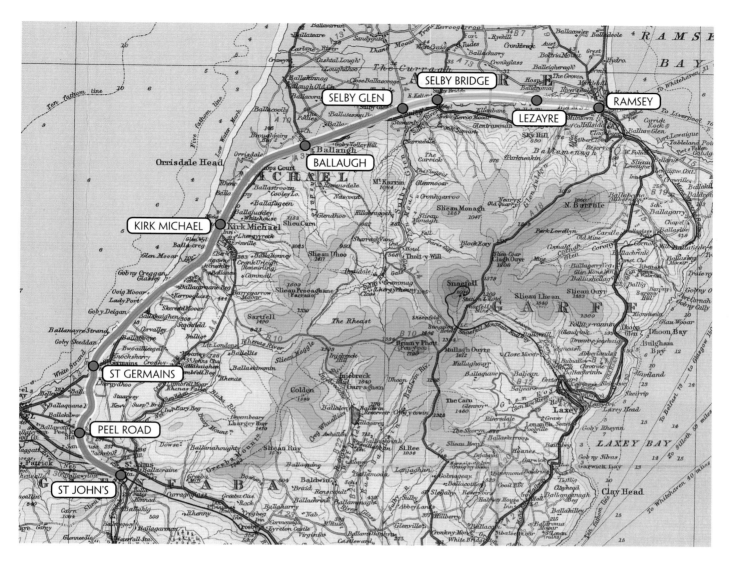

A fter opening its railway from Douglas to Peel in 1873 (see pages 188–193), the Isle of Man Railway's (IOMR) decision not to build the extension from St John's to Ramsey left the townsfolk and businessmen of the latter town fuming. In the end they dealt with this problem by promoting their own 3-ft-gauge railway, the Manx Northern Railway (MNR). Due to the difficult terrain along the east coast of the island, its route necessitated a long detour to the west coast before it could link up with the IOMR's line at St John's. Construction of the 16½-mile route started in 1878 and involved the building of viaducts across Glen Mooar and Glen Wyllin – these substantial structures were built with stone stanchions supporting latticework girders. Along the west coast, near St Germains, the railway was built in an exposed position high above the coastline; this section became prone to subsidence in later years.

The railway opened on 23 September 1879 but, as the MNR were still awaiting delivery of its locomotives, the IOMR operated the trains until November 1880. Through passenger trains between Ramsey and Douglas began operating the following year when MNR trains were given running rights over IOMR track. At Ramsey a branch line was opened in 1883 to serve the harbour.

The MNR was taken over by the IOMR in 1905, creating a network of 46 miles of steam-operated lines across the island. With ever-increasing numbers of holidaymakers visiting the island, the line from St John's to Ramsey was kept busy during the summer months

LEFT: Built by Beyer, Peacock in 1874, Isle of Man Railway 2-4-0T No. 5 *Mona* departs from Crosby with the 10 am Douglas to Peel train on 28 August 1967. The locomotive is currently stored at Douglas awaiting preservation.

although it did face competition from the more direct Douglas to Ramsey Manx Electric Railway (MER) that opened in 1893 – the 17-mile 3-ft-gauge MER was 8 miles shorter than the railway route, with a consequent saving of journey times. This fascinating line with its vintage tram cars is still open for business today.

Passenger traffic on the island's railways peaked in the 1920s with over 1.5 million passengers carried.

But economic recession coupled with increased competition from motor buses saw this figure nearly halved by the 1930s. In the end the IOMR set up its own bus company to complement its railway services and in doing so bankrupted the rival bus operator. All this ended in 1939 with the outbreak of the Second World War but, despite the loss of holidaymakers, the railways of the island were kept busy transporting prisoners of war and service personnel until 1945.

By 1947 holidaymakers had returned and the railways were busy once again but before long the worn-out system, with its vintage locomotives and old rolling stock, was struggling to survive. The 1950 timetable shows five return passenger services operating between Ramsey and Douglas on weekdays only, the 25-mile journey taking a leisurely 75 minutes.

By 1961 passenger numbers had declined and the passenger service between St John's and Ramsey was withdrawn for the winter months. In a bid to reduce operating costs two diesel railcars were purchased from the closed County Donegal Railway in Ireland in 1961 – and the island's railways struggled on until November 1965 when they were all abruptly closed. The Marquess of Ailsa then leased all three routes, which were reopened

BELOW: Built by Beyer, Peacock in 1910, Isle of Man Railway 2-4-0T No. 13 *Kissack* crosses Kirk Michael Viaduct with the 12.18 pm St John's to Ramsey train on 12 June 1959. The locomotive is still in service on the Douglas to Port Erin line.

briefly for the summer months of 1967 and 1968 but this renaissance was short-lived as the Douglas to Peel and the St John's to Ramsey lines closed for good in September of 1968. Following complete closure the track was eventually lifted between St John's and Ramsey in 1974.

Since closure 12 miles of the railway trackbed between St John's and Sulby has been reopened as footpath, with the scenic coastal section between St Germain's and Bishopscourt forming part of the 95-mile long-distance path around the coast of the Isle of Man. There is still much to interest lovers of lost railways along this route: at Peel Road station the overgrown platform survives alongside the footpath; St Germain's station building is now a private residence; the crossing keeper's cottage at West Berk is now a private residence; the stone stanchions of Glen Mooar and Glen Wyllin viaducts survive, although the latticework girders have long been dismantled; complete with level crossing gate and a short length of track, the station building and goods shed at Kirk Michael are now in use as a fire station; the site of Bishop's Court Halt is marked by a bench; the goods shed, goods platform and cattle dock survive at Ballaugh amidst a landscaped park. Although the railway footpath ends here, to the east the station buildings at Sulby Glen, Sulby Bridge and Lezayre have all survived as private residences although, sadly, the terminus building at Ramsey has been demolished.

Groudle Glen Railway

Built by Richard Maltby Broadbent and opened in 1896, this 2-ft-gauge railway was built to carry visitors from Groudle Glen to Sea Lion Rocks, a headland on the east coast of the Isle of Man. The ¾-mile line closed in 1962 but has since been reopened by preservationists. The original 1896 steam locomotive, Sea Lion, has been restored to working condition and operates trains alongside several more recent additions to the motive power. Open Easter and Sundays from May to September, also Wednesday evenings from 21 June to 30 August.

LEFT: This distinctive bridge once carried the St John's to Ramsey line over Glen Balleira near Kirk Michael. A footpath now follows this route as far as Sulby.

BELOW: Affording glorious views of the coastline and the Irish Sea, a clifftop footpath now follows the route of the railway near Glen Mooar.

Foxdale Branch

St John's to Foxdale

Open to passengers 1886–1943 | **Original length** 2½ miles
Original route operator Manx Northern Railway
Length currently open for walkers 2½ miles

Built to serve lead mines, the 2½-mile narrow-gauge railway from St John's to Foxdale opened in 1886 but soon fell on hard times when the mining ceased. The minimal passenger service ended in 1943 and the line closed completely in 1960. Since then this steeply-graded route has been reopened as a footpath.

Built primarily to serve lead mines, the 3-ft-gauge Foxdale Railway opened between St John's and Foxdale, a distance of 2½ miles, on 17 August 1886. The line was worked from the outset by the Manx Northern Railway (MNR), which then went on to take it over in 1891. To cope with the extra traffic forecast to originate from the mines a unique 0-6-0T locomotive, *Caledonia*, was supplied to haul lead-spoil trains on the steeply-graded line – it saw little use, instead being employed on the MNR for hauling heavy cattle trains. Lead mining in the area was soon in decline and it ceased altogether in 1911, by which time the MNR had been absorbed by the Isle of Man Railway.

A minimal passenger service was also operated – the 1922 timetable shows only two return trips each weekday, the journey taking 14 minutes with an optional stop at the only intermediate station, Waterfall. Trains consisted of one coach, made specifically for the branch, hauled by a Beyer, Peacock 2-4-0T but this was replaced by a bus service in 1940 with passenger trains being officially withdrawn in 1943. Both the unique 'Foxdale Coach' and *Caledonia* have fortunately survived and can be seen at work on the Isle of Man Steam Railway.

Sporadic goods trains continued to climb up from St John's to Foxdale until January 1960 when the line closed but the track remained *in situ* until it was eventually lifted in the mid-1970s. Today, the entire route of the Foxdale Railway is an official footpath while the station building at Foxdale has survived in various guises as a private residence and more recently as a club house. The simple wooden hut provided at Waterfall station in Lower Foxdale has gone to the great railway graveyard in the sky!

LEFT: The steeply-graded branch line from St John's to Foxdale lost its passenger service in 1943. Affording glorious views of unspoilt countryside, a footpath now follows the entire route of this railway.

BELOW: Henry Casserley's wife, Kathleen, poses at diminutive Waterfall Halt, the only intermediate station on the Foxdale banch. Facing St John's, this view was taken on 3 July 1933.

Trans-Pennine Trail

Hadfield to Wortley via Woodhead Tunnel

Open to passengers 1845–1970/83 | **Original length** 41½ miles
Original route operator Sheffield, Ashton-under-Lyne & Manchester Railway
Length currently open for walkers 10½ miles **& cyclists** 6½ miles | **NCN** 62 & 627

One of the earliest main line railways built in Britain, the Manchester to Sheffield route involved the building of the 3-mile Woodhead Tunnel, at that time the longest tunnel in the world. Primarily a coal-carrying line, it was electrified and modernized after the Second World War but with the slow decline of the coal industry its days were numbered, finally closing in 1983. Since then, the two sections on either side of the tunnel have been incorporated into the Trans-Pennine Trail.

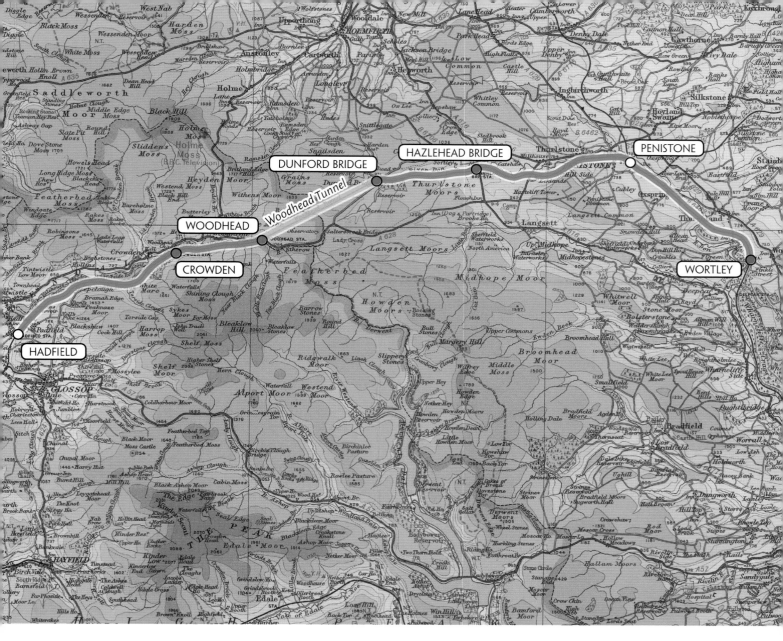

Authorized in 1837 and one of the earliest main railway trunk routes to be built in Britain, the Sheffield, Ashton-under-Lyne & Manchester Railway (SA&MR) was an amazing feat of early Victorian engineering. Linking the two major industrial centres of Manchester and Sheffield on either side of the rugged Pennine Hills, the 41½-mile double-track line featured long viaducts at Dinting and Etherow and the 3-m-13-yd single-bore Woodhead Tunnel, which at the time of its opening was one of the longest single-bores in the world. The tunnel took eight years to complete and cost the lives of twenty-six navvies. Engineered by Charles Vignoles and Joseph Locke, the railway opened for business via Penistone in 1845 and before long it became obvious that the single-bore Woodhead Tunnel had become a bottleneck on this busy line. A second parallel bore was opened in 1852 but its construction cost the lives of twenty-eight navvies who died from an outbreak of cholera. Despite this improvement to traffic flows, the tunnels were always appalling places for drivers and firemen of steam locomotives who were often nearly asphyxiated by the smoke.

In the meantime, the SA&MR had merged with two other companies in 1847 to become the Manchester, Sheffield & Lincolnshire Railway (MS&LR). For all of its life coal was the lifeblood of the railway, linking as it did the coalfields of South Yorkshire with the ports of Manchester and Liverpool. Heavy coal trains always needed rear-end banking assistance, while passenger expresses were normally double-headed. The MS&LR changed its name to the Great Central Railway (GCR) in

1897 in anticipation of the opening of its London Extension to Marylebone, which was completed in 1899. Under its general manager, Sir Sam Fay, this go-ahead railway went on to open the giant Wath Marshalling Yard near Sheffield in 1907 and vast coal-handling docks at Immingham in 1912.

The problems in operating heavy coal trains over the Woodhead route eventually led to proposals to electrify the line after the First World War. Finally, in 1936, the London & North Eastern Railway (L&NER), successor to the GCR, started work on installing an overhead 1.5 kV DC system but progress on this was halted by the outbreak of the Second World War in 1939. Work restarted on the electrification in 1945, a new double-track tunnel at Woodhead was constructed and new Class EM1 and more powerful Class EM2 electric locomotives were built at Gorton Works. Work on the line was completed on 14 June 1954 and the new electric locomotives were universally welcomed by drivers of the heavy coal trains through the tunnel. Sadly, any euphoria was short-lived as, within fifteen years, the coalfields of South Yorkshire had gone into terminal decline and technological advances had made the 1.5 kV DC system obsolete.

PREVIOUS SPREAD: Walkers and cyclists now enjoy using the scenic and traffic-free Longdendale Trail along the route of the former electrified railway between Hadfield and Woodhead.

BELOW: LNER Class O4 2-8-0 No. 6272 heads an eastbound freight through Dunford Bridge station soon after exiting the 3-mile-long Woodhead Tunnel on 15 September 1945. Although this line was electrified in 1954 it was closed in 1981.

The writing was on the wall for the Woodhead line and all passenger services between Manchester and Sheffield were withdrawn in January 1970 – all that remained were electric suburban trains between Manchester, Glossop and Hadfield (these still operate today) and a local diesel multiple unit service between Huddersfield and Sheffield that used the route between Penistone and Sheffield. Coal traffic continued to be electrically-hauled but this ended on 17 July 1981 leaving just the local diesel multiple unit service between Penistone and Sheffield until May 1983 when it was diverted via Barnsley. The mothballed main line and its electrification masts were finally ripped up in the mid-1980s, ending any hope that it might reopen. Hailed by the British Railways Board in 1955 as 'Britain's First All-Electric Main Line', the modernized Woodhead line only had a working life of twenty-seven years.

Since closure two distinct sections of this railway have been incorporated into the Trans-Pennine Trail, a 207-mile long-distance footpath and cycleway stretching across northern England from Southport in Lancashire to Hornsea in East Yorkshire. The old railway route

southeast of Penistone forms part of the 70-mile branch of the Trail that runs between Leeds to Chesterfield. The section from Hadfield to the eastern portals of the Woodhead Tunnels is also known as the Longdendale Trail. One of the two original single-bore Woodhead Tunnels has been used since 1963 by the National Grid to carry the Trans-Pennine 400 kV electricity cables under the Peak District National Park, but despite much controversy, the cables have been relocated to the newer double-track tunnel, thus preventing any possible reopening in the future.

Opened in 1992, the 6½-mile traffic-free Longdendale Trail starts close to Hadfield station and heads up the valley alongside three enormous reservoirs that were completed in 1884 by Manchester Corporation. Despite the traffic on the A628 on the opposite side of the valley and the striding line of pylons this is a highly scenic route that ends at the western portals of the Woodhead Tunnels – above the portal of the modern tunnel a stone commemorates its opening by British Railways in 1954 while, nearby, the platforms of Woodhead station are remarkable survivors. While the Longdendale Trail ends

here the Trans-Pennine Trail takes to side roads across moorland above the 3-mile tunnel, rejoining the old railway route at Dunford Bridge.

From the car park at Dunford Bridge this 10½-mile section of the Trans-Pennine Trail heads east through the Wogden Foot Nature Reserve, an amazing grassland rich with over eighty-six plant species that has been developed on former railway sidings. Continuing eastward the Trail passes the site of Hazlehead station and the Bullhouse Minewater Project before reaching Penistone where the railway station is still served by trains on the scenic Penistone Line between Huddersfield and Barnsley. The Trail now heads southeasterly to Oxspring where the main Pennine Trail (NCN Route 62) branches off to the east – the railway trackbed from here is used by the 70-mile branch of the Pennine Trail (NCN Route 627) that runs between Leeds to Chesterfield. En route to the end of the railway path at Wortley, the Trail passes through the 1947-single-bore of the 308-yd curving Thurgoland Tunnel, which is lit up between 6 am and midnight. The railway path ends at Wortley where the station has survived despite closure in 1955 – the nearest car park here is at Cote Green.

Kirklees Light Railway

This 15-in-gauge passenger-carrying railway operates along the route of the Clayton West branch line, which closed in 1983. The line was originally opened by the Lancashire & Yorkshire Railway in 1879 and features the 511-yd Shelley Woodhouse Tunnel. Today's miniature railway features two articulated 0-4+4-0 locomotives and enclosed heated passenger coaches. Open weekends and Bank Holidays throughout the year, and daily during school holidays.

LEFT: LNER 4-4-2 No. 3284 exits Woodhead Tunnel and approaches Dunford Bridge station with the 2.50 pm express from Manchester London Road to Sheffield Victoria on 15 September 1945.

BELOW: As part of the new electrification scheme of the line after the Second World War the second single-bore 308-yd-long Thurgoland Tunnel was built by the LNER in 1947 and completed by the new British Railways in 1948. It is now used by walkers and cyclists on the Trans-Pennine Trail.

Cinder Track

Scarborough to Whitby West Cliff

Open to passengers 1885–1965 | **Original length** 23½ miles
Original route operator North Eastern Railway
Length currently open for walkers & cyclists 21 miles | **NCN** 1

After a long and drawn-out construction period during which it was nearly abandoned, the scenic 21¾-mile coastal route between Scarborough and Whitby West Cliff was finally opened in 1885. The steeply-graded single-track line was difficult to work and journey times between the two towns were painfully slow. The line became a victim of the 'Beeching axe' in 1965 but has since become a highly popular footpath and cycleway known as The Cinder Track.

WHITBY

WHITBY WEST CLIFF

HAWSKER

ROBIN HOOD'S BAY

FYLING HALL

RAVENSCAR

STAINTONDALE

HAYBURN WYKE

CLOUGHTON

SCALBY

SCARBOROUGH

The fishing port of Whitby was one of the first towns in Britain to be served by a railway when the horse-drawn Whitby & Pickering Railway (W&PR) opened in 1836. Its route across the North Yorkshire Moors was engineered by George Stephenson and, until 1847, included a rope-worked incline at Goathland. To the south, Scarborough had been reached by the York & North Midland Railway in 1845. A second route to Whitby opened in 1865 when the Esk Valley line from Battersby was completed, linking up with the W&PR route at Grosmont.

The third railway to serve Whitby was the coast-hugging Whitby, Redcar & Middlesbrough Union Railway, which opened throughout in 1883. The fourth and final railway to reach Whitby, the Scarborough & Whitby Railway (S&WR), had a very long gestation period after receiving parliamentary authorization in 1871. Closely following the Yorkshire coastline, construction of the steeply-graded railway started in 1872, but progress was painfully slow and by 1878 it had virtually ceased owing to lack of funds. In the nick of time a local benefactor, William Hammond of Raven Hall, stepped in and saved the project from abandonment but he insisted that the railway should disappear from his view through a tunnel where it passed his estate! The railway was finally opened in 1885 – its crowning glory was (and still is) the thirteen-arch Larpool Viaduct that carried the line high over the Esk Valley to West Cliff station, just north of Whitby. At a height of 120 ft, the viaduct was built with more than five million bricks and is even mentioned in local author Bram Stoker's *Dracula*. The working of trains from Scarborough into Whitby was complicated with trains having to change direction down a steeply-graded spur from West Cliff to Town station. The working arrangements in Scarborough were equally complicated with trains having to reverse in and out of Central station. Consequently, journey times were slow with trains taking about 80 minutes for the 23½-mile journey between Scarborough Central and Whitby Town.

The North Eastern Railway (NER) worked the S&WR line from the outset, eventually taking over the company in 1898. Its scenic qualities were heavily promoted in the company's advertising material and during the summer months the line was used by trains taking holidaymakers on circular tours via Scarborough, Whitby and Pickering. The NER's successor, the London & North Eastern Railway, introduced Sentinel steam railcars on this route in the 1920s and even experimented with a pioneering diesel-electric railcar.

Camping coaches also became a familiar sight at many of the intermediate stations and these remained popular with holidaymakers until the closure of the line. Working the steeply-graded line was hard work for drivers of steam locomotives and, much to their relief, these were replaced by new diesel multiple units in 1958. But by then declining traffic meant that the writing was on the wall for all four railways that served Whitby – the first one to close was the line from Redcar and Loftus, which closed on 5 May of that year. Then along came the Beeching Report (1963), which recommended closure of all of the remaining railway routes to Whitby – in the end the Esk Valley line was reprieved but both the Scarborough and Pickering lines closed on 8 March 1965. While the Pickering route was ultimately saved and reopened as the North Yorkshire Moors heritage railway (see box), the Whitby to Scarborough line was not so lucky and the track was lifted in 1968.

Since closure the entire length of the railway route between Whitby West Cliff and Scarborough has been reopened as a footpath and cycleway known as the Scarborough to Whitby Rail Trail or, alternatively, the Scarborough to Whitby Cinder Track. It also forms part of National Cycle Network Route 1 and although most of it is traffic-free, it does have long gradients and is often muddy after heavy rain, making it unsuitable for anything but mountain bikes. The Cinder Track starts in a supermarket car park in Scarborough and immediately joins the railway trackbed, soon reaching open country at Scalby – the first station on the line here has been demolished to make room for modern housing. The Track continues to climb northward to Cloughton where the station building, the remains of platforms and a goods shed have all been beautifully restored as a bed and breakfast establishment and tea room – there is even a British Railways (BR) Mk 1 coach sitting on a short length of track that provides self-catering accommodation. Continuing its climb north, the Track reaches Hayburn Wyke where the platform has survived along with the stationmaster's house, which is now a private residence. Stainton Dale station follows, and both platforms and station buildings have survived, the latter is also now a private residence.

After Stainton Dale the Cinder Track approaches the coast at Ravenscar where the station platform has survived and where there is a car park; the nearby Raven Hotel is open for refreshments. Between here and Robin Hood's Bay there are superb views of the coastline from the Cinder Track, with the old railway trackbed taking an inland loop through the site of Fyling Hall station. The station buildings at Robin Hood's Bay have survived and are now used as holiday accommodation and from here the Trail touches the coast before turning inland to Hawsker. The station here has been beautifully restored and is now used by Trailways, a cycle hire centre for users of the Cinder Track, while several BR coaches provide an information centre and deluxe self-catering accommodation. Beyond Hawsker the Track crosses the beautiful Esk Valley on the iconic Larpool Viaduct before heading down to end at Whitby Harbour.

North Yorkshire Moors Railway

Originally built by George Stephenson as a horse-drawn railway with a rope-worked incline, the Whitby & Pickering Railway opened in 1836. The line was rebuilt to allow the operation of steam locomotives in 1845 and the incline bypassed in 1865, by which time the railway had been taken over by the North Eastern Railway. Crossing the North Yorkshire Moors and serving only a few small villages en route, the railway became a victim of the 'Beeching axe' and was closed on 8 March 1965. It was reopened as a heritage railway in 1973 and today the North Yorkshire Moors Railway is one of the most popular in Britain. Trains are normally steam-hauled and connect with Esk Valley Line trains at Grosmont – certain trains continue their journey along this route to and from Whitby, making this, at 24¼ miles, the longest standard-gauge heritage railway journey in Britain. Open from February half-term, and daily from late March to the end of October, and the Christmas period.

Mentioned in Bram Stoker's *Dracula* and featuring in a TV *Heartbeat* episode, the magnificent thirteen-arch, 120-ft-high Larpool Viaduct near Whitby is now enjoyed by users of the Cinder Track from Scarborough.

Whitehaven, Cleator & Egremont Railway

Whitehaven to Rowrah

Open to passengers 1856/81–1931/35 | **Original length** 32¼ miles
Original route operator Whitehaven, Cleator & Egremont Railway
Length currently open for walkers & cyclists 8½ miles | **NCN** 71 & 72

Transporting iron ore and coal from local mines, the highly profitable Whitehaven, Cleator & Egremont Railway was eventually taken over as a joint concern by its two bigger neighbours – the London & North Western Railway and the Furness Railway. Mine closures in the 1930s led to the cessation of passenger services but sections remained open to serve quarries, mines and iron and steel works until the late 1970s. In recent years the trackbed between Whitehaven and Rowrah has been reopened by Sustrans as a footpath and cycleway.

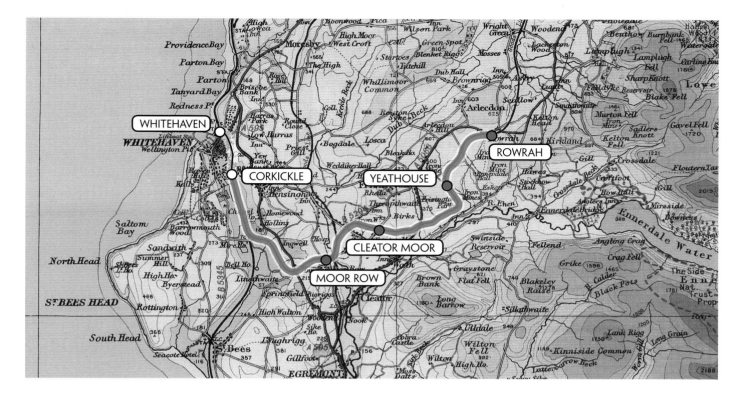

Originally built to transport coal and iron ore from the many mines to the south and east of Whitehaven down to the town's harbour, the Whitehaven, Cleator & Egremont Railway (WC&ER) was formed in 1853. Forming a steep junction with the Whitehaven & Furness Junction Railway (W&FJR), 2 miles to the south of Whitehaven at Mirehouse, the 4½-mile railway was opened via Moor Row to iron works and iron ore mines at Frizington in 1856. A year later the 2½-mile line from Moor Row to Egremont, serving iron ore mines at Woodend, was opened and passenger services, on both lines, to and from Whitehaven were introduced. The WC&ER had obtained running powers over the W&FJR northwards from Mirehouse Junction to Whitehaven via Corkickle station and the single-bore 1,333-yd Whitehaven Tunnel. Mining subsidence, which plagued the railway throughout its life, soon reared its ugly head when a viaduct at Woodend needed to be replaced in 1859 by an embankment. However, the railway soon proved to be very profitable with large amounts of iron ore being shipped from Whitehaven Harbour to iron works in South Wales.

Mineral traffic was so heavy that the Mirehouse Junction to Frizington line was doubled and an extension to Collier Yeat, near Rowrah, was opened in 1862. Passenger services were introduced on the extension in 1864, by which time the line was handling over 600,000 tons of iron ore per year. The Frizington line was again extended 11 miles through Rowrah to Marron Junction, where it connected with the Cockermouth & Workington Railway, allowing WC&ER mineral trains to operate directly to the iron and steel works at Workington. The line opened to mineral and passenger traffic in 1866, although the latter was very much of secondary importance. Mineral traffic was so heavy that the line was doubled in 1871.

To the south, the Egremont branch was later extended to Sellafield, where it met the Furness Railway's (FR, successor to the W&FJR) coastal route from Barrow-in-Furness to Whitehaven. A joint enterprise between the WC&ER and the FR, the 5-mile extension opened via Beckermet in 1869.

The 'big brother' from Euston, the London & North Western Railway (L&NWR) already had its sights on taking over the WC&ER but its offers were turned down on several occasions. Increasingly angry over the high profits being made at their expense by the WC&ER,

LEFT: The soot encrusted road overbridge at Winder Brow bears testament to the hard slog experienced by steam locomotives climbing up to Rowrah. Today walkers and cyclists can enjoy the eastern section of the Sea to Sea (C2C) National Cycle Route as it follows the old railway route from Whitehaven to Rowrah.

the owners of iron and steel works in this part of Cumbria proposed their own line – competing head-on with the WC&ER, the first part of the Cleator & Workington Junction Railway (C&WJR) opened in 1879. However, by this time, the WC&ER had finally been taken over as a joint enterprise by the L&NWR and the FR. The final piece in this complicated jigsaw came in 1881 when the 7-mile Gilgarran Branch was opened throughout from Ullock Junction (on the Rowrah to Marron Junction line) to Parton (north of Whitehaven) via Distington. Serving a colliery and ironworks, the new line had been built to compete directly with the encroaching C&WJR. It carried very little passenger traffic and was closed in stages between 1932 and 1965.

Both the L&NWR and FR went on to become part of the newly-formed London, Midland & Scottish Railway

(LMS) in 1923. On the original WC&ER routes the closure of mines led to passenger services being withdrawn from Moor Row to Marron Junction in 1931, and from Whitehaven to Sellafield via Egremont in 1935. Mineral traffic continued north of Rowrah until 1954, while the line south of here to Moor Row remained open to serve a quarry until 1978. The last vestige of the WC&ER to remain operational was the line from Mirehouse Junction to Egremont, which remained open to serve an iron ore mine until 1980 although the track remained *in situ* until the 1990s.

In more recent years the trackbed of the railway from Mirehouse Junction to Rowrah has been reopened as a footpath and cycleway that forms the eastern part of the challenging Sea to Sea (C2C) National Cycle Route – making use of many closed railways the route finally ends

on the east coast at Sunderland. Classified as Route 72 of the National Cycle Network, the railway path starts at Whitehaven Harbour with just one short on-road section here. From there onwards the path is traffic-free as it climbs gradually up through Mirehouse to Moor Row – here there is a junction (as in railway days) with Route 72 continuing south to Egremont and Beckermet to reach the Cumbrian Coast at Sellafield station – in parts this route also follows the trackbed of the railway.

Resuming our journey at Moor Row, the footpath and cycleway becomes Route 71 of the NCN, following the railway trackbed through Cleator Moor to Rowrah – beyond here the railway route is left behind as the cycle path heads east to Penrith. There are many sculptures and artworks along this route reflecting the industrial heritage of the area as well as physical reminders of its railway past. At Moor Row the road overbridge and a platform still remain while the station house at Frizington is now a private residence. Although nothing remains of the station at Yeathouse, the station at Winder, along with the platform, and the station at Rowrah are also private residences. Although Route 71 of the NCN heads off eastwards at Rowrah, a footpath follows much of the course of the remaining railway route northwards through Lamplugh, Ullock and Branthwaite to the site of Marron Junction.

Ravenglass & Eskdale Railway

Opened in 1875 as a 3-ft-gauge mineral line, the 'Ratty', as it is affectionately known, closed in 1913. It was reopened in 1915 as a 15-in-gauge miniature railway by model engineer W. J. Bassett-Lowke and flourished transporting granite and summer visitors until the Second World War. The railway narrowly escaped closure after the closure of the quarries in 1960 but was rescued by a group of enthusiasts. Today steam trains haul passengers along the picturesque 7-mile route between Ravenglass and Dalegarth. Open daily from mid-March to the end of October.

LEFT: Immaculately turned out No. 43006 has reached the end of the line at Rowrah with an enthusiasts' brake van special from Whitehaven on 7 May 1966. Designed by George Ivatt, this Class 4F 2-6-0 locomotive was built at Horwich Works in 1948 and withdrawn in 1968.

BELOW: The Cleator to Woodend road overbridge at the former Moor Row station on the C2C National Cycle Route in Cumbria, looking towards Whitehaven. Moor Row was once the junction for the railway to Sellafield, which lost its passenger service in 1935.

Bowes Railway Path

Dipton Colliery to Jarrow

Open 1826–1974 | **Original length** 15 miles
Original route operator Pontop & Jarrow Railway
Length currently open for walkers & cyclists 10½ miles | **NCN** 11

Engineered by George Stephenson and one of the earliest railways in the world, the standard-gauge coal-carrying Pontop & Jarrow Railway opened in 1826. Serving numerous collieries, it remained privately owned until 1947 when the National Coal Board took over operations. Steam operations continued until 1970 and the railway closed in 1974. Since then a short section has been reopened as a working museum while much of the trackbed has been reopened as the Bowes Railway Path.

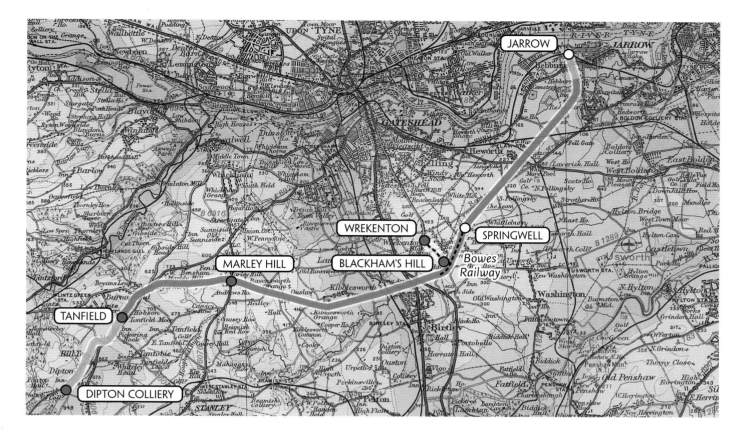

From as early as the 17th century simple horse-drawn wooden waggonways were being used to transport coal from collieries in north Durham to staithes on the River Tyne. Here the coal was loaded onto barges for transfer to seagoing colliers. Before Acts of Parliament became the norm for railways to be built, the operators of waggonways required permission from landowners to cross their land – these financial agreements were known as wayleaves. By the 18th century there were a number of these waggonways operating in northeast England, notable among them being the Beamish, Chopwell, Garesfield, Tanfield Washington, Lambton, and Londonderry waggonways. Wooden waggonways were gradually replaced by plateways with the introduction of cast iron rails in the 1780s.

Built to connect Springwell and Mount Moor collieries in northwest Durham to staithes on the River Tyne at Jarrow, the Pontop & Jarrow Railway was one of the first railways in the world. The plan for the line was first put forward by a group of local colliery owners known as the 'Grand Allies' who soon handed the project over to up-and-coming local railway engineer George Stephenson. After refining the 'Grand Allies' plan, he went on to design an 11½-mile line using three inclined planes and a level locomotive-worked section. The railway opened across the Team Valley, climbing to a height of 567 ft before descending again, on 17 January 1826 and was extended to collieries at Kibblesworth in 1842, Marley Hill in 1853, and Dipton in 1855. This was the furthest extent of the railway, 15 miles, with two gravity-worked inclines, four powered inclines using stationary steam engines and two locomotive-worked sections at each end – at its peak the railway carried over one million tons of coal a year.

Springwell Colliery closed in 1932 and the Pontop & Jarrow Railway was taken over by another group of colliery owners, notable among them being members of the Bowes-Lyon family, and it was then renamed the Bowes Railway. The colliery buildings at Springwell became the workshops for the new railway. The nationalization of Britain's coal industry in 1947 saw the railway becoming part of the newly-formed National Coal Board (NCB).

LEFT: Marley Hill Colliery in 1968 as Austerity Class 0-6-0 saddle tank '83' (Works No. 3688, built in 1949) shuffles through the yard, its exhaust whipped away on the cold north-easterly wind. Marley Hill Colliery was served by sidings from the Bowes Railway until July 1971. The present-day Tanfield Railway running shed and workshop now occupies part of this site in the foreground, while the former colliery site is now a nature reserve.

Modernization followed in 1950 with the stationary steam winding engines at the top of the inclines being replaced by electric power and, five years later, a new line was built to connect the Bowes Railway with the nearby Pelaw Main line. With the decline in coal mining and the closure of collieries the railway eventually succumbed to closure at the end of 1974, apart from a 1-mile section between Jarrow and Springwell Bankfoot, which remained open to serve a coal washing plant until 1986.

Fortunately the 1½-mile section of the Bowes Railway between Springwell and Black Fell, including the workshops at Springwell and a number of coal wagons, were purchased by Tyne & Wear Council and reopened as a working museum. The Bowes Railway Museum site includes the Blackham's Hill East and Blackham's Hill West inclines, which are worked by the 300-hp Blackham's Hill winding engine. The museum is open to the public on Tuesdays, Thursdays and Saturdays with special open days on the first weekend of each month (March to December).

At the western end of the line the engine shed at Marley Hill was also saved by preservationists and today forms part of the Tanfield Railway (see box).

The 10½-mile section of the railway from Tanfield to Jarrow has also been reopened as a footpath and cycleway and is designated as National Cycle Network Regional

BELOW: The Great North Forest Heritage Trail at Burnopmoor, near Andrew's House, County Durham. This is looking towards the site of the former Blackburn Fell Drift Mine, which was located to the north side of the Bowes Railway running line, to the left of this photograph. This mine, located between Marley Hill and Birkheads Bank Top, supplied coal for the Bowes Railway locomotives at Marley Hill and in latter years coal for coking. Coal production from the drift commenced in July 1937 and the mine was finally closed in February 1979.

Route 11. As the railway included inclined planes on its route certain sections are far from level, with the Newcastle Bank to Springwell section being the steepest. Known as the Bowes Railway Path, this traffic-free route straddles the Great North Forest and offers panoramic views across the Team Valley and County Durham. En route watch out for the five pieces of modern sculpture between Tanfield and Kibblesworth, Anthony Gormley's iconic *Angel of the North* overlooking the Team Valley, and the Bowes Railway Museum at Springwell.

BELOW: Vulcan Foundry 1945-built Austerity Class 0-6-0ST No. 28, working from the NCB's Marley Hill shed, drifts down the 1-in-35 Hobson bank on the Bowes Railway at Burnopfield village with a loaded train from Burnopfield Colliery towards Marley Hill in the summer of 1968.

Tanfield Railway

Located on the site of the coal-carrying Tanfield Waggonway, which opened in 1725, the Tanfield Railway features 3 miles of running track from Sunniside to East Tanfield and the world's oldest surviving railway bridge, Causey Arch, reached via a woodland walk from Causey station. Once used by the Bowes Railway, the engine shed at Marley Hill dates from 1854 and was in use until the end of steam in 1970. Passengers are carried in restored 19th-century coaches hauled by a collection of small, mainly steam, industrial locomotives, the oldest of which dates from 1873. Open on Sundays, some Saturdays, and bank holiday weekends all year, also on Thursdays and Saturdays during school summer holidays.

Tees Valley Railway Walk

Middleton-in-Teesdale to Barnard Castle

Open to passengers 1868–1964 | **Original length** 8¾ miles
Original route operator North Eastern Railway
Length currently open for walkers 6 miles

Built primarily to serve stone quarries along the upper Tees Valley, the branch line to Middleton-in-Teesdale opened in 1868. While stone traffic kept the line busy until the 1930s, passenger numbers were fairly minimal and even the introduction of modern diesel multiple units in 1957 failed to boost traffic. Following complete closure in 1965, 6 miles of the trackbed has reopened as a footpath.

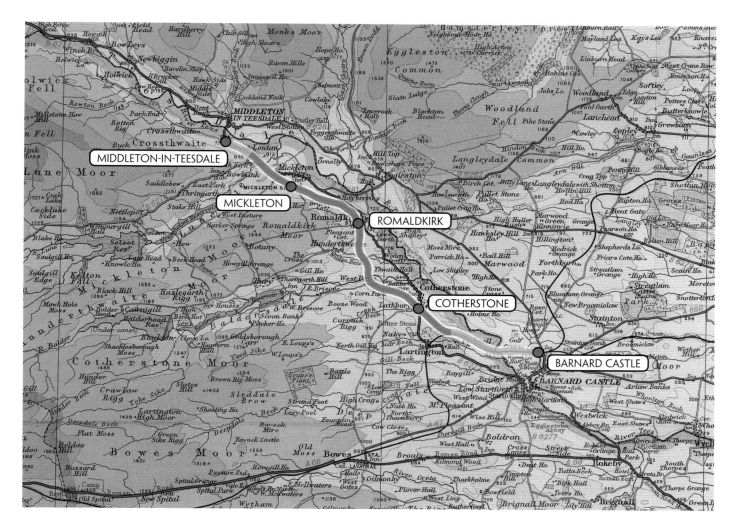

Railways first reached the market town of Barnard Castle in Teesdale, County Durham, in 1856 when the Stockton & Darlington Railway's (S&DR) route from Darlington opened. Within six years the S&DR had absorbed two newer railways – the South Durham & Lancashire Union Railway and the Eden Valley Railway – that linked Bishop Auckland and Barnard Castle with Tebay and Penrith via Stainmore Summit. The S&DR was absorbed by the North Eastern Railway (NER) in 1863.

The final railway to serve Barnard Castle was the Tees Valley Railway, which was incorporated in 1865 to build a single-track line from the town up the Tees Valley to serve stone quarries around Middleton-in-Teesdale. Featuring two viaducts and with intermediate stations at Cotherstone, Romaldkirk and Mickleton, the line opened on 12 May 1868 – it was worked from the outset by the NER but remained independent until 1882. Stone quarries at Greengates, Crossthwaite, Park End and Middleton were all served by their own sidings and a 4-mile narrow-

gauge line was opened in the early 20th century to aid the construction of large reservoirs at Grassholme and Selset. A proposed extension across the hills designed to serve coal and lead mines around the town of Alston (see pages 226–231) failed to materialize – the 25-mile Cumberland & Cleveland Junction Railway would have climbed from the Tees Valley to a height of 1,900 ft above sea level before descending to the South Tyne Valley.

Passenger traffic on the Middleton-in-Teesdale branch was never heavy with the 1950 timetable listing just six return journeys each weekday – trains originated from, or returned to, Newcastle, Sunderland, Durham and Darlington.

LEFT: The double-headed nine-coach RCTS 'The North Yorkshireman Rail Tour' crosses the viaduct over River Lune on the approach to Middleton-in-Teesdale on 25 April 1964. The train engines are ex-LNER Class V3 2-6-2T No. 67646 and ex-LMS Class 4P 2-6-4T No. 42639 – the line from Barnard Castle closed and both locos were withdrawn later that year.

While passenger traffic was of secondary importance, the scenic branch line was once used by day-trippers visiting the famous High Force waterfall – in the summer charabancs carried them from Middleton-in-Teesdale station to this beauty spot. Following the end of the Second World War much of the stone traffic was lost to road transport and, with passenger numbers also in decline, British Railways introduced diesel multiple units as a cost-saving measure in 1957. A new timetable was introduced with six out of the seven trains each weekday starting or ending their journey at Darlington. But this was all to no avail as there were very few passengers and the line was recommended for closure in the Beeching Report (1963) – even before this was published, Barnard Castle had lost its railway across the Pennines via Stainmore Summit in January 1962. Passenger services from Darlington to Barnard Castle and Middleton-in-Teesdale ceased on 30 November 1964 and freight services ended on 5 April 1965.

The track was lifted in 1967 and since then 6 miles of this scenic branch line has been reopened as the Tees Valley Railway Walk. While the station at Middleton-in-Teesdale has survived in the midst of a caravan park, the level railway path starts a ½-mile east of here, reached along the river bank via Lonton. Heading southeasterly, the path soon crosses the River Lune on the five-arch Lunedale Viaduct, completed in 1868, before reaching the former site of Mickleton station with its car park and picnic site. The traffic-free path is a superb way of leisurely exploring glorious Teesdale, offering far-reaching views from what is now a green corridor rich in plant, butterfly and bird life. Two miles further on the

path reaches Romaldkirk where the old station building is a private residence presided over by a NER signal. After a short detour through the village the path heads south to cross the River Balder on the tall nine-arched Baldersdale Viaduct before reaching Cotherstone, where the station building is also a private residence. After a short detour around the station, the path continues to Lartington, where it ends. To reach Barnard Castle walkers can continue their journey on the Teesdale Way Long Distance Path from Cotherstone.

LEFT: Following the course of the railway from the outskirts of Middleton-in-Teesdale to Cotherstone, the 6-mile Tees Valley Railway Walk is a peaceful green corridor rich in plant, butterfly and bird life.

BELOW: A Barnard Castle to Middleton-in-Teesdale train hauled by ex-LNER Class G5 0-4-4T No. 67284 has just arrived at Romaldkirk station on 26 April 1954. The old station building is now a private residence.

'Head of Steam' Railway Museum

Formerly known as the Darlington Railway Centre and Museum, the Head of Steam is located in the 1842-built North Road station, goods shed and the Hopetown Carriage Works in Darlington. Exhibits include the original Stockton & Darlington Railway locomotive Locomotion No. 1, dating from 1825, Darlington-built 0-6-0 Derwent, dating from 1845, and historic rolling stock. The museum also houses the Ken Hoole Study Centre. The historic station is still served by trains on the Darlington to Bishop Auckland branch line. Open Tuesday to Sunday from April to September, and Wednesday to Sunday from October to March.

South Tyne Trail

Haltwhistle to Alston

Open to passengers 1852–1976 | **Original length** 13 miles
Original route operator Newcastle & Carlisle Railway
Length currently open for walkers & cyclists 13 miles | **NCN** 11

Built to serve collieries and lead mines in the South Tyne Valley, the steeply-graded 13-mile Haltwhistle to Alston branch line was opened by the Newcastle & Carlisle Railway in 1852. Featuring the graceful Lambley Viaduct, the railway finally closed in 1976 but since then the entire route has been reopened as a footpath and cycleway, while the southern section has also been reopened as a narrow-gauge railway.

Coal had been mined on a small scale in east Cumberland since Roman times. By the 17th century the primary landowner, the Earl of Carlisle, started to develop collieries at Tindale Fell but transporting the coal by packhorse was a slow and tedious business. It is known that towards the end of the 18th century the then Earl of Carlisle had opened a wooden horse-drawn waggonway from the collieries to staithes at Brampton. The wooden rails on this 5½-mile railway were soon replaced by wrought iron rails and the network expanded to serve other collieries and limeworks. In 1838 the completion of the Newcastle & Carlisle Railway (N&CR) provided a much more efficient outlet for the Earl of Carlisle's coal with an interchange at Milton station – from here the Earl opened a short railway to the nearby town of Brampton, providing a passenger service operated by a horse-drawn coach.

The opening of the N&CR soon led to proposals for a railway to be built up the South Tyne Valley to serve collieries and lead mines around the town of Alston. Both the N&CR and the Stockton & Darlington Railway had their sights set on reaching Alston – the latter company was already progressing up the Wear Valley but only managed to reach Wearhead, where work stopped due to the high cost of continuing. However, the N&CR's proposal for a branch line from Haltwhistle, on that company's main line between Carlisle and Newcastle, to Alston received parliamentary approval in 1846. Involving the creation of nine viaducts, the steeply-graded line climbed over 500 ft over its 13-mile length – elegant 850-ft-long Lambley Viaduct was (and still is) the major feat of engineering, with nine arches carrying the railway 105 ft above the South Tyne River. The Alston branch line was opened throughout on 17 November 1852 but later proposals to extend it to Middleton-in-Teesdale (see pages 222–225) did not materialize.

The Earl of Carlisle's Railway (also known as the Brampton Railway) was extended eastward to serve Lambley Colliery and link up with the newly-opened Alston branch at Lambley. Britain's coal industry was nationalized in 1947 and the Brampton Railway became part of the newly-formed National Coal Board. But by

LEFT: Although not on the official South Tyne Trail, graceful Lambley Viaduct can still be accessed via a footpath offering pedestrians far-reaching views of the South Tyne Valley and the surrounding countryside.

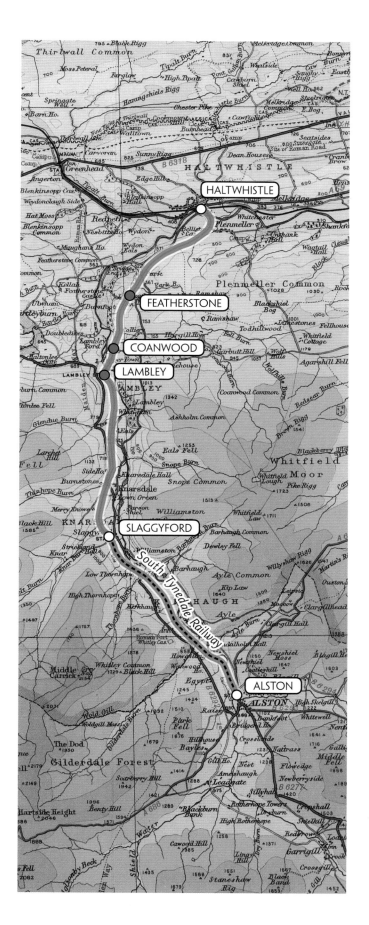

then coal mining in east Cumberland was in decline and this historic railway closed in March 1953.

Passenger train services on the Alston branch were never generous – in 1922 they amounted to only four trains each way on weekdays but by 1950 this figure had risen to six with an additional late evening service for pub-goers on Saturdays. The journey time for the 13-mile trip was 35 minutes. Economies were introduced in 1955 when the intermediate stations of Featherstone Park, Coanwood, Lambley and Slaggyford became unstaffed halts. Diesel multiple units replaced steam-hauled trains in 1959 and freight services had all been withdrawn by 1965. By then closure of the branch had been recommended in the Beeching Report (1963) but, due to the poor state of the

roads in the area, the obligatory replacement bus service could not be operated. Eventually the roads were improved, the railway closed, and the buses introduced – closure for the Alston branch came on 3 May 1976, one of the last railways in the country to fall victim to Dr Beeching's 'axe'. Since closure the entire route of the line has become a footpath and cycleway, forming part of the South Tyne

Trail and National Cycle Network Route 68 (Pennine Cycleway). Between Alston and Slaggyford the Trail shares the old trackbed with the South Tynedale Railway (STR, see box on page 231).

The Trail offers superb views of the surrounding countryside, especially from the top of Lambley Viaduct, which is reached via a footpath from the Trail – the

cycleway follows a diversion around it. Refreshments can be taken at the Wallace Arms near the site of Featherstone Park station – the nearby Featherstone Castle was used as a German POW camp during the Second World War. Car parking is available in Alston, Slaggyford, Coanwood, Featherstone Park and Haltwhistle. Haltwhistle station, on the Carlisle to Newcastle line, with its staggered platforms, decorative footbridge and superb cantilevered signal box is still open for business.

There is still much of interest for lovers of lost railways along the South Tyne Trail today: the station house and platform with name board at Featherstone Park; the station house, platform and trackbed of a colliery tramway at Coanwood; station buildings and platform at Lambley, now a private residence, immediately followed by the stunning Grade II*-listed Lambley Viaduct; the station building and platform at Slaggyford, which is now the terminus of the newly-extended STR;

the platform at Kirkhaugh, which is now used by the STR; the Grade II-listed station building, platform and goods shed at Alston, which now form the Headquarters of the STR.

PREVIOUS SPREAD: Beautifully restored Slaggyford station is the northern terminus of the narrow-gauge South Tynedale Railway, and the station is also convenient for users of the South Tyne Trail. At time of writing the railway extension from Lintley to Slaggyford, installed on the former standard-gauge line, was not yet open but its completion is likely in 2018. When open the station will have a café, toilets, engineering workshops and a discovery centre.

BELOW: The 2-ft-gauge South Tynedale Railway and the South Tyne Trail, seen here near Alston, run side by side for 6¼ miles between Alston and Slaggyford.

RIGHT: A two-car Gloucester RC&W Co/Metro Cammell diesel multiple unit calls at Lambley station with the 5.40 pm Haltwhistle to Alston train on 27 June 1968. The station building is now a private residence.

South Tynedale Railway

Opened in stages from 1983 onwards, this 2-ft-gauge railway operates along the route of the former Haltwhistle to Alston branch line between Alston and Slaggyford, a distance of 6¼ miles. With intermediate stations at Gilderdale, Kirkhaugh and Lintley, the railway crosses three viaducts including Gilderdale Viaduct, which is the boundary between Northumberland and Cumbria. Trains are diesel- and steam-hauled with examples of the latter originally at work in Germany, Poland and South Africa. The former London & North Eastern Railway signal box from Ainderby (on the Northallerton to Hawes line) has been re-erected at Alston station and controls all movements in the station. Services between Lintley and Slaggyford are not yet operational but are likely in 2018. The Alston to Lintley section of the line is open Tuesdays, Thursdays, weekends and bank holidays from the end of March to the end of October, and daily from the end of July to early September.

SCOTLAND

Lochwinnoch Loop
Cart Junction to Brownhill Junction
via Lochwinnoch

Open to passengers 1905–1966 | **Original length** 13 miles
Original route operator Glasgow & South Western Railway
Length currently open for walkers & cyclists 10¾ miles | **NCN** 7

Opened by the Glasgow & South Western Railway in 1905 to provide an alternative route for rail traffic on the congested Glasgow to Ayr main line, the Lochwinnoch Loop had a short working life. Once popular with Glaswegian day-trippers visiting Castle Semple Loch, it closed to passengers in 1966 and completely in 1977. Since closure much of this route has been reopened as a footpath and cycleway.

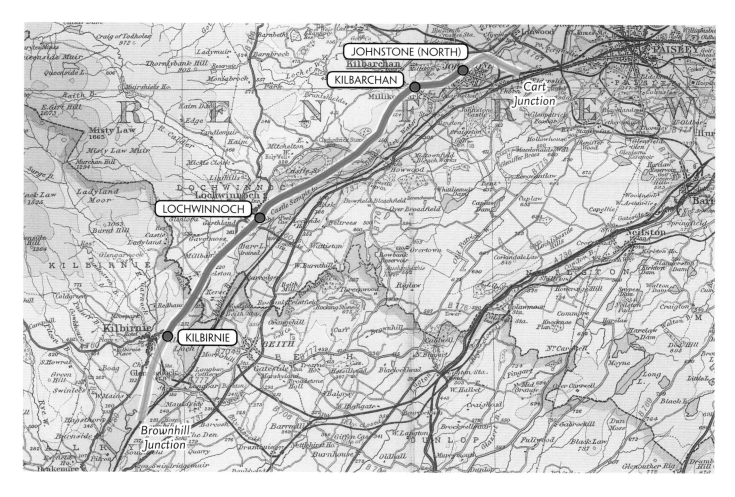

When it was completed in 1840, the Glasgow, Paisley, Kilmarnock & Ayr Railway's 33-mile line linked Scotland's biggest city with the port of Ayr along the Black Carr Water and Garnock valleys, for nearly 5 miles skirting the eastern shores of three small lochs – Castle Semple Loch, Barr Loch and Kilbirnie Loch. The company merged with the Glasgow, Dumfries & Carlisle Railway in 1850 to form the Glasgow & South Western Railway (G&SWR). The Glasgow to Ayr route had become increasingly congested by the end of the century but doubling the line's capacity was not possible due to the cramped confines of the valleys. The G&SWR's answer to this was to bypass the section between Elderslie Junction, near Johnstone, to Brownhill Junction, north of Dalry, by building a new double-track line on the western side of the lochs. Serving intermediate stations at Johnstone North (a terminus since 1896), Kilbarchan, Lochwinnoch and Kilbirnie, the 13-mile line opened between Cart Junction and Brownhill Junction on 1 June 1905. An unusual feature of the new stations was that they all had one wide island platform with a substantial, attractive wooden waiting room, connected to the road below by a subway and stairs.

For the whole of its short life the line was served by a frequent service of trains running between Glasgow St Enoch and Ardrossan, Ayr, Largs or Kilmarnock. At weekends and bank holidays in the summer the station at Lochwinnoch could be very busy handling hordes of Glaswegian day-trippers heading for Castle Semple Loch. Competition from road transport started to bite in the 1950s and Johnstone North station closed to passengers on 7 March 1955. With falling passenger numbers, more

PREVIOUS SPREAD: Glorious autumn colours highlight the remoteness and wild beauty of the Dava Way between Dunphail and Dava (see pages 262–267). Note the old railway fence posts either side of the track that have survived for over fifty years since closure in 1965.

LEFT: BR Standard Class 4MT 2-6-0 No. 76094 passes through Kilbarchan station with the 6.22 am Kilmarnock to Glasgow train on 2 August 1965. Closure to passengers came less than a year later while the locomotive, which was built at Horwich Works in 1957, was withdrawn in 1967.

cost-effective diesel multiple units were introduced in the early 1960s but this was all to no avail and the line was recommended for closure in the Beeching Report (1963). Closure to passengers came on 27 June 1966 although freight services continued until 3 February 1971, when the line north of Kilbirnie closed completely. The southern section from Brownhill junction to Kilbirnie remained open to serve Glengarnock Steel Works until 19 December 1977.

Since closure 10¾ miles of the Lochwinnoch Loop line between Johnstone and Kilbirnie has been reopened alongside the three lochs as a level, traffic-free footpath and cycleway, the latter forming part of National Cycle Network Route 7. Still popular with Glaswegians, Castle Semple Loch now has a modern visitor centre with car parking, café, bike hire, water sports and fishing facilities. The path can be accessed from the railway stations at Johnstone, Lochwinnoch and Glengarnock that are still served by trains on the Glasgow to Ayr main line that still operate along the opposite side of the lochs. Apart from cuttings, embankments, overbridges and the stone bridge across the River Calder near Lochwinnoch, little now remains of the railway infrastructure. The old wooden waiting rooms with their wide awnings have long gone,

but there are still some remains at the stations along this route: the railway bridge, street entrance and the island platform at Kilbarchan; the bricked-up station entrance and railway bridge at Lochwinnoch; the island platform at Kilbirnie.

LEFT: A surviving railway bridge over a lane at Millbank, southwest of Lochwinnoch.

BELOW: Kilbirnie station as seen from a northbound train on 4 July 1957. Today National Cycle Network Route 7 passes through on the trackbed alongside the surviving island platform.

Strathaven Miniature Railway

The Strathaven Model Society operates a dual-gauge ground-level and a triple-gauge raised miniature railway in George Allan Park, Strathaven. Steam-hauled ride-on passenger trains operate for the public on open days. The park also contains bowling and putting greens, a café and a boating pond. The railway is open on weekend afternoons from April to September.

Paisley & Clyde Railway Path

Johnstone to Princes Pier, Greenock

Open to passengers 1864/69–1965/83 | **Original length** 15¾ miles
Original route operators Bridge of Weir Railway/Glasgow & South Western Railway
Length currently open for walkers & cyclists 13 miles | **NCN** 75

The opening of the railway to Princes Pier in Greenock in 1869 led to an
all-out price war between two rival railway companies competing for the
lucrative Clyde steamer traffic. Local services to Princes Pier ended in 1959
but trains carrying trans-Atlantic liner passengers continued until 1965.
Meanwhile Kilmacolm continued to be served by local trains from Glasgow
until 1983, when the line closed. Since then much of the route
has been reopened as a footpath and cycleway.

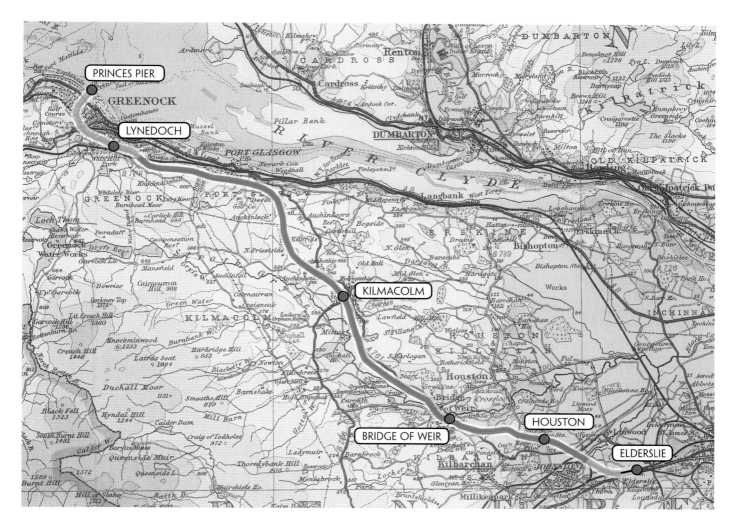

The success of Henry Bell's 'Comet', the first successful steamboat service in Europe, which started operating between Glasgow and Greenock in 1812, soon led to hundreds of Clyde steamers operating up, down and across the river. Soon, getting away from industrial Glasgow 'doon the watter' to resorts along the Firth of Clyde was to become a favourite pastime at weekends and bank holidays for Glaswegians. Railway companies latched on to this lucrative traffic with the Glasgow, Paisley & Greenock Railway (GP&GR) opening from Glasgow Bridge Street to what is now Greenock Central station in 1841 – passengers for the steamers had a ¼-mile walk from this station to Custom House Quay. The GP&GR became part of the Caledonian Railway (CR) in 1847.

LEFT: BR Standard Class 4MT 2-6-4T No. 80112 leaves Bridge of Weir with the 6.45 am Glasgow St Enoch to Kilmacolm train on 2 August 1965. Steam haulage on this service was soon to end but the line did not close to passengers until early 1983.

For over twenty years the CR had a stranglehold on this profitable traffic until its rival, the Glasgow & South Western Railway (G&SWR), invaded its territory. The G&SWR did this by backing the Greenock & Ayrshire Railway (G&AR), which had been authorized in 1862 to build a 11¾-mile line from Bridge of Weir to Greenock – the former station had already been served from Glasgow by the Bridge of Weir Railway since 1864, the latter being absorbed by the G&SWR a year later. The G&AR opened in 1869 and was worked from the outset by the G&SWR, the latter absorbing the former in 1872. Originally named Albert Harbour, the G&SWR station at Greenock was renamed Princes Pier in 1875 – the station was replaced by a much enlarged Italianate-style building in 1894. It was reached from the penultimate station at Lynedoch by two tunnels that burrowed under the streets of Greenock.

The opening of this new route to Greenock from Glasgow St Enoch started a vicious price war between the

G&SWR and its arch-rival, the Caledonian, operating out of Glasgow Central. Despite increasing their Clyde passenger traffic, neither of the companies really won although the G&SWR had the edge as its station at Princes Pier in Greenock allowed passengers to board the steamers directly from their train. In the end the two companies came to an agreement to fix their fares and share the revenue from the two routes. Both the CR and G&SWR had fleets of passenger steamers, with those of the latter company serving many destinations along the Clyde Estuary including the islands of Great Cumbrae, Bute and Arran.

There was also a three-road engine shed with a turntable, water tank and coal stage at Princes Pier that was opened by the G&AR in 1869. The shed was rebuilt by British Railways in 1952 and closed in May 1959 – thereafter the heavy boat trains from Glasgow St Enoch, usually double-headed, were worked tender first in one direction due to the lack of a turntable. The October 1950 timetable shows thirteen return passenger services from Monday to Friday but on Saturdays this was increased to fourteen – this included a late-night arrival at Princes Pier of 23.53 no doubt laid on to get folks home after the pubs closed!

Nationalization of the railways and Clyde steamer services in 1948 finally ended the competition. Following the withdrawal of Clyde steamers from Princes Pier, local passenger services were withdrawn between Kilmacolm and Greenock on 2 February 1959 (with the closure of Lynedoch and Port Glasgow Upper stations) although the route continued to be used for trans-Atlantic liner passengers – these trains ran non-stop to and from Glasgow St Enoch until ceasing on 30 November 1965, although freight traffic continued until 29 September 1966. The line had already been recommended for

closure in the Beeching Report (1963) but local passenger services from St Enoch (this station closed in 1966, after which trains used Glasgow Central) to Kilmacolm continued for another twenty years before ending on 3 January 1983, thus becoming the last line in Britain to succumb to Dr Beeching's 'axe'.

Since closure almost the entire route of the railway has been reopened as part of a 21-mile footpath and cycleway – forming part of National Cycle Network Route 75 – known as the Paisley & Clyde Railway Path (P&CRP). The path starts at Paisley Canal station and shares the route of National Cycle Network Route 7 as far as Johnstone where the latter branches off westward along the railway path to Lochwinnoch (see pages 234–237). The P&CRP heads northwesterly to Bridge of Weir where it crosses the River Gryfe on a stone viaduct. Heading up the Gryfe Valley into open countryside, the path reaches Kilmacolm where the station is now a pub. Beyond here it continues through cuttings and along embankments to Port Glasgow from where the traffic-free railway section ends and the P&CRP continues to Greenock and Gourock along public roads.

Riverside Museum, Glasgow

Opened in 2011 and now one of the most popular attractions in Scotland, this modern museum is located on the north bank of the River Clyde near Kelvingrove. Among its extensive collection are railway exhibits that were formerly on show at the Glasgow Museum of Transport in Kelvin Hall including steam locomotives from the main Scottish railway companies and also from the North British Locomotive Company of Glasgow. Open daily throughout the year.

LEFT: The Paisley & Clyde Railway Path as seen from a road bridge near Quarriers Village, south of Kilmacolm.

BELOW: A fascinating band of red Roman legionnaires made out of old gas tanks lie in wait for walkers and cyclists on the Paisley & Clyde Railway Path near Kilmacolm.

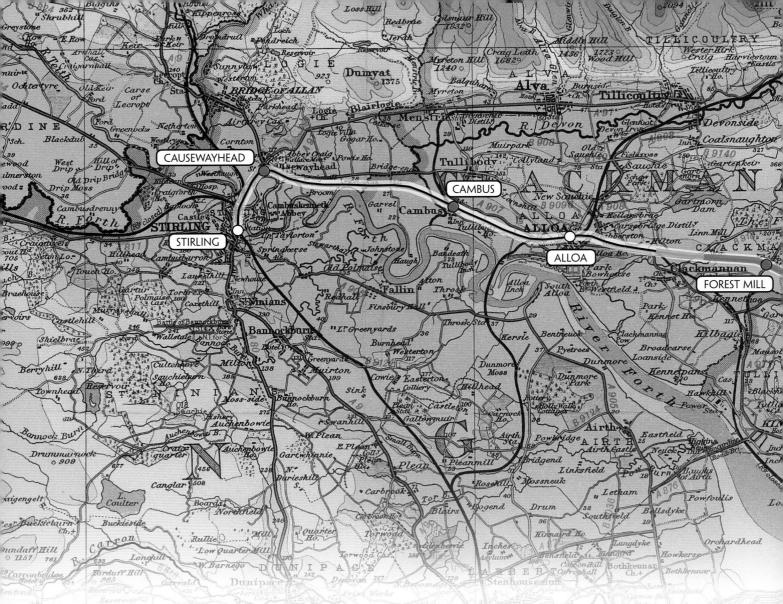

West Fife Way

Dunfermline Upper to Stirling

Open to passengers 1852–1968 | **Original length** 20½ miles
Original route operator Stirling & Dunfermline Railway
Length currently open for walkers & cyclists 14 miles | **NCN** 764

Built to serve the coalfields of West Fife, the Stirling & Dunfermline Railway opened throughout in 1852. Closure to passengers came in 1968 although the eastern and western stubs remained open for coal traffic until the 1980s. Passenger services between Stirling and Alloa were reinstated in 2008 and the 14-mile section of trackbed between Dunfermline and the outskirts of Clackmannan has been reopened as a footpath and cycleway.

BOGSIDE

EAST GRANGE

OAKLEY

DUNFERMLINE UPPER

243

Promoted by the Edinburgh & Glasgow Railway (E&GR) to serve the coalfields of West Fife, the Stirling & Dunfermline Railway (S&DR) opened westwards from Dunfermline to Alloa and Stirling in stages between 1849 and 1852. Branches were also opened to Alloa Harbour and from Alloa to Tillicoultry along the route of a 3-ft-3-in-gauge horse-drawn wooden waggonway that had been built to serve coal mines in the latter half of the 18th century.

The fairly level double-track route of the S&DR main line featured the eight-arch Comrie Dean Viaduct and served intermediate stations at Oakley, East Grange, Bogside, Forest Mill, Alloa, Cambus and Causewayhead. The railway was absorbed by the E&GR in 1858, which was in turn taken over by the North British Railway (NBR) in 1865. Serving textile mills and a distillery, a 3½-mile branch line from Cambus to Alva via Menstrie was opened

by the Alva Railway in 1863 – the company was taken over by the E&GR in the following year. A short branch line was also opened from Oakley, home to an ironworks and colliery, to serve Comrie Colliery and the Roxio Cokeworks – this line became much busier in the 1930s when the Fife Coal Company started extracting coal from a large underground seam between Comrie village and Dollar.

The Tillicoultry branch from Alloa was eventually extended by the Devon Valley Railway to Kinross via Dollar and Rumbling Bridge, opening throughout in 1871 – the company was taken over by the NBR in 1875. The Caledonian Railway (CR) eventually reached Alloa from Larbert in 1885 via Alloa Viaduct (nineteen steel spans plus a lifting section) across the River Forth which, until the opening of the Forth Bridge in 1890, was the lowest crossing of the river. The final link in the chain of associated branch lines was the Forth coastal route

between Alloa and Dunfermline Lower via Kincardine, which opened in stages between 1893 and 1906.

Coal remained the lifeblood of the railways for their entire life, and passenger services between Dunfermline and Stirling were of secondary importance, although most trains started or ended their journeys at Edinburgh. This route would have taken trains across the Forth Bridge to Dunfermline Lower station and then on a 2½-mile trip around the town to Dunfermline Upper station, all very time consuming and probably perplexing for passengers! Steam haulage for these passenger trains was replaced by diesel multiple units in the early 1960s but by then many of the intermediate stations had already closed. The timetable for the summer of 1964 shows only Oakley, Alloa and Cambus remaining of the intermediate stations still open and they were served by nine trains each way on weekdays – the Alloa to Stirling service had an additional five journeys.

Closure of the connecting lines started early with the coastal route via Kincardine losing its passenger service in 1930, although the line remains in-situ after it was used by coal trains to Longannet power station until 2016. The Alva branch lost its passenger service in 1954 and the Devon Valley line via Dollar similarly in 1964, although by that time only one return train each weekday completed the final part of the journey between Dollar and Kinross. Coal trains continued to leave Dollar Colliery bound for Alloa until 1973. The former CR route from Larbert to Alloa via the Alloa Viaduct closed to passengers in January 1968.

Facing increased competition from road transport and with an alternative route available between Edinburgh and Stirling via Larbert, the passenger service between Dunfermline Upper and Stirling was withdrawn on 7 October 1968. The line remained open for freight until 1979 when it was closed west of Oakley, with the connection from Dunfermline Upper staying open until the closure of Comrie Colliery in 1986. At its western end Alloa was served by freight trains from Stirling until 1988. This section reopened in 2008 not only for merry-go-round coal trains destined for Longannet power station but also for passengers to a new station at Alloa.

Since closure, the 14-mile section of trackbed between Dunfermline Queen Margaret station and the eastern outskirts of Clackmannan, via the site of Dunfermline Upper station, has been reopened as a mainly traffic-free footpath and cycleway known as the West Fife Way.

Sadly nothing remains today of the extensive station and sidings at Dunfermline Upper, despite it surviving fairly intact until demolition in 1990. Just to the west of the station site a remarkable survivor is a cast-iron lattice footbridge that once crossed the railway and now faces an uncertain future. Apart from a number of double-track-width road bridges and the Comrie Dean Viaduct, the rest of the route to the outskirts of Clackmannan is virtually devoid of any surviving railway infrastructure apart from one shining example at Bogside – here the signal box still stands in a wooded cutting, complete with imitation painted windows.

LEFT: Ex-North British Railway Class J37 0-6-0 No. 64623 runs light engine through Alloa on 9 August 1965. The locomotive was built by the North British Locomotive Company of Glasgow in 1921 and withdrawn in November 1966.

BELOW: A wooden milepost on the West Fife Way, west of Dunfermline.

Bo'ness & Kinneil Railway

Operated by the Scottish Railway Preservation Society (SRPS), this 5-mile heritage railway was reopened between 1984 and 2010 and operates mainly steam-hauled trains along the route of the former Slamannan & Borrowstouness Railway between Bo'ness and Manuel Junction. The railway's terminus station and associated structures at Bo'ness comprise historic buildings that originally stood at Edinburgh Haymarket, Wormit, Garnqueen and Murthly. Intermediate stations are provided at Birkhill and Kinneil, the latter the site of a colliery until 1989. The railway owns a large collection of historic rolling stock while the fascinating SRPS Exhibition Museum is located adjacent to Bo'ness station. At Manuel Junction there is a physical link to the Glasgow to Edinburgh via Falkirk main line. Open Tuesdays, weekends and bank holidays from April to October, daily from the end of July to the end of August, and weekends in December.

The signal box, platform and road overbridge have all survived at the site of Bogside station. Not to be confused with Bogside in Ayrshire, this intermediate station between Dunfermline Upper and Alloa closed to passengers on 15 September 1958.

Tayport to Tay Bridge Cycle Route

Leuchars Junction to Wormit via Tayport

Open to passengers 1849/79–1956/69 | **Original length** 10¼ miles
Original route operators Edinburgh & Northern Railway/Newport Railway
Length currently open for walkers & cyclists 4¾ miles | **NCN** 1

This is the story of two railways that met on the southern shore of the
Firth of Tay at Tayport. The future of both railways was inextricably linked to
the opening of the Tay Bridge in 1878, but while the railway from Leuchars
Junction became a sleepy byway with an infrequent service of trains, the other,
from Wormit, became a lifeline for commuters working in Dundee.
The opening of the Tay Road Bridge in 1966 brought an end to this traffic
and the line was progressively closed over the next three years.
Since closure, the Tayport to Wormit route has become a footpath and cycleway.

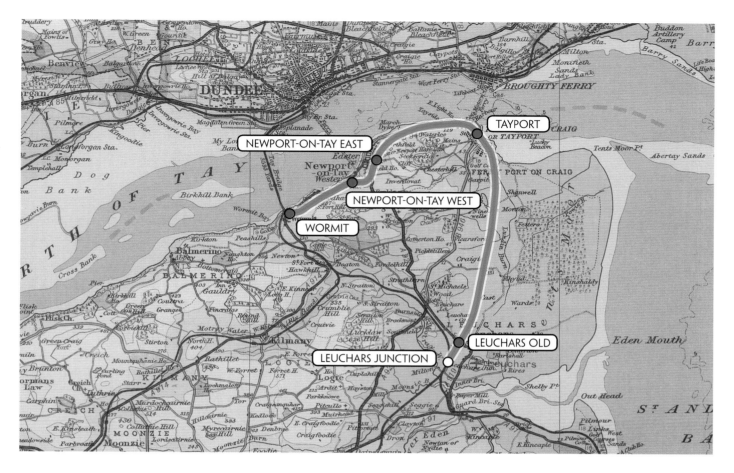

The first railway to reach Tayport, a village on the south shore of the Firth of Tay opposite Dundee, was built by the Edinburgh & Northern Railway. Opened via Cupar and Leuchars in 1849, this railway, later renamed the Edinburgh, Perth & Dundee Railway (EP&DR), linked the Firth of Forth at Burntisland with the Firth of Tay at Ferry-Port-on-Craig (soon to be renamed Tayport). Passengers travelling between Edinburgh and Dundee were carried across the two wide firths by company-owned ferries – 5 miles across the Forth between Granton and Burntisland and 2 miles across the Tay from Tayport to Broughty Ferry – and from here the Dundee & Arbroath Railway took over for the last few miles into Dundee. It was a very slow and often uncomfortable journey between Edinburgh and Dundee! Goods were carried separately in the world's first railway wagon ferries, which also started operation in 1849.

Leuchars station became the junction for the line to St Andrews in 1852 until it was resited about ¾-mile to the south in 1878. The new station was known as Leuchars Junction while the original station became Leuchars Old until it was closed to passengers in 1921.

The EP&DR was absorbed by the North British Railway in 1862. The opening of the 2¼-mile Tay Bridge in 1878, reached via a shorter route from Leuchars Junction to Wormit, should have seen the demise of the railway north of Leuchars to Tayport but the bridge's dramatic collapse, with the loss of 75 lives, the following year brought the line back to life again. The second Tay Bridge opened in 1887 and, with the opening of the Forth Bridge in 1890, the North British Railway finally had its direct route between Edinburgh and Aberdeen. The 5½-mile line from Leuchars Junction became quiet again – by 1922 there were only five trains each weekday to Tayport while from Tayport to Dundee there were twenty. It finally closed in 1956.

Meanwhile the 4¾-mile Newport Railway had opened from Wormit, south of the Tay Bridge, to Tayport in 1879.

LEFT: Ex-North British Railway Class J37 0-6-0 No. 64577 awaits departure from Tayport with a short freight train for Dundee on 30 September 1965. This locomotive was built by the North British Locomotive Company of Glasgow in 1918 and withdrawn in August 1966.

Intermediate stations were provided at Newport East and Newport West and the railway was absorbed by the North British Railway in 1900. Served by trains over the Tay Bridge to and from Dundee, Tayport became an important commuter town but lost this passenger service on 23 May 1966 – the opening of the Tay Road Bridge in that year killed off most of the traffic. The line was then cut back to Newport-on-Tay, which lost its goods service on 2 January 1967 and passenger service on 5 May 1969.

Since closure the entire section of the old railway route along the southern shore of the Firth of Tay between Tayport and Wormit, thence across the Tay Road Bridge to Dundee, has been reopened as a footpath and cycleway. Cyclists use the elevated cycle path in the centre of the bridge and on the Dundee side use a lift to reach ground level. While the station at Tayport has long been demolished, the station buildings at Newport East and Newport West have both survived as private residences. The Edinburgh to Dundee main line still runs through Wormit and across the Tay Bridge although there is no station here any more – the station building was dismantled and re-erected by the Scottish Railway Preservation Society at Birkhill on the Bo'ness & Kinneil Railway (see page 247).

Kerr's Miniature Railway

Opened in 1935, this historic family-run 10¼-in-gauge miniature railway operates passenger trains for ½-mile alongside the Dundee to Aberdeen main line in West Links Park at Arbroath. Trains are hauled by a mixture of steam- and petrol-engine locomotives, including the 1936-built Atlantic steam outline *Auld Reekie.* Open weekends and school holidays from April to September

BELOW: Newport-on-Tay East station building is now a private residence. Before closure there were two platforms connected by a cast-iron footbridge and a passing loop, signal box and small goods yard.

RIGHT: A two-car diesel multiple unit stands at Tayport station after having arrived from Dundee on 30 September 1965. The line from here to Wormit closed in 1969 following the opening of the Tay Road Bridge.

Formartine & Buchan Way 1

Dyce to Peterhead

Open to passengers 1862–1965 | **Original length** 37¾ miles
Original route operator Great North of Scotland Railway
Length currently open for walkers & cyclists 37½ miles | **NCN** 1 (Dyce to Newmachar/Auchnagatt to Maud)

Opening in 1862, this long and winding railway to the busy fishing port
of Peterhead served only small villages and farming communities along
its 37¾-mile route. The eastern half closed to passengers in May 1965 and,
despite the booming local offshore gas and oil industry, to freight in 1970 –
the southern half soldiered on with freight trains for Fraserburgh
until 1979. Since then the entire trackbed has been reopened
as a footpath and cycleway.

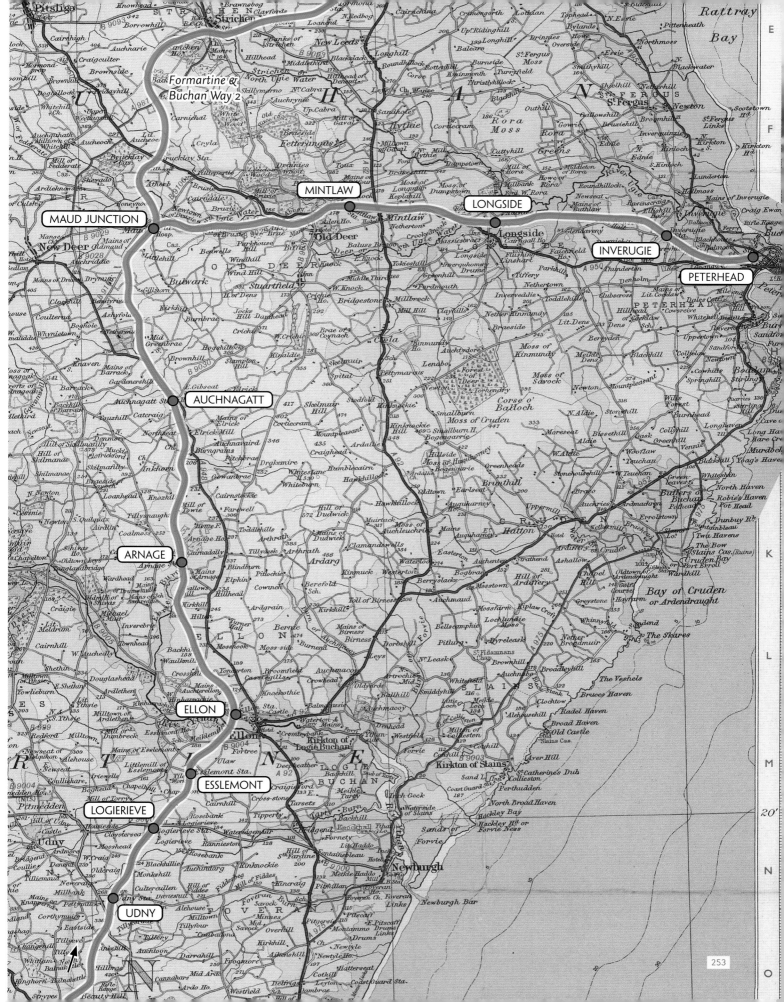

Formartine & Buchan Way 2

MAUD JUNCTION

MINTLAW

LONGSIDE

INVERUGIE

PETERHEAD

AUCHNAGATT

ARNAGE

ELLON

ESSLEMONT

LOGIERIEVE

UDNY

Incorporated in 1846, the Great North of Scotland Railway's (GNoSR) ambition to build a 40½-mile line from Aberdeen to Huntly was delayed by shortage of capital. Construction work eventually started in 1852 and the line opened between Kittybrewster and Huntly in 1854. A new station was opened at Aberdeen (Waterloo) in 1856.

There then followed several unsuccessful proposals to build a line from Dyce, north of Aberdeen, to the fishing ports of Peterhead and Fraserburgh. Finally the GNoSR-backed Formartine & Buchan Railway (F&BR) received authorization in 1858 to build the line. Construction was held up by severe weather in February 1860 when the newly-built viaduct across the River Ythan at Ellon collapsed, with the line eventually opening between Dyce and Mintlaw in July 1861. Peterhead, 37¾ miles from Dyce, was reached one year later and a branch line to the important fishing harbour was opened in 1865. The railway was worked from the outset by the GNoSR and a

16-mile extension from Maud to the fishing port of Fraserburgh (see pages 258–261) was also opened in 1865. The GNoSR then went on to absorb the F&BR in the following year.

A 15½-mile branch line from Ellon to Boddam opened in 1897, primarily to serve the railway company's new hotel and golf course at Cruden Bay. In its latter years it was worked by Sentinel steam railcars, closing to passengers as early as 1932 but remaining open for freight until 1945. A short branch line was built from Longside to Lenabo to service a Royal Naval Air Service airship station between 1916 and 1920.

For a century both the Peterhead line and the Fraserburgh line were served by through passenger trains to and from Aberdeen, with most of them splitting or joining at Maud. Apart from their final destinations, the long and winding railway passed through farming country serving only small villages en route. The 1950 timetable is fairly typical of services with six northbound

and five southbound trains operating between Aberdeen and Peterhead on weekdays; the 44-mile journey took about 1 hr 45 mins.

Maud became an important centre for the sale of livestock transported there by train but fish traffic was the lifeblood of the line, especially during the herring season, with fish catches landed at Peterhead being dispatched to distant markets such as Billingsgate in London in overnight refrigerated trains. Diesel multiple units were introduced in 1959 but with declining passenger numbers the railway was recommended for closure in the Beeching Report (1963). The Maud Junction to Peterhead section lost its passenger service on 3 May 1965 (Dyce to Fraserburgh was closed to passengers in the following November), although freight trains continued to serve Peterhead until 7 September 1970 – even the rapid growth of the local offshore gas and oil industry failed to halt the closure. Freight trains continued to run from Dyce to Fraserburgh until 1979, when the route was closed.

Following closure, the trackbed between Dyce and Peterhead and from Maud to Fraserburgh was purchased by what is now Aberdeenshire Council and has been reopened as a footpath and cycleway known as the Formartine & Buchan Way. Much of the infrastructure, such as bridges, viaducts and stations, has survived, the latter mainly used as private residences.

The main route from Dyce to Peterhead travels north from Dyce station, which is still served by trains operating between Aberdeen and Inverness. The first station to be

BELOW: The Formartine & Buchan Way crosses the River Ythan on this railway viaduct at Ellon. It was constructed originally with three arches but had to be rebuilt with an extra arch following a collapse during construction.

reached is at Parkhill, which closed in 1950 and where the platforms and the viaduct over the River Don have survived. Further north the screened-off Newmachar station is a private residence while a short distance further on is a deep cutting at the summit of the line. Descending from here, the Way passes through Udny, Logierieve and Esslemont stations, which are all now private residences. At Ellon the Way passes over the River Ythan on a substantial four-arch viaduct before continuing north past Arnage and Auchnagatt stations (both private residences) to arrive at Maud Junction.

The well preserved station buildings, platforms and turntable pit at Maud is where the Fraserburgh section of the Formartine & Buchan Way heads north (see pages 258–261), while the route to Peterhead turns eastward. En route, the Way first passes the ruins of Mintlaw station followed by the stations at Longside and Newseat, which are both private residences. Not much remains now of the penultimate station at Inverugie, and nothing at all remains of the once-extensive station site and extensive goods yard at Peterhead, which was completely bulldozed and redeveloped in the 1970s.

Alford Valley Railway

The standard-gauge Alford Valley Railway in the Don Valley opened in 1859, closed to passengers in 1950 and to freight in 1966. A 2-ft-gauge railway opened from the old terminus station at Alford to Murray Park in 1980 with equipment originally used at a peat works. With trains hauled by diminutive industrial locomotives, the line currently operates between Alford and Haughton Country Park, a distance of just less than a mile. The excellent Grampian Transport Museum is also located at Alford. The railway is open on weekends from April to October, and daily in July and August.

LEFT: BR Standard Class 4MT 2-6-4T No. 80112 is seen here at Maud Junction with a Peterhead train in June 1959, shortly before the introduction of diesel multiple units.

BELOW: This wooden lineside hut has survived alongside the Formartine & Buchan Way for over forty years since complete closure of the railway.

Formartine & Buchan Way 2

Maud Junction to Fraserburgh

Open to passengers 1865–1965 | **Original length** 16 miles
Original route operator Great North of Scotland Railway
Length currently open for walkers & cyclists 16 miles

Connecting with the Dyce to Peterhead line, the 16-mile railway between Maud Junction and the fishing port of Fraserburgh was opened in 1865. Fish and livestock traffic were its lifeblood as passenger trains only served intermediate villages along the meandering route. Passenger services ceased after a century of service but freight traffic continued until 1979. Since closure the entire length of the trackbed has been reopened as a footpath and cycleway.

Sponsored by the Great North of Scotland Railway (GNoSR) and built by the Formartine & Buchan Railway, the single-track line from Maud Junction, on the Dyce to Peterhead line (see pages 252–257), to the fishing port of Fraserburgh opened in 1865. The railway was worked from the outset by the GNoSR, which went on to absorb the F&BR a year later. A 5-mile branch line from Fraserburgh to St Combs was built as a Light Railway and opened in 1903.

For a century both the Peterhead and Fraserburgh lines were served by through passenger trains from and to Aberdeen with most of them splitting or joining at

PREVIOUS SPREAD: The St Combs branch locomotive at Fraserburgh engine shed on 17 June 1949. As the 5-mile branch was a light railway, locomotives using it had to be fitted with cowcatchers. Still sporting its LNER livery, Class F4 No. 67164 was built by the Great Eastern Railway at Stratford Works in 1907 and withdrawn in 1951.

BELOW: Seen here in the 1920s Maud Junction was the busiest intermediate station between Dyce and Fraserburgh/Peterhead. Here trains from Aberdeen were spilt with one half going to Fraserburgh via the line on the left and the other half going to Peterhead via the line on the right. The platforms and station building have survived closure while the Formartine & Buchan Way now splits here and follows the separate trackbeds to Fraserburgh and Peterhead.

Maud Junction. Fish traffic was the lifeblood of the line, with catches landed at Fraserburgh being despatched to distant markets such as Billingsgate in London in overnight refrigerated trains. The pattern of passenger train services remained fairly constant until closure – for example, in the summer of 1964 there were five return services each weekday between Aberdeen and Fraserburgh, the 47-mile journey taking about 1 hr 30 mins. The Fraserburgh to St Combs branch line, by comparison, had no less than eleven return services on weekdays, plus an extra working on Saturdays, with trains taking 20 minutes for the 5-mile journey.

Diesel multiple units were introduced in 1959 but with declining passenger numbers the railway was recommended for closure in the Beeching Report (1963). The St Combs branch was closed on 3 May 1965, the same day that the Maud to Peterhead line closed to passengers, while the line from Dyce to Fraserburgh soldiered on with its passenger service until 4 October of that year. Freight trains continued to serve Fraserburgh until 8 October 1979.

Following closure, the trackbed of the Dyce to Peterhead and Fraserburgh lines was purchased by what is now Aberdeenshire Council and reopened as a

footpath and cycleway known as the Formartine & Buchan Way. Much of the infrastructure, such as bridges, viaducts and stations, has survived, the latter mainly used as private residences.

The 16-mile Fraserburgh section of the Formartine & Buchan Way continues north from the well-preserved station at Maud on the Peterhead line (see pages 252–257). The first station en route was at Brucklay, which is now a private residence. On the approach to the village of Strichen, the Way winds eastward over the tall girder bridge across the North Ugie Water, while the station building and two platforms in the village have all survived. Now heading northeasterly, the Way passes the stations at Mormond, Lonmay and Philorth, all of which still have platforms and are now private residences – the latter station was built for the use of the 18th Lord Saltoun, a Scottish Representative Peer who lived at nearby Philorth House. The Way ends near to the site of Fraserburgh station but apart from the goods office building and engine shed, the rest of the once-extensive station and yard here has been demolished to make way for a road and commercial redevelopment.

Keith & Dufftown Railway

Opened in 1862, the original Keith & Dufftown Railway served the Glenfiddich Whisky Distillery until complete closure in 1991, although passenger services had already ceased in 1968. With an intermediate station at Drummuir, the 11-mile heritage line between the restored stations at Keith Town and Dufftown is now run by a group of preservationists. Diesel railcar services normally operate on weekends and bank holidays from March to September, as well as during the Christmas period.

BELOW: The Formartine & Buchan way crosses the North Ugie Water on the old railway viaduct at Strichen on its route between Maud Junction and Fraserburgh.

Dava Way

Forres to Aviemore

Open to passengers 1863–1965 | **Original length** 35¾ miles
Original route operator Newcastle & Carlisle Railway
Length currently open for walkers & cyclists 13 miles | **NCN** 11

Forming part of what became the Highland Railway's main line from
Inverness to Perth, the 35¾-mile railway between Forres and Aviemore via
remote Dava Moor opened in 1863. The opening of a more direct railway
between Inverness and Aviemore in 1898 led to its downgrading as
a secondary route. Since closure in 1965, when it was a victim of
Dr Beeching's 'axe', the northern section has come back to life as the
Dava Way footpath and cycleway. In the south the Strathspey Railway
operates steam trains between Aviemore and Broomhill.

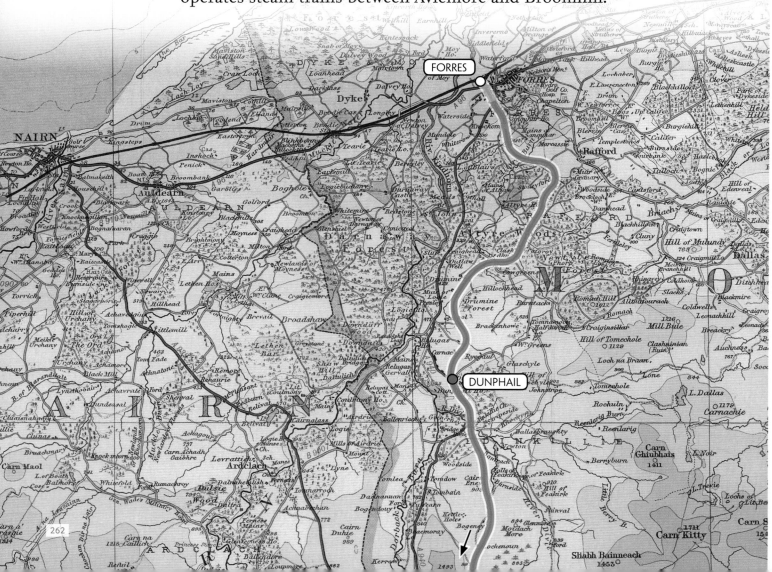

DAVA

GRANTOWN-ON-SPEY WEST

Grantown

BROOMHILL

Nethybridge

BOAT OF GARTEN

Strathspey Railway

AVIEMORE

Carrbridge

263

At the height of 'Railway Mania' in 1845 the townsfolk and businessmen of Inverness were clamouring for a railway that would connect them with the lowlands down south. Conquering the Highlands was seen as well nigh impossible at that time and, for a while, the only solution seemed to lie in building a railway eastwards across easier terrain to Aberdeen. From here both Glasgow and Edinburgh beckoned but it was a truly circuitous route. In the end the Great North of Scotland Railway (GNoSR), intent on reaching Inverness, only got as far Keith when its main line from Aberdeen via Huntly opened throughout in 1856.

Meanwhile the Inverness & Nairn Railway had opened its line between those two towns in 1855. The company was taken over by the Inverness & Aberdeen Junction Railway (I&AJR) in 1861, by which time the latter company had constructed the missing link between Nairn and Keith. This had opened in 1858 and for the first time there was a railway – albeit owned by three companies – between Inverness and Aberdeen.

However, the dream of conquering the Highlands was left to the ambitious Inverness & Perth Junction Railway (I&PJR), which received Parliamentary approval for its 113½-mile line between Forres and Dunkeld in 1861. The route of the new line struck southwards from Forres (where it met the I&AJR) and across remote Dava Moor to Grantown-on-Spey and Aviemore and then up and over Druimachdair (Drumochter) Summit (1,484 ft above sea level) to Pitlochry and Dunkeld – here it would meet the Perth & Dunkeld Railway (P&DR), which had opened in 1856. The I&PJR was rapidly constructed across the Highlands and opened throughout in 1863, going on to absorb the P&DR a year later. The next chapter in the complicated story of what became the Highland main line came in 1865 when the I&PJR merged with the I&AJR to form the

BELOW: Complete with an ex-Highland Railway cast-iron latticework footbridge, remote Dava station is seen here from an Aviemore to Forres train on 18 June 1937. At 985 ft above sea level, the station was opened in 1864 by the Inverness & Perth Junction Railway and closed on 18 October 1965. The stationmaster's house (now a private residence), station building and platforms have all survived.

RIGHT: The seven-arch Divie Viaduct, which carries the Dava Way 170 ft above the River Divie near Dunphail, is the major engineering structure on this highly scenic route.

Highland Railway, an Inverness-based company whose tentacles would eventually extend to Perth in the south, Kyle of Lochalsh in the west, Keith in the east and Wick and Thurso in the Far North.

The next stage in the development of the Highland main line came in 1898 with the completion of a more direct route between Inverness and Aviemore. This steeply-graded line via Culloden Moor, Daviot, Moy, Tomatin, Slochd Summit and Carr Bridge was 28 miles shorter than the original route via Forres and cut journey times by 1 hour. Engineering highlights of this new route included the 600-yd-long twenty-eight-arch Nairn Viaduct and the 445-yd-long steel viaduct over the River Findhorn.

The opening of this shorter route inevitably led to the downgrading of the Forres to Aviemore line – with intermediate stations at Dunphail, Dava, Grantown-on-Spey (West), Broomhill and Boat of Garten it was served on weekdays by trains to and from Inverness. The line was recommended for closure in the Beeching Report (1963) and by then there were six northbound services each weekday with one originating in Glasgow; southbound, there were only four including one that only ran on Saturdays. Curiously, in 1964, there were two

through trains in each direction on Sundays, one a Glasgow/Edinburgh to Inverness service and the other an Inverness to London (Euston) sleeping car train. This all came to an end on 18 October 1965 when the line closed.

Since closure much of the route of this railway has been reborn – the northern 22½-mile section between the southern outskirts of Forres and Grantown-on-Spey has been reopened as the Dava Way footpath and cycleway, while the southern 8¾-mile section between Aviemore and Broomhill has been reopened as a heritage railway by the Strathspey Railway (see box).

In addition to its remoteness and wild beauty, the highlights of the Dava Way include, from north to south: the Dallas Dhu Distillery and visitor centre, now owned by Historic Scotland, alongside the path 1 mile south of Forres; the seven-arch Divie Viaduct 170 ft above the River Divie, near Dunphail; the wild, remote section between Dunphail and Dava that takes walkers and cyclists around the Knock of Braemoray (1,496 ft) – trains often got stranded along this exposed stretch during heavy snowfall; the ornate station (known as Lady Catherine's Halt) and castellated railway bridge at Castle Grant.

Strathspey Railway

The former Highland Railway main line between Aviemore and Forres was opened in 1863 before being downgraded in 1898 by a more direct route from Inverness. Following closure in 1965, the 8¾-mile section from Aviemore to Broomhill was reopened as a heritage railway by the Strathspey Railway. With its headquarters and museum at Boat of Garten, the railway operates passenger trains hauled mainly by steam locomotives. A 3¾-mile extension from Broomhill to Grantown-on-Spey (West) via a new bridge over the River Dulnain is currently on hold due to rising construction costs. Open daily excluding Mondays, Tuesdays and Fridays from the end of March to the end of May, and in October; daily excluding Mondays and Tuesdays in June and September; daily in July and August; at weekends during the Christmas/New Year period.

With snow fences either side of the line, ex-LMS Class 5MT 4-6-0 No. 44978 heads the RCTS/SLS Scottish Rail Tour special train across Dava Moor on the Forres to Aviemore line on 16 June 1962. Built in 1946 at Crewe Works, this locomotive was withdrawn in 1965, the same year that this remote route closed.

Index

Acknowledgements

l = left; r = right; t = top; b = bottom

Photo credits:
Ben Abel: 149
Alamy Stock Photo: 8/9 (David Forster); 54 (Ian Redding); 106/107 (John Worrall); 120 (Richard Wayman); 135 (Dick Makin); 143 (Roy Childs); 152 (Frank Irwin); 154/155 (greenwales); 173 (Keith Morris); 178 (itdarbs); 202 (Andrew Kearton); back endpaper (David Hall)
Hugh Ballantyne: 53
Bill Boaden: 175
Jack Boskett: 126; 128
Henry Casserley: 14; 36/37; 56/57; 62/63; 66; 68/69; 80; 82; 86/87; 92; 114; 121; 124/125; 132/133; 134; 142; 150; 153; 156; 158; 162; 164; 166/167; 201; 204/205; 206; 208; 210; 225; 237; 258; 264
Richard Casserley: 22; 29; 74/75; 96/97; 116/117; 136; 172
Richard Casserley Collection: 76/77; 129; 183/183; 196/197 (R. J.Buckley)
Colour-Rail: 23 (G. F. Bloxham); 28 (M. Dart); 30; 32 (J. Cramp); 49 (R. Mason); 84; 89; 111; 127 (R. Patterson); 144/145; 148 (P. Moffat); 176 (L. V. Reason); 179 (R. Patterson); 216 (R. Patterson); 266/267
Simon Douglas: 4/5; 138
Gordon Edgar: 12; 112/113; 186/187; 214; 217; 218; 220; 221
Mike Esau: 17; 180
John Furneval: 250
Getty Images: front cover (Science & Society Picture Library); 72 (Patricia Hamilton)
John Goss: 18; 44; 64; 79; 160; 188; 190/191; 194; 234; 238; 244; 248; 251
Andrew Graham: 16; 20
John Gray: front endpaper; 232/233; 254/255; 261
Tony Harden: 104; 260
Bob Hodgson: 13t
Julian Holland: 7; 19; 24t; 24b; 25; 26; 33; 42/43; 45; 46; 48; 52; 55; 60; 61bl; 61br; 65; 67; 71b; 88; 90; 91; 94; 95; 100; 101; 110; 118; 119; 122; 123; 159; 163; 168; 169; 184; 185; 236; 240; 245; 246/247
Neal Jennings: 38/39
Damien Knowles: 85
Michael Mensing: 231
Milepost 92½: 224
Gavin Morrison: 174; 222; 256
Pallot Steam & Motor Museum, Jersey: 13b
John Parkes Photography: 212/213
Ray Pettit: 265
Ian Quiggin: 192; 193; 198; 199

Brian Sharpe: 105
John Shepley: 226; 228/229; 230
Paul Simpson: 139
Hugh and Uisdean Spicer: 241
Andrew Swift: 71t
Wee Yellow Bus: 200
Whitstable Community Museum: 78; 81
John Williamson: 257
Stephen Woodcock: 207

Map credits:
Page 5 © Collins Bartholomew Ltd 2018
Historical maps © HarperCollins Publishers and National Library of Scotland

With thanks to:
Gordon Edgar; Chris Fleet at NLS

Author's note:
I was saddened to hear of the death of Richard Casserley during the making of this book. Richard and his father, Henry, have contributed vast amounts of railway photographs of great historic value to publishers over many years. Their photographs grace the pages of this book, bringing back to life railway scenes which have now gone forever.

Front cover:
In this stylised Southern Railway poster a steam train is seen approaching the bridge over Little Petherick Creek near Padstow. The line closed in 1967 and the Camel Trail now follows its route from Padstow to Wadebridge, Bodmin and Wenford Bridge alongside the beautiful Camel Estuary.

Front endpaper:
The Dava Way, seen here as it crosses remote Dava Moor, now follows the route of the closed railway from Forres to Grantown-on-Spey.

Back endpaper:
Following the route of the closed railway between Afon Mawddach (Barmouth Junction) and Dolgellau, the Mawddach Trail is one of Britain's most scenic lost railway routes as it closely follows the south shore of the beautiful Mawddach Estuary.